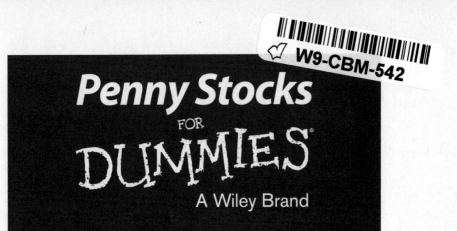

Penny Stocks

FOR

DUMMIES

A Wiley Brand

by Peter Leeds

FOR

DUMMIES

A Wiley Brand

Penny Stocks For Dummies®

Published by
John Wiley & Sons, Inc.
111 River St.
Hoboken, NJ 07030-5774
www.wiley.com

About the Author

Peter Leeds is the most widely recognized and trusted personality in penny stocks. Major media outlets such as NBC, CBS, Fox, CNNfn, Russia Today, and the Associated Press have covered Peter.

Also known as The Penny Stock Professional, he and his team publish the world-famous Peter Leeds Penny Stock newsletter (located at www.peterleeds.com), which has sold more than 35,000 subscriptions. Leading with integrity, honesty, and a commitment to ethics, never has Peter or any of his staff taken any compensation of any kind from the companies they analyze and profile.

Peter is the author of *Invest in Penny Stocks,* also published by John Wiley & Sons, Inc. His comments are often published through various sources, such as *Forbes, Business Excellence Magazine,* Yahoo! News, and numerous others.

Peter speaks publicly on various investing topics and has led panels at various stock market seminars, including the prestigious Arch Investment Conferences in Manhattan.

Peter attributes his success and love of penny stock investing to his foolish start. Losing all his money in one trade at the age of 14, Leeds was able to develop the Leeds Analysis method to make back those funds hundreds of times over. He is now focused on helping people sidestep the easily avoidable pitfalls while identifying in the highest quality companies with growing revenues, expanding market share, and massive upside potential.

Dedication

One constant leading every success. One light guiding every path. My wife.

Author's Acknowledgments

A project of this size is not the achievement of an individual. Of those who enabled *Penny Stocks For Dummies,* none was tested more than DRC, and I thank you.

To my parents, your support has been wonderful and appreciated.

John Wiley & Sons, Inc. has been an excellent organization to work with. They are professional and motivated, and their unmatched reach is certainly well-deserved. The opportunity to be supported by the Wiley team can not be replicated.

Among the many individuals at Wiley, I would point out a few. Stacy Kennedy, thank you for believing in the project. Jennifer Moore, it has been a pleasure working with you. Debra Englander, who represented my first book, deserves my gratitude for introducing me to the Dummies team.

Lisa, good call. Thank you for lending me your brain power. I hope to repay the favor one day.

A most special thank you to each member of the Peter Leeds team. Tammy, Jeremy, Roman, Lisa, Matt: You have each taken turns making me sound good, look sharp, be smart, and generally stay on track. Thank you for a job well done.

Al Ries and Jack Trout developed many of the concepts related to the marketing strategies of businesses, and I draw on their work for my discussion of them in Chapter 11.

Publisher's Acknowledgments

We're proud of this book; please send us your comments at http://dummies.custhelp.com. For other comments, please contact our Customer Care Department within the U.S. at 877-762-2974, outside the U.S. at 317-572-3993, or fax 317-572-4002.

Some of the people who helped bring this book to market include the following:

Acquisitions, Editorial, and Vertical Websites

Project Editor: Jennifer Moore

Acquisitions Editor: Stacy Kennedy

Copy Editor: Jennifer Moore

Assistant Editor: David Lutton

Editorial Program Coordinator: Joe Niesen

Technical Editor: Erik Falconer

Editorial Managers: Jennifer Ehrlich and Carmen Krikorian

Editorial Assistant: Alexa Koschier

Cover Photos: © Ralf Hettler / iStockphoto

Composition Services

Project Coordinator: Patrick Redmond

Layout and Graphics: Jennifer Creasey, Joyce Haughey

Proofreaders: Lindsay Amones, Bonnie Mikkelson

Indexer: Valerie Haynes Perry

Publishing and Editorial for Consumer Dummies

Kathleen Nebenhaus, Vice President and Executive Publisher

Kristin Ferguson-Wagstaffe, Product Development Director

Ensley Eikenburg, Associate Publisher, Travel

Kelly Regan, Editorial Director, Travel

Publishing for Technology Dummies

Andy Cummings, Vice President and Publisher

Composition Services

Debbie Stailey, Director of Composition Services

Contents at a Glance

Table of Contents

Introduction

- -

Some of the greatest companies started out very small, with their stocks valued at less than five dollars per share. In other words, they started out as what the investment world calls "penny stocks." As those businesses grew in size, many of their shareholders grew in wealth along with the companies.

Few paths to significant and rapid wealth creation are as effective as investing in the right kinds of low-priced penny stocks. Excellent companies, regardless of their size, will always be able to provide their shareholders with impressive investment gains.

With increased opportunity, though, you have increased risks. Many people have been stung by those risks, and subsequently penny stocks have gotten a bad name in some investment circles. In almost all situations in which investors lost money, however, they could have easily avoided the downside if they had only followed the tips and suggestions in this book.

By showing you how to sidestep the risks, I clear the way for investors like you to profit from high-quality penny stocks. I help you find companies that have low debt loads, strong management teams, expanding market share, growing revenues, and game-changing intellectual property.

I wrote *Penny Stocks For Dummies* for two reasons. First, I want to help you — and investors like you — steer clear of the common (and easily avoidable) mistakes in penny stock trading. Second, I want to show you how wonderful it can feel to get in on a great company early and build significant wealth from a small investment as the shares multiply in value many times over.

About This Book

In this book, you get the straight goods, free of any boring theories, complicated strategies, or inane details. In short, I tell you what you need to know to become a successful penny stock trader. Among the topics I cover are:

- ✔ Why penny stocks have a bad reputation among many traders
- ✔ Why avoiding the pitfalls is the first step to major profits

- ✔ How to trade risk-free with no money
- ✔ What the best penny stock investments look like and where you can find them
- ✔ Why proper trading strategies will turn into money in the bank
- ✔ How effective due diligence takes out all the guesswork
- ✔ Why fundamental analysis is the most important step to truly investing well — and in solid companies
- ✔ How technical analysis helps you narrow down your buying opportunities
- ✔ How financial ratios make for better comparisons and, by extension, better investment returns
- ✔ Why an abstract review gives you a major trading advantage

You can zip straight to the sections that interest you. I promise you that will find what you want to know very quickly, and I won't subject you to financial mumbo jumbo or unnecessary details along the way.

Whether you benefit from sidestepping all the junky investments out there or you profit big by finding really excellent (yet still undiscovered) stocks, this book has something for you. And the beauty is that the information you need is just a few page-flips away!

Conventions Used in This Book

To help you navigate this book as you navigate the world of penny stocks, I use the following conventions:

- ✔ *Italic* text highlights new words and defined terms.
- ✔ **Boldfaced** text indicates keywords in bulleted lists.
- ✔ `Monofont` text highlights a web address.

What You're Not to Read

Feel free to skip the sidebars that appear throughout the book; these shaded gray boxes contain interesting info that isn't essential to your understanding of penny stocks. The same goes for any text I mark with the Technical Stuff icon.

Foolish Assumptions

We haven't met, but I bet you've made some assumptions about me. For instance, you probably think that I'm a nerdy financial type and that, because I'm involved in the stock market, I've always been a good investor. Believe me, I really wish that were true. (The part about being a good investor, not the nerdy part).

Well, I've made a few assumptions about you, too. Here they are:

- ✔ You're logical and make decisions quickly.
- ✔ You're willing to take the steps needed to better your situation, and you don't shy away from excitement.
- ✔ Someone you know (possibly you) has invested in penny stocks before — and almost certainly lost money!
- ✔ You're new to investing or have limited experience in trading penny stocks.
- ✔ You have limited funds available to invest and you want to make the most of them.
- ✔ You're willing to accept a little risk in exchange for the potential to have greater returns.
- ✔ You know that many of the best companies started small, and you realize that the shareholders in those companies reaped massive financial rewards.

How This Book Is Organized

If you peeked at the table of contents, you know that I divide this book into four parts. Here's a breakdown of what you find in each one.

Part 1: Getting Started with Penny Stocks

Penny stocks are victims of their own popularity. Because of their potential for great financial gain, they draw many naïve investors who fall for all the hoopla surrounding penny stocks, make rash and ill-informed investment decisions, and end up losing out big-time in the process.

In this part, I set the record straight about many preconceived notions surrounding penny stocks. I tell you how the tiny shares are defined and help you see the ways in which they're different than (and often superior to) stocks from larger companies.

Part II: Research and Investment Strategies

Anyone who has had sustained success in any aspect of life knows that a big part of that success comes from practice. For example, world-class tennis players don't just pick up their racquets and start beating their opponents with no preparation. Before they ever step on a court to play a match, they spend hours honing their strokes and working on their strategies.

In this part, I tell you how you can develop your own investing strokes and strategies before you spend even a single penny on low-priced stocks. I also reveal the best ways to do effective research and show you how to interpret your findings to uncover those life-changing investments.

Part III: Trading Penny Stocks

With penny stocks, it all comes down to buying shares that multiply in value. In this part I clue you in on how you can capture some exciting gains by using important trading methodologies and effective (yet simple) fundamental analysis techniques. Taking your analysis a step farther, you can use financial ratios and an abstract review to eliminate almost all the guesswork and turn a small investment into a tidy profit. I also explain why most technical analysis doesn't work with penny stocks, but that the aspects that are useful often reveal significant short-term profit opportunities.

Part IV: The Part of Tens

Readers have come to expect short and snappy top-ten lists at the end of every For Dummies guide. So as not to disappoint you, I offer three such lists of my own: ten rapid result tactics that should instantly improve your trading; ten key considerations when considering investing in any company; and ten trading truths that will put you in a much better investing position.

Icons Used in This Book

To make this book even easier to read, I include a few icons to highlight certain types of information.

Abide by these quick points to save yourself time and hassle.

This icon identifies fundamental points that focus on basic rules and concepts of trading low-priced shares.

Heed these warnings to protect yourself from some of the pitfalls surrounding penny stocks.

You can easily skip over the content flagged by these icons without missing out on any benefits the book provides. However, for those who really want to know everything, give these a look.

Where to Go from Here

This book is set up so you can get right to the information you want. By all means, start at the very beginning if you feel like it, but if you're like most people and have only so much time to devote to investing, flip right to the sections that interest you.

Decide what approach works best for you, and use this as a reference for anything you could possibly want to know about penny stocks. The table of contents and the index will help with that, or just visit the specific parts that will provide you with the most benefit.

Part I

getting started with **penny stocks**

In this part . . .

✔ Find out what characteristics distinguish penny stocks from other types of shares.

✔ Uncover the truth about common assumptions — both positive and negative — about low-priced shares.

✔ Get the scoop on which stock markets are the best for penny stock investors.

✔ Examine the differences between investments of various sizes.

✔ Become acquainted with events that can impact a company and its shares.

✔ Learn how to protect yourself from scams and low-quality companies.

Chapter 1

Getting to Know Penny Stocks

• •

• •

*P*enny stocks are shares of companies that trade at low prices — typically anywhere from one cent to five dollars per share. The low-priced shares are usually associated with very small companies that are just getting started. When the companies grow, the value of their shares increases, making money for anyone who owns the stock.

I just described the upside of trading in penny stocks, and it's this potential for making money that explains the growing popularity of this type of investment vehicle. Of course, not all small companies thrive or even stay in business — which brings me to the downside of penny stocks: Should the company shrink, or run into any number of other problems that I describe later in this chapter, stockholder shares will decrease in value, leaving investors with a loss.

Many investors are drawn to penny stocks because they find the upside compelling. They're intrigued by the idea of investing in a tiny company in its early stages and watching that money grow along with the company. After all, many companies that started out as penny stocks have gone on to become household names, making their early investors very wealthy in the process. Few other investment vehicles offer the possibility of turning a small amount of cash into a small fortune without even having to work at the company or break a sweat.

To succeed as a penny stock investor, you need to be able to maximize the upside (making money), while minimizing the downside (losing money). Unfortunately, far too many investors treat penny stock trading more like a get-rich-quick scheme or a trip to the casino than they do a legitimate investment strategy. But as I explain in this book, there is a right way to trade penny stocks and a wrong way. Said more directly, there is a profitable way and a costly way. In this book I give you all the information and tools you need to avoid the downside, while benefiting from owning small shares that have the potential to grow exponentially.

The first step to reaping the rewards of penny stock investing is to understand the basics, and the process of gaining that knowledge begins in this chapter. I begin by separating fact from fiction, exposing the truth about penny stocks and letting you know which rumors and innuendos have some basis in reality (spoiler alert: A lot of the negative things that you may have heard about penny stocks are actually true). I also offer a clear definition of penny stocks and fill you in on the ways that they're unique investment vehicles.

A Big, Fat, "Tiny" Penny Stock Summary

Companies usually need to raise money to operate, and the most common way to generate that cash is for them to sell shares of their corporation on the stock market. If they need more money at a later time, they can issue even more shares (see Chapter 3 for details on this process). The company gets money to operate; in exchange, the shareholders get part or all of the company.

The shareholders will see the value of their investment in the company change based on what the share price does. If the company does well and grows, the shares typically increase in value. But if the business shrinks or runs into detrimental issues such as weak sales numbers, lawsuits, or new competitors, its shares will likely decrease in value.

Although the aim for most companies is to get bigger and bigger, the majority of them start out very small, with only a handful of employees or a total company value of a couple million dollars or less. Their shares may trade for a few dollars or even pennies. However, those penny stocks may become worth much more if the companies grow. If everything goes according to plan, the stock won't actually be a "penny" stock for long, and both the value of the shares and your investment in them will be dramatically higher.

A lot of quality companies trade as penny stocks and many of these will perform very well for their investors. Of course, because share price is a reflection of perceived value, many downright awful companies with no prospects, or even on the verge of bankruptcy, trade as penny stocks as well.

Unfortunately, the number of low-quality companies outweighs the good ones. In fact, only 5 percent of penny stocks I review pass my analysis. Combined with the propensity for promoters and shady characters to provide misleading information (more on the shadowy side in a bit), penny stocks have earned a bad name.

Some of the negative connotations surrounding penny stocks suggest that they are

- ✓ **Hard to buy and sell:** This is true for lightly traded shares on many of the penny stock markets. You won't have this problem if you stick to shares trading on the better stock exchanges, which I detail in Chapter 3.

- ✓ **Subject to scams:** Unfortunately, penny stocks are the focus of many scam artists because of the opportunity to make money by manipulating the prices of the underlying shares. Dishonest promoters try to push up the prices of the penny stocks they own by tricking unsuspecting investors through free newsletters and message boards.

- ✓ **Based on low-quality companies:** The majority of penny stock companies are not strong — and that's putting it kindly. The key is to avoid those lackluster stocks and instead find the top 5 percent that will be extremely profitable. This book details how you can do exactly that.

- ✓ **Very volatile:** Penny stocks are volatile, but that's part of their appeal. Although such volatility isn't appropriate for everyone, low-priced shares can move quickly and significantly, which can generate profit potential that isn't available elsewhere.

You need to be aware of the negative connotations surrounding penny stocks. That awareness, combined with appropriate knowledge, will enable you to sidestep the dangers while remaining open to all the opportunities that low-priced shares can provide.

Defining Penny Stocks

No universally accepted definition of the term *penny stock* exists. Instead, folks in the financial sector categorize these low-priced shares in a variety ways, depending on who is doing the defining and why. What one trader may consider a penny stock may not qualify as such under another person's definition.

In the following sections I walk you through the three major ways that investors typically distinguish penny stocks from their more expensive counterparts.

Price per share

Price per share is the most common (and simplest) criteria for identifying penny stocks. Many people apply the tag to any shares trading at one dollar or less. For others, the price range includes stocks trading as high as three or even five dollars per share.

The closest definition to actually being "official" is that of the Securities and Exchange Commission (SEC), which identifies shares trading at five dollars or less as a penny stock. Following the SEC's lead, almost all stockbrokers and professional investors have adopted the same criteria, and I have as well. So, for the purposes of this book, I consider penny stocks to be any shares that trade at five dollars or less.

The primary drawback with using this definition is that price fluctuations can move the stock below and above the threshold level. What started out as a penny stock in the morning could trade above the threshold price at noon and then fall back below it an hour later.

Market capitalization

Market capitalization (*market cap,* for short), refers to the total value of a company, which is derived by multiplying the total number of shares available by the price per share. For example, if a company has two million shares valued at two dollars each, the market cap of the company is four million dollars. Some investors like to consider companies with market caps of less than $10 million to be penny stocks, while others use a cutoff point of $25 million, or $100 million, or an even great number.

Using market capitalization to define penny stocks is more involved than simply looking at the price per share. Also, because the underlying share prices and the total market cap continually change, it can make for more work when identifying penny stocks. Using market cap may also lead to situations in which a company trading at one cent per share isn't considered a penny stock (due to the company having an extraordinarily large number of shares outstanding).

Most investors don't use market capitalization as a method to define penny stocks. However, some prefer to focus their holdings on companies of a certain size for the implied stability that comes with larger businesses, and in such a case they may find the market capitalization approach helpful.

A Penny Stock in Their Past

Many people are surprised to find out just how many successful companies have been considered penny stocks at some point in their past.

Penny stocks have included the Ford Motor Company, Sirius satellite radio, American Airlines, Nokia, Lucent Alcatel, and many other recognizable names. In other words, these low-priced shares aren't necessarily the junky companies you may have been led to believe!

Stock market

Some choose to label all companies trading on lower-quality stock markets (see Chapter 3 for details) with the penny stock moniker. For example, any company listed on the Pink Sheets may be considered a penny stock, even if its shares are trading at $90 each and its market cap is in the billions.

Mix and match

In some cases, investors may combine more than one of the previous criteria when defining a penny stock. For example, they may decide that any company trading on the Pink Sheets *and* with a share price of less than two dollars is a penny stock.

Why does it matter?

You may wonder why the definition of penny stock matters at all. For most people, and in most cases, it doesn't. However, the distinction can have significant implications in certain circumstances:

- ✔ **Broker restrictions and fees:** Stockbrokers often have special rules for low-priced shares. Some don't allow their customers to purchase any penny stocks, while others charge much higher commissions for penny stock trades. Because most brokers define penny stocks as shares trading at five dollars or less, these parameters have implications on a significant number of investments.

- ✔ **Option eligibility:** Certain shares are considered "option eligible" by the stock exchanges and stockbrokers. The criteria is usually based on a share price of at least five dollars, and it allows trading on margin (buying the stock with borrowed money), short selling (selling the shares and then buying them back later), and options trading in the particular company. Flip to Chapter 6 to find out more about these concepts.

✓ **Portfolio balancing:** An individual investor, or a professional such as a hedge fund trader or mutual fund manager, may only want a certain portion of her total portfolio to be in more speculative or volatile shares such as penny stocks. If she realizes that she has too much or too little of a percentage in one investment size or type, she will rebalance her holdings through the appropriate trades. Of course, she needs to have a criterion for what constitutes a low-priced share in order to manage her holdings.

✓ **Listing requirements:** The stock exchanges have very specific requirements for any company whose shares are traded on them. Those requirements vary from one exchange to the next and generally get more demanding the better the exchange. Some of the criteria involve share price and market cap, and they typically exclude penny stocks. Penny stocks usually start trading on lower-level exchanges with easier parameters for inclusion. (I discuss the various stock exchanges for penny stocks in Chapter 3.)

Comparing Penny Stocks to Their Blue-Chip Cousins

Many differences exist between penny stocks and higher-priced shares. By being aware of how smaller companies and their lower-priced shares behave, you can position yourself in the right kinds of companies and make better trading decisions. More important, you'll have an idea of whether this type of investment is for you.

Investors typically organize stocks into the following categories:

✓ **Large cap companies, also known as blue-chip stocks:** Any company whose shares value them at $5 billion or more are known as *large capitalization companies,* or *large caps* for short. Some investors use the value of $10 billion as criterion for the large cap criteria moniker while others use different criteria.

Shares of the biggest companies, which are valued at billions of dollars, are known as *blue-chip stocks.* Many of these companies are household names, such as IBM, McDonald's, Disney, and Exxon, and trade on the New York Stock Exchange (NYSE) or on other major stock markets (see Chapter 3 for details on the various markets).

Educating the market

Imagine standing before a huge group of people who don't like live music. They've had bad experiences at concerts before, whether because the speakers were too loud, the venue had poor acoustics, or they just picked the wrong band.

But you know that some live music can be great. You know that they will love concerts if they just attend the right ones. Now imagine that it's your job to convince them to give concerts another try. Substitute the word *concert* with *penny stocks*, and you get a sense of what I face when trying to persuade people that trading in penny stocks can be a positive investment experience.

Many people have invested in penny stocks at some point. Almost all of them have lost money on those shares, and they've let their negative experiences with low-quality penny stocks scare them away. However, to conclude that penny stocks are foolish investments means that people aren't taking responsibility for the mistakes they've made. They have painted the entire investment class with one brush just because of their singular experience, but that's like assuming all live concerts are bad just because you picked a bad seat at the only concert you ever attended.

My first task when speaking about penny stocks is to explain that there is a difference between low- and high-quality penny stocks. After I address the negative connotations surrounding the topic and explain how easy it is to avoid the pitfalls and junk, people always become more interested.

Low-quality penny stocks traded in the wrong ways are foolish investments. High-quality companies trading for pennies at the right time, in my opinion, are far and away the best investment choice available.

The good news is that everything you need to know to trade penny stocks successfully is included in this very book. I have no doubt that you will become a phenomenal investor in low-priced shares if you follow the suggestions in this book.

However, my biggest hope is that you go a step farther and help protect your friends and family from getting burned by the wrong kinds of penny stocks. They'll never know that you saved them thousands. They'll never thank you. But isn't that the best kind of reward?

- ✔ **Mid cap companies:** The term *mid cap* is short for *middle capitalization*, but you'll probably never hear the long version of the name. These companies are typically valued between $500 million and $5 billion, but again this depends on who is providing the definition.

- ✔ **Small cap corporations:** These companies have total values of between $50 million and $500 million.

- ✔ **Micro caps, also known as penny stocks:** Any company whose total value is less than $50 million is considered a *micro cap.* Because penny stocks typically represent smaller, growing corporations, they're often in the micro cap category. This category of stocks reacts to situations that are unique and material to it, even when the same events would have little impact on much larger companies.

Although micro caps are much like blue-chip shares, only smaller, they play by their own set of valuation and price behavior rules. To become consistently successful trading penny stocks, you need to understand this concept and the specific ways in which these micro cap shares behave.

Volatility and speed

In terms of percentage of the share price, penny stock shares make greater moves, and more quickly, than their better-capitalized counterparts. Several factors cause faster and larger price changes:

- **Starting from lower prices:** The lower the price of the shares, the greater any moves in them will be, proportionately. If a penny stock increases from 20¢ to 30¢, that's a 50 percent gain. The same ten-cent jump in a stock priced at ten dollars per share only represents an increase of 1 percent.

- **Earlier phase of corporate life cycle:** When a company is new, its potential is wide open. It may end up at point A or point Z, or anywhere in between. Any event or shift in the mind-set of investors can result in major changes in expectations for the company's future. With any early shift in that anticipation comes significant adjustments to what investors are expecting from it, and those adjustments directly impact the share price.

- **Thinly traded:** As penny stocks are generally traded by fewer people, and in smaller amounts, a large buy or sell order can move the price significantly. If there is a limited supply of shares for sale at lower prices, any significant buying demand may push the price up into higher prices.

- **Changes in speculation and potential:** The prices of penny stock shares have a much greater basis in speculation and potential. In other words, what a company theoretically "could" do has a lot more value when it is just getting started or is in the early phase of its life cycle. Unlike quarterly financial reports, or gradually improving client lists, for example, massive shifts in speculation can occur quickly and have a dramatic impact on the potential for the underlying company and its share price.

- **Fewer, more meaningful events:** Newer and smaller companies typically experience fewer major events. When they do have something to report, such as a new client win or a patent approval, that event will have a proportionately greater impact on the company.

To invest in penny stocks well, you need to understand the reasons behind the larger, and more rapid, price moves. Proper knowledge leads to improved anticipation, clarity, and wiser trading choices.

Safety and risk

Most people in the financial world consider larger companies to be safer investments, and for the most part they are correct. Because companies tend to grow in size as they become successful (as expressed by a higher share price and larger market cap), the bigger they get, usually the more stable their position. In contrast, newer, smaller, or less-successful companies generally see their stock trading for low prices. From this perspective, penny stocks are typically riskier or lower-quality investments than larger companies.

The risk and perceived lack of safety associated with penny stocks are what create the opportunities for penny stock investors to reap substantial rewards. If they weren't risky, penny stocks wouldn't trade as penny stocks at all, but would instead be priced at much higher levels.

Investors who can identify and accept areas of concern for a company, or anticipate improvements in those risk factors, can find numerous values among low-priced shares.

Opportunity exists for those penny stock investors who can

- ✔ **Accept the risk.** As long as you're aware of the greater perceived risk and are willing to accept it in exchange for the potential of greater returns, you can find numerous opportunities among penny stocks.

- ✔ **Find overblown risk perceptions.** When investors are over-reacting to a company's risk factors, they may greatly undervalue the shares. Investors who recognize that the concerns are overblown can accumulate shares at very low prices. For example, if a drug development company with 12 products fails to get FDA approval for one of them, the shares often collapse in response. But investors who remember that the company has another 11 drugs in development will scoop up the shares for a fraction of what they're actually worth.

- ✔ **Identify shrinking degrees of risk.** Often the risk factors keeping the shares of a company down eventually abate or change for the better. Usually there is a delay of weeks or months between when circumstances improve for the company and the resulting share price increases. That delay represents an opportunity for investors to invest in a penny stock that's being held down by perceived risk that's no longer a factor.

Investor following and visibility

Larger companies generally trade on bigger stock exchanges (I tell you all about stock exchanges in Chapter 3). Those companies have more investors, a greater number of people following their shares, and larger amounts invested in them.

And so, when a massive company trading on the New York Stock Exchange needs to raise money, it generally doesn't have a problem getting that cash. Given its high level of visibility among investors and its large following of institutional investors and analysts, it is able to generate the funds it requires.

Penny stock companies, on the other hand, have far fewer involved parties and are usually listed on lower-quality stock exchanges with easier listing requirements and fewer serious investors. When they need to raise money, they often have to sell their concept first. They need to convince individuals, banks, and other creditors that they represent a good investment. Part of the job of a tiny company — and a potential distraction to operations — invariably becomes generating investor interest and expanding its base of shareholders. Insiders and key executives often front a major portion of any money a penny stock company needs; they know the potential the business holds, but the company doesn't have enough of a following or history of operations to generate the money from a bank or outside investors.

Any penny stock has the responsibility to increase the visibility of its shares and its company. As it becomes more successful at this task, whether by listing on a more widely followed stock market or expanding the number of shareholders who are invested in it, the company may find that the price of its shares increases, perhaps even to the point where it no longer qualifies as a penny stock.

Larger stones take more force to move

The bigger something is, the more effort it will require to move or lift. This is not only true in the physical world, but in the stock market as well.

Multibillion-dollar corporations might encounter issues that they barely even notice, while those same events could derail or dramatically impact any micro cap company. While small events don't tend to affect the prospects or direction of a blue-chip stock, everything matters when a company is new, tiny, or more vulnerable.

Larger corporations are also more diversified. They may have several business lines, thousands of customers, offices in dozens of countries, and a legal team capable of intimidating even the fiercest plaintiff. Penny stocks, on the other hand, often have a select few clients and revenue streams, so while any advances can really increase the share price, they're also significantly more vulnerable to any losses or lack of improvement.

In the following sections, I describe some types of events that can dramatically affect penny stocks but that may not be significant to large cap companies.

The bigger a company becomes, such events will have proportionately less of an impact on the shares. Until that point, however, many issues will be of greater importance to penny stocks than mid cap and large cap companies. Although this vulnerability can represent massive downside potential if things go against the smaller business, it also clears the way for dramatic and lasting upside price gains when events play out as hoped.

Lawsuits

Besides being very costly and a distraction for the executives and shareholders alike, the outcome of a lawsuit can have a major impact on a small company.

Suits brought against a penny stock are usually a massive financial drain and, if the company loses, can mean lights out. When the penny stock is the one launching the suit, the action may demonstrate the company's commitment to defending its products or patents through the courts; and if it comes out in the end with a good settlement or a victory, the results may be very beneficial. This assumes that it has the funds to see the litigation to the end.

Larger corporations devote a smaller percentage of their income to pay legal bills and have the financial luxury and insulation to launch or defend numerous court battles as they see fit.

Regulatory approvals or denials

FDA approval, a trademark grant, or a regulatory body award will have a much more significant impact on the share price of smaller companies. With some single-product corporations, a clearance or allowance is everything — without it, they go out of business; with it, they could change the world. On the other hand, a large cap corporation with 55 patents may not see a major impact when it wins its 56th patent.

Employee poaching or brain drain

Losing key employees is a very common problem for penny stock companies, especially among specialized technology companies. Bigger nanotech corporations, for example, often lure employees away from smaller nanotech businesses. The large cap companies can pay more and head-hunt more aggressively, while struggling and new penny stocks have a tough time thwarting these efforts. In some cases, a larger company will buy an entire smaller company for the sole purpose of gaining the employees.

Intellectual property events

The development and subsequent legal defense of trademarks, patents, and other intellectual property is very costly and time consuming, but such protections can help tiny companies level the playing field. Being granted the right patent can suddenly make a $500 billion corporation stop certain activities, pay royalties, or negotiate various aspects of its business. As such, intellectual property awards can have proportionately more impact on the shares of a smaller company.

Financial results

Penny stocks are often so new and small that the financial results demonstrate a lot more than just the numbers. Implied within the data is the validity of the product, the demand among customers, the growth trend, and client retention levels. When a micro cap company says that its sales increased by 20 percent, it's also saying that its product or service has value and that more customers are buying or coming back for more. Financial results early in a company's life cycle can reveal a lot more in terms of upside potential for the share price — and early viability of the business concept — than those released after years of operations.

Customer changes

When a company has fewer customers, winning or losing one will have more impact. Customer changes could be really great (such as a penny stock going from two to three big clients), or very detrimental to the company and its stock price (such as losing one of only two big clients).

Changes in competitors

When a penny stock loses a competitor, it may be able to pick up the market share that has become available as a result, and that benefit may be very significant for a small company. When that same penny stock sees new (and sometimes massive) competition enter its space, its best option is often to get bought out or taken over (see Chapter 3 for details), unless the company has the patents and trademarks it needs to defend itself and its sales channels.

Chapter 2

Deciding If Penny Stocks Are Right for You

In This Chapter

▶ Finding out why penny stocks are so popular

▶ Understanding the big business of tiny companies

▶ Getting a grip on the bad press surrounding low-priced shares

▶ Determining whether penny stocks are right for you

*Y*ou've probably heard both sides of the argument about the value of trading penny stocks. Many investors are afraid of penny stocks because of their risk, the low quality of the companies, and the potential for fraud and price manipulation. Others point out that penny stock trading is one of the few channels in which a small amount of money has the potential to turn into significant wealth so quickly.

The truth happens to fall between these extremes. Sure, any information that's available about the stocks is less reliable, and the underlying company may be newer and more risky than bigger, more established stocks. But compared to bigger and more established stocks, that company may provide much greater returns as it grows.

You may have heard numerous horror stories about penny stocks, and get just as many warnings about them from professionals, friends, and family members. Yet, at the end of the day, you may decide to invest in these speculative shares anyway. That investment could be a big mistake, but if you get involved in fundamentally solid penny stocks by using the methods I detail throughout this book, you could also be making a very profitable move.

In this chapter, I explore the growing popularity of penny stocks. I also reveal the big business of tiny stocks and detail the numerous negative connotations surrounding low-priced shares. My aim in providing you with all this information is to help you decide if penny stocks are appropriate investment vehicle for you.

Gauging the Popularity of Penny Stocks

As the world goes increasingly digital, researchers can more easily track people's interests based on their online activity. And although I don't find the news surprising, data from top sources indicates that people's interest in penny stocks is on the rise.

The term "penny stocks" is one of the most popular financial queries on the major search engines, topping such phrases as "stock pick," "stock quote," "New York Stock Exchange," "NYSE," and "stock-broker." Such searches represent millions of people worldwide actively looking for tips or guidance about low-priced shares, and that broad-based interest is growing.

I offer some reasons for the increasing interest in penny stocks in the following sections.

A high risk/reward ratio

You've heard the old adage, "the higher the risk, the higher the reward." This saying is especially apt when it comes to penny stocks. Investing in speculative shares is always very risky.

However, you can dramatically reduce your risk in penny stocks — while maintaining your higher reward potential — by abiding by the various concepts I detail in this book.

I've personally lost $15,000 on a penny stock (risk), but I have also turned $30,000 into $500,000 (reward). After having traded all types of investments, from real estate to options and from currencies to derivatives, I've never found a more lucrative or reliable method for building wealth than buying fundamentally solid penny stocks.

The risk-reward ratio increases as you move down the list of these investment vehicles:

- **Hiding money under your mattress:** Barring a house fire, you won't lose anything with this savings strategy, but you won't gain anything, either. Of course, even cash stuffed in your pillow will decrease in value due to inflation, because the purchasing power of each dollar will diminish.

- **Certificates of Deposit (CDs):** These investment vehicles have very low risk, but you get paid very minimally for the security of it. An investment of $100 may be worth only $102 a year later.

✔ **Bonds:** Government or corporate bonds expose you to minimal risk but have very low payouts. If you invest in bonds issued by riskier countries or companies, you increase the possibility of losing your money.

✔ **Real estate:** Property ownership has generally been profitable over time in most areas. However, the risk-reward ratio depends greatly on the area and your timing. Florida condo ownership was very profitable for a long time — until home prices collapsed and many people lost their shirts. Real estate investments also entail significant carry costs (property tax, insurance, condo fees), and when you sell you face numerous disposition fees (real estate agent commissions, land transfer tax).

✔ **Blue-chip stocks:** Big name companies are generally considered to be safe investments, but they can drop in value and very often do. Although blue chips generally provide better returns than CDs or bonds, they can also go down in price, and so the potential for greater returns comes hand in hand with increased risk.

✔ **Midrange and small cap stocks:** These investment vehicles are riskier than blue-chip stocks and safer than penny stocks, making them a good option for people who aren't quite ready to trade very small, highly speculative companies associated with penny stocks.

✔ **Penny stocks:** Penny stocks offer the perfect mix of risk and reward for many individuals. You can push the odds of making money strongly in your favor by using the techniques I describe in this book. Plus, penny stocks are easier to understand than complex strategies required for options trading and they have the potential for bigger returns from smaller investments than other investment types.

✔ **Options and derivatives:** These extremely risky investment vehicles are only appropriate for complex hedging strategies. If you don't understand what I mean by "complex hedging strategies," then you shouldn't trade options.

I've made money from each of these investment vehicles and I've also lost money from most of them. If you seek absolute safety for each dollar you invest, then penny stocks aren't appropriate for you. However, if you want to take on some risk in the hopes of creating some more money from your portfolio, you've come to the right place.

Limited funds

Of the many reasons why an individual may be attracted to penny stocks, the most popular is that the investor has limited funds.

Whether you have only a few hundred, or a couple thousand, dollars to invest, low-priced shares afford you an opportunity to turn that small amount of cash into something much more substantial.

Investors with small amounts of start-up cash also tend to be more interested in taking a shot at something, almost like they're buying a lottery ticket, partially because they feel that they don't have a lot to lose. This is precisely the wrong approach, especially if you have limited funds.

I always suggest that investors with limited funds, or even those with no funds at all, start off by paper trading, as I detail in Chapter 5. Only after you discover how to find penny stocks of great fundamental quality, and to trade them well, should you venture into using your limited amount of real money.

The upside of investing well, especially with small amounts of starting cash, is that it can grow quickly. Instead of taking a chance because you have a limited amount of money, I suggest that you turn it into a more significant amount by investing well!

Risky misconceptions

Unfortunately, traders are prone to a number of misconceptions about penny stocks, many of which can expose them to unnecessary risk:

- **They can't fall much lower.** If a stock falls to pennies from several dollars or more, some investors wrongly believe that the shares can't go much lower. Don't make the mistake of comparing any stock to where it was before, because the stock has no memory, and past levels have no bearing as to where it may go from here. For example, even a stock that fell 99 percent — from $5 to 5¢ — can go a lot lower, and might just be on its way to 0.

- **It's not a big investment.** If you invest $500 in a stock rather than $5,000, you're risking less money (or, to use investment lingo, your downside is limited to $500). But the size of your downside has no bearing on whether the underlying shares are a good investment. If your reasoning is that you didn't invest a lot, you're gambling. If you buy a stock because it has an outstanding management team, low debt load, and expanding market share, you're investing.

- **The downside is smaller than on blue-chip stocks.** Just because penny stocks are closer to zero than large blue-chip stocks or more expensive shares, it doesn't mean that they are less risky. A $455 stock can go to 0. A 4¢-penny stock can go to 0. In either case, you can lose 100 percent of your investment.

My aim in addressing these risky assumptions is to help you approach penny stocks in the most knowledgeable, and therefore most profitable, way. Every dollar put into the market is at risk, and by being fully aware of that risk, you are in a better position to make wise trading choices.

Taking Stock of the Big Business of Penny Stocks

Small businesses are the source of the majority of economic growth in the United States, and this is probably true in most nations worldwide. In addition, the small-business sector is America's largest employer.

When small businesses need to raise capital, they often go public by listing stock on the market (I describe this process in Chapter 3). Some of these companies are tiny, or just getting started, and their value is still low, so they often trade as penny stocks. As such, penny stocks are a big part of the economy.

In addition to making significant contributions to the economy, some penny stock companies eventually grow up and become huge corporations with hundreds of employees and share prices of $10 or $50 or more. Most people don't realize that many corporations that used to be penny stocks helped build the economy from the bottom.

You're not alone

Buying penny stocks isn't as unusual of a practice as you may think. You may not realize all the people around you who have invested in penny stocks.

The main reason that you don't hear about people investing in penny stocks is that most novice or new penny stock investors lose money. They don't want to talk about the $1,000 they threw away, and so they sweep their mistakes under the rug.

You will hear, or course, from the office jerk who is making money on a penny stock. And you probably heard about it yesterday, and will again tomorrow.

Despite the taboo nature of the subject among investors who have been burned, a quiet and significant army of penny stock traders is busy building personal wealth through these low-cost shares.

Next time you're at a wedding reception, family reunion, or office party, bring up the topic of investing. See if you can find people who will admit to trading penny stocks. You will certainly find a few, and probably more than you would expect. My guess is that many of them lost money.

Room to grow

In addition to the growing interest in penny stocks, many of the underlying companies are also expanding, making the economic footprint of smaller corporations more significant.

A small company can grow in a variety of ways, including through

- ✓ **Market share:** A growing market share is a great indicator for the success of the underlying company. If that market share is being taken from direct competitors, a growing market can be an even better sign. Keep in mind, though, that a growing market share may not show up right away in the earnings or share price of a penny stock company.

- ✓ **Revenues/sales:** Known as the *top line number* because it's displayed on the first line of the income statement, the revenues (sometimes called *sales*) shows you exactly how much money a penny stock is bringing in by selling their product or service.

- ✓ **Employees:** Growth in employees sometimes demonstrates an increased focus on capturing more sales. Other times it shows that the company is requiring a greater workforce to meet the increased demands of its customers. In either case, as a company grows, so will its headcount.

- ✓ **Mergers, acquisitions, and amalgamations:** When two or three companies merge into one, or they are bought out by a bigger corporation, a 10¢-penny stock can quickly increase in value. Of course, the original business model of the smaller company will be significantly changed. These events are also quite costly at first, and thus place an additional expense on the corporation. As well, keep in mind that such events are not always great for investors because, while the company may be bigger and worth more, the original shareholders may be given approximately equivalent value in the new corporation (for example, shareholders in the smaller company may get one share of the new company for every eight shares of the old one).

- ✓ **Recurring billing:** You can easily analyze the growth in penny stocks that derive revenues from recurring billing and subscription fees. Track the number of recurring billing customers to have a clear representation of the underlying growth and upcoming revenues.

> ✔ **Average order size:** When the average order size per customer doubles, total revenues should theoretically double as well.

Growth is the biggest indicator of potential increases in the prices of penny stocks. If a company is enjoying higher revenues, hiring more workers, or fulfilling larger average order sizes, you can anticipate that the share price may perform very well.

Making Sense of What You've Heard (Much of Which Is True!)

You know that penny stock investing is risky. You've probably heard some pretty scary stories about scam artists and investment dollars disappearing overnight. Although investing well in fundamentally solid penny stocks can be very lucrative, the unfortunate fact is that many of the negative things that you've heard about penny stocks are all too real.

Whether you've heard about an elderly widow being swindled out of her life's savings by some con artist over the phone, or some 14-year-old child running a pump-and-dump scheme out of his mother's basement, such awful stories have some basis in reality. By recognizing this fact, you will be able to sidestep potential pitfalls much more easily.

Penny stocks represent low-quality companies

Stocks rise in value when a company does well and fall in value when a company does poorly. Therefore, more successful companies typically have higher share prices, while the majority of troubled companies become penny stocks, if they aren't trading at those levels already.

When a penny stock company does really well, its shares tend to move higher and eventually may rise above five dollars per share. And as soon as the price rises above five dollars, the stock is no longer considered a penny stock. As a consequence, the universe of penny stocks is made up of only the companies that have not yet done well enough to rise above penny stock territory. The result is that penny stocks are lower-quality companies, and lower-quality companies tend to be penny stocks.

If you want to play . . .

If you want to play in the universe of penny stocks, you will need to have at least two characteristics:

- ✓ **A good filter.** The better you are at screening out the lower-caliber companies, and the more effective you are at finding the up-and-coming corporations, the more impressive your results will be.

- ✓ **A strong stomach.** You need to be able to handle the higher volatility and potential downside if you're going to be involved with penny stocks.

You may not have a good filter at first. You may not have a strong stomach when you start out. However, you can gain these attributes over time in direct proportion to how involved you become with trading speculative, low-priced shares.

Penny stocks are subject to price manipulation scams

Because penny stocks are more thinly traded, and prices are much lower per share, they tend to be easy targets for price manipulation. They also tend to represent lower-quality companies and trade on markets with fewer manipulation controls and governmental oversight.

Pump-and-dump artists may drive up the shares of near bankrupt companies through their free online newsletter, only to take their profits and walk away to let the stock crash back down. Dishonest promoters may paint a very weak company in a positive light, a process called *putting lipstick on a pig*.

In any case, the prices of shares may rise well above what they are realistically worth. This price manipulation puts investors (who haven't done proper due diligence) at significant risk, because shares always return to their appropriate valuations. The good news is that you can avoid these types of price manipulation pitfalls pretty easily by following the guidance I offer in Chapter 4.

Trading penny stocks is a game of chance

For some investors, penny stock investing can be like a playing a one-armed bandit at the casino or buying a lottery ticket. Such investors have resigned themselves to the fact that they are taking a chance on a big gain, but will probably lose. The house odds are stacked against them.

But traders who perform proper due diligence never consider penny stock investing like gambling. They only invest their money when the "odds" are stacked in their favor. They have a clear understanding of which penny stocks to avoid, and which are likely to increase in price, and why, and when.

Whether or not penny stock trading is like playing at the casino depends on how you approach your trades.

Making a Fast Million . . . Not!

The number-one reason people get involved in penny stocks is to get rich quick. They have a few hundred dollars, which they need to turn into several million before the weekend so they can buy a yacht and pay their telephone bill.

The likelihood of getting rich quickly from penny stocks is slim (although it is possible). My experience has shown me that those who want to get rich quickly never do. Those who focus on investing well, and perform their own due diligence, tend to do dramatically better.

 Enjoy the process, and you will come much closer to reaching your end goal. Focus on the end goal alone and you will never reach it. Like the turtle taught us when he raced the hare, slow and steady wins the race.

Penny stocks appeal to the impatient

I am an impatient investor. Perhaps that's why I was drawn to penny stocks myself. In fact, a significant proportion of investors who follow me, as well as those who seek out low-priced shares through other channels, tend to embrace the volatility of the underlying shares. The potential to make significant moves very rapidly appeals to them, even as it exposes them to equivalent downside risks.

While impatience may be the reason why many investors seek out penny stocks, this character trait can cause investment problems. Impatient investors may sell shares at inopportune times, such as just before the stock begins reflecting stronger operational results. They may jump from investment to investment in a constant hunt for profits, which can lead to many poor trading choices (not to mention excessive brokerage commission fees).

To succeed with penny stocks, you need to substitute contemplation for impatience. Give the underlying company time to let its business plan play out. As long as it's making progress, however slow, and the reasons you got involved with it in the first place still hold true, let the shares gradually reflect the improving operational results.

Keep in mind that the slower and more gradual the move up, the more sustainable the higher prices will be. Rapid and sudden price spikes typically don't last.

The greatest gains in penny stocks come over years, not days. Shares that balloon from 5¢ to $5 only do so over the course of longer time frames, and one winner of this magnitude will trump all the 5 percent and 20 percent profits you may see from decades of trading. But only patient investors have the wherewithal to enjoy these kinds of benefits.

Newer investors gravitate to penny stocks

Typically, newer investors are interested in penny stocks because they believe there is less downside. They find smaller and newer companies less intimidating, and they expect such investments to be more attainable and appropriate for their minimal level of trading experience.

Although such reasoning isn't without merit, it can be dangerous. There is just as much downside risk in a 1¢ stock as in a $99 stock (100 percent in each case). Also, finding high-quality penny stocks is much more difficult than uncovering good investments among larger shares, mainly because low-priced stocks have fewer companies of high caliber and a greater percentage of lackluster options.

Despite the aforementioned pitfalls, newer investors may find many benefits to starting off with low-priced shares:

- ✔ **Broader diversity of investments.** Newer investors will learn much more from trading numerous types of investments, rather than just buying one or two. With penny stocks, you can spread a small investment among several stocks.

- ✔ **Greater volatility.** Larger and ostensibly more boring investments will not teach their shareholders much. Penny stocks will display greater volatility and, as such, be more educational for the newer investor.

> ✔ **Price moves happen much more quickly.** Whether your investment is going to go up or down, it will happen over a much shorter time period than with larger stocks. Newer investors tend to be attracted to these faster price moves.

> ✔ **Steeper learning curve.** Newer investors have the most to learn. The combination of greater volatility in penny stocks, rapid price moves, bigger magnitudes of those moves, and the potential to own several different stocks at once, enables inexperienced traders to get up to speed very quickly.

For newer or less-experienced investors to quickly learn about trading, or to develop their own styles to afford them the greatest opportunity to profit, penny stocks may be the perfect outlet.

When I talk about *high-quality penny stocks,* I'm referring to specific criteria that add to the strength of the investment. Among other factors, these include a strong and respected management team, low debt loads, plenty of positive cash flow, positive earnings, growing market share, and low customer attrition rates. Other criteria include having a solid position within an industry with high barriers to entry, strong alliances with top customers, improving financial ratios, and very effective branding and marketing. You can find out more about all these ways to analyze penny stocks when you flip to chapters 8, 9, and 10.

Penny stocks appeal to smaller portfolios

Individuals with less money to invest may only be able to afford a few shares in a larger company. They also may not be too impressed by 5 or 10 percent gains, especially if that adds up to only $50 over the course of an entire year.

Given their situation, many investors with minimal portfolio values opt to not invest at all. Others gravitate to penny stocks.

Investors who believe in the power of penny stocks, yet who do not have a significant portfolio, understand that low-priced speculative shares may be the best way to increase their financial standing. Of course, not all traders who buy and sell penny stocks have a small portfolio, but a significant portion of traders with small portfolios do trade penny stocks.

Being Honest with Yourself: Are Penny Stocks Right For You?

Penny stocks appeal to millions of investors or potential investors. Low-priced shares have probably caught your attention, too, as evidenced by the fact that you are reading this book.

Take a moment to consider if trading penny stocks is actually appropriate for you.

Penny stock investing may be more appropriate for individuals who

- ✔ **Are willing to do the work required.** Investing in speculative shares requires effort on your part. Proper analysis, performing due diligence, and monitoring the shares you purchase, all require work. Investors who put in the time garner the greatest rewards.

- ✔ **Possess a high tolerance for risk.** You will enjoy penny stock investing more if you can tolerate risk and volatility well. If you are going to lose sleep over 20 percent price swings, safer investments may be more appropriate for you.

- ✔ **Intend to invest "play" or risk money.** It would be a mistake to invest money you need for your child's education or to buy groceries in speculative stocks. Penny stocks are best traded with money you have set aside to have some fun with rather than with funds you will need for the important things in life.

- ✔ **Are skeptical of what they read.** The penny stock industry is filled with hidden motivations and misleading reviews of the companies. Don't believe most of what you read, and always perform your own due diligence.

- ✔ **Have realistic expectations.** You might make some good money trading penny stocks. However, if you're expecting to become a millionaire from a $300 investment, you will be disappointed.

- ✔ **Have time available for research and trading.** Unlike day trading or options trading, you won't need to be glued to multiple computer screens all day long. However, the more time you can set aside to research your shares and monitor them, the greater the level of success you will probably enjoy in penny stocks.

If you decide that penny stock investing makes sense for you, I encourage you to keep reading. In the rest of this book I go over every concept I know for investing well in low-priced shares.

Chapter 3

Buying and Selling Penny Stocks

· ·

· ·

Companies list their shares on the stock market (also know as *going public* or *becoming publicly traded*) for a number of reasons, but the most common involves raising money. They need the fundsto facilitate growth in revenues, earnings, and market share. The more effective and successful a company is at creating growth, typically the more valuable its shares become, and the greater the profits produced for the shareholders.

To take full advantage of the potential share price increases, the company needs to make sure that investors can easily buy and sell its stock, and the best way to ensure easy access is to list the stock on a good stock exchange. Penny stocks trade on a few different stock exchanges, and each exchange has unique advantages and disadvantages.

In this chapter, I explain the various stock markets and tell you how investors can gain an understanding of the merits of a company just by knowing which exchange it trades on. I also discuss some of the possible events that can affect publicly traded stocks and how each will affect shareholders.

The Ins and Outs of the Stock Market

When a company goes public, it lists its shares on a stock market, also called an *exchange*. Investors buy and sell those shares through their stockbrokers. Although the New York Stock Exchange (NYSE) is the biggest stock exchange, numerous other exchanges are in business in North America and around the world.

Getting listed on a stock exchange, also known as being *publicly traded,* can have numerous benefits for a company. Likewise, it can be detrimental to lose the listing, or to be on an inappropriate stock exchange.

Penny stocks trade on numerous exchanges, and which exchange can be your first clue as to the quality or legitimacy of the underlying company. Although you'll rarely find a penny stock listed on the high-quality large cap exchanges, such as the New York Stock Exchange (NYSE), certain penny stock markets are vastly superior to the few questionable markets filled with questionable penny stock companies. (Later in this chapter I tell you which exchanges are known for handling quality penny stocks.)

Companies enjoy listing on a reputable stock market because it gives them credibility and the greater visibility for the shares that comes with more popular markets makes it easier to raise funds when required. As well, being listed on a quality exchange usually results in a greater number of investors trading the shares, and this increased activity is typically beneficial to the share price.

Factors influencing what exchange a company lists on

The majority of publicly traded companies, and certainly all the more serious and professional ones, have a listing on a stock exchange. Before they trade, however, or before they work to move from one market to another, they must take several factors into account:

- ✔ **Fees:** The greater the benefit from the listing, the higher the fees will be for listing on the exchange. Companies may pay hundreds of thousands of dollars to be listed initially on the New York Stock Exchange, along with $5,000 to $40,000 in fees annually, depending on the company. A listing on markets with lower visibility costs considerably less.

- ✔ **Listing requirements:** Each exchange has its own requirements for any company interested in being listed. These requirements are not only for initial approval but are also ongoing. For example, some exchanges require that companies maintain minimum share price, minimum number of unique shareholders, or even a certain makeup of their board of directors. If a company fails to meet the requirements, the exchange won't allow the company to list with it in the first place; if the company is already listed on the exchange, the exchange may take action to remove the company from the exchange.

✔ **Corporate obligations:** Publicly traded companies must meet the obligations of the exchange upon which they trade. These obligations include meeting filing deadlines for financial reporting and having a board of directors. They are also required to work with an investor relations firm or individual who answers shareholder questions and performs related tasks. (Investor relations representatives are very important to any penny stock investor, and I explain why in Chapter 6).

✔ **Visibility:** A company should know what level of visibility it is trying to attain and the type of investors it wants to attract. If it wants to attract billions of dollars in investments from mutual funds, it needs to list on one of the major American stock exchanges. If it's a Canadian penny stock, listing on the smaller and more relevant Toronto Venture Exchange may make more sense.

✔ **Appropriate peers:** Certain types of companies gravitate to specific stock markets. For example, the NASDAQ (which stands for National Association of Securities Dealers Automated Quotations, a name nobody ever uses) houses the majority of technology companies, while the American Stock Exchange (AMEX) includes many resource corporations. Although these divisions aren't obligatory, a company may find better results when listed with its peers. I describe each of these stock markets in detail later in this chapter.

Any penny stock needs to weigh the benefits of a stock market listing with the added costs and obligations. A smaller company may need much wider investor visibility but could have difficulty paying the fees or even being approved in the first place.

Fortunately, the sheer number and variety of exchanges usually means that a company can find an appropriate exchange to house its shares. In addition, as a company grows (or shrinks) it can leave one listing tier or stock market for another, to ensure that it strikes a good balance between requirements and benefits.

Many companies, especially volatile penny stocks, have difficulty maintaining their listing requirements. The result can be that they lose that listing, in which case they generally trade on another stock exchange with easier requirements. For example, a company that can't maintain the minimum share price for the NASDAQ may switch to the Over The Counter Bulletin Board (OTC-BB), which also happens to be owned by the same corporation. Before being delisted however, companies have a certain amount of time to meet the requirements and, therefore, maintain their listing.

A who's who of stock exchanges

Not all stock exchanges are created equal, but neither are all stocks. As you can see from the following discussion, each stock market is unique, and companies will find some exchanges more appropriate and effective for their goals than others.

New York Stock Exchange (NYSE)

Also called "the big board," the NYSE is the largest equity market in the world. While some penny stocks do actually trade here, they are few and far between, and they are continually at risk of being dropped off the exchange if they fail to meet certain requirements, such as minimum corporate size, number of unique shareholders, or a minimum per share trading price of one dollar.

Be cautious with any penny stocks listed on the NYSE. They are paying astronomical membership fees, may be dumped onto the lower markets at any time, and should more than likely be listed on another exchange.

American Stock Exchange (AMEX)

The AMEX was bought by the NYSE but continues to operate independently. You will find many penny stock companies listed here, especially in the mining and resource sectors.

The AMEX is a good place to find high-caliber penny stocks, and the listed companies are generally very legitimate. However, due to this market's strictly enforced listing requirements, such as the number of unique shareholders and minimum trading volume requirements, penny stock companies tend to be at greater risk of losing their listing than the larger cap companies listed on the exchange. When this happens, the companies generally seek to be listed on an exchange with easier requirements, such as the OTC-BB (described later in this chapter). Although the shares are almost always successful in obtaining a new listing on a market with easier listing requirements, the transition can sometimes negatively impact the share price. As well, during the transition, the shares may not be available to trade for a few days.

National Association of Securities Dealers Automated Quotations (NASDAQ)

The NASDAQ market is a great place to find mid-range penny stocks (those trading for between three and five dollars per share). The NASDAQ has a heavy concentration of technology companies, both among blue chips and penny stocks, but other types of companies also list on the exchange.

The NASDAQ has different listing tiers, each with different fees, potential exposure to investors, and minimum share price requirements. To be considered for inclusion on the NASDAQ in the first place, depending on which tier the company is interested in attaining, the shares must be trading at two dollars, three dollars, or four dollars per share at a minimum.

Companies must also maintain a one-dollar minimum share price on an ongoing basis, among other requirements. For this reason, you will see some mid-range penny stocks trading for a couple dollars apiece but will find fewer shares trading close to or below the one-dollar threshold.

When a company is delisted from the NASDAQ, it is typically demoted to the OTC-BB, which NASDAQ owns.

Over the Counter Bulletin Board (OTC-BB)

Owned by the NASDAQ, the OTC-BB is a legitimate exchange with easier listing requirements than its parent company, making it a more appropriate venue for smaller companies. For instance, the OTC-BB has no minimum price threshold or other strict regulations and mainly only requires that the company file financial reports regularly.

This structure makes the OTC-BB a wonderful market for penny stocks because it requires the companies to regularly report their financial results. At the same time, those stocks don't need to worry about getting kicked off the exchange just because their shares trade at very low levels. The majority of penny stocks I research and select for my newsletter, and the vast majority of companies with shares trading at less than two dollars apiece, have their home on the OTC-BB.

Be careful not to confuse stocks traded on the Over the Counter Bulletin Board (OTC-BB) with stocks traded over the counter. The former are generally legitimate stocks on a regulated market owned by the NASDAQ. When a stock is traded *over the counter,* the company isn't listed on any stock exchange at all and is instead sold over the phone by promoters.

Selling a stock over the counter is no different than selling your old golf clubs or used car. You simply need to find someone who you can talk into buying it. The price per share is somewhat arbitrary, and the buyer will be unable to sell the stock unless she finds someone else to purchase it directly from her. Don't buy over the counter shares.

OTC Markets (Pink Sheets, QX, QB and others)

The OTC markets aren't actually stock markets at all, and they represent a very inefficient method to trade shares. That's because transactions on the OTC markets are on a one-to-one basis — a buyer is purchasing directly from a seller, not unlike if you are buying your uncle's old golf clubs when you see him over the holidays. This transaction differs from proper stock exchanges, where the price of the shares is based on every buyer and every seller coming together to ensure the best prices.

The OTC markets have different tiers for the companies, with the Pink Sheets having basically no listing requirements whatsoever. The companies listed on "the Pinks" don't even have to report financial data.

Companies that can meet stricter (although still very lax) listing requirements, such as reporting their financials, can trade via the OTCQB. Businesses that meet even higher reporting standards can move up to the OTCQX.

I have always been a very vocal opponent of trading shares that are listed on the Pink Sheets, or other OTC markets such as the QX, or QB. These are not technically stock exchanges, per se, and the companies that list on them are generally of lower quality.

Although the shares of some of these companies can increase or decrease in value, my experience has been that the potential for losses outweighs the opportunity for gains with companies listed on these venues. If you choose to ignore my opinion and buy stocks listed on these markets, proceed with extreme caution.

Note: I want to make one exception to my caution against trading stocks on Pink Sheets. Sometimes high-quality Canadian penny stocks traded on the Toronto Exchange (described in the next section), also list on the Pink Sheets (this process is called *interlisting*). By interlisting their stocks on an American exchange, these Canadian companies eliminate any currency exchange difficulties and so make themselves much more attractive to American investors. In cases where companies are interlisted on Pink Sheets as well as a proper international stock exchange, they are more likely to be legitimate stocks worthy of your consideration.

Toronto Stock Exchange (TSX) and Toronto Venture Exchange (TSX-V)

Numerous Canadian penny stocks trade on exchanges based in Toronto, Canada. The larger companies gravitate to the main Toronto Stock Exchange (TSX), while the rest find a home on the Toronto Venture Exchange (TSX-V).

The listing requirements and reporting regulations on the TSX and TSX-V are legitimate and demanding. Penny stock investors in Canada can find many high-quality companies trading on these markets.

Many investors suggest that penny stocks were "invented" in Canada, or at least rose to popularity there while they generated funds for the thousands of mining exploration companies based on the West Coast. For many years, the Vancouver Stock Exchange housed penny stocks almost exclusively, until it merged with the Toronto Stock Exchange, to become the TSX-V, or Toronto Venture Exchange. Canada's thousands of penny stocks still trade there.

International markets

Most countries around the world have stock exchanges. My philosophy is that if you're unable to find high-quality and profitable investments on your home soil, you probably won't be able to do better by looking farther afield.

If you're not a good investor close to home, nothing about stocks several thousand miles away is going to make you a better investor. Thousands of penny stocks are within close reach of you right now and many of them may represent good value.

Issuing Shares

The main benefit of being listed on a stock market is that it makes raising money easier. A company may start off with an initial public offering (IPO), which sells a portion or all of the corporation to shareholders in exchange for the money they pay for the shares.

Penny stock companies issue shares more frequently than larger corporations because they are

- **Newer:** At the early stages for any company, the funds required need to be generated from investors and supporters. An IPO or subsequent public offering is a common way to accomplish this end.

- **Not making money:** After a company is "off the ground," it is likely to be operating at a loss, at least for the first few years. While the funds to continue aren't coming from its own revenues, the company often looks to investors to buy into its vision.

- **Launching big plans:** Often a penny stock company wants to take some big, aggressive steps. If it wants to buy a factory, acquire another company, or double its sales force, it may need to sell more shares to obtain enough funds.

✔ **Unable to obtain funding:** Small, new companies have a hard time convincing banks to loan them millions of dollars. When taking on loans is too difficult or simply unrealistic, many penny stocks turn to selling shares to generate the funds.

Issuing shares can be a great way for small companies to get up and running. Many of the greatest corporations in America started by issuing shares, and did so again whenever they needed more cash.

Diluting a good thing

If the company needs more money after its initial public offering, it can sell even more shares to generate the funds it needs. Those new shares could represent a portion of the company that wasn't released in the original IPO. Any newly issued shares are sold to investors, and the company uses the money for working capital, or to pay debts, or make an acquisition.

Issuing new shares can decrease the proportionate value of each existing and new share, a result that investors call *dilution*. If a company doubles the total number of shares, the amount of money each share represents drops in half.

Every company needs to balance the ability to raise funds with the concerns caused by dilution.

The most obvious reason for issuing more shares is to raise funds, but companies issue new shares for other reasons, too. For example, companies may use new shares to entice or reward key personnel.

Here are more reasons that a company may issue new stock to investors or key personnel:

✔ **Raising money:** Whether an IPO or a subsequent offering, this is an efficient way for any publicly traded company to generate funds.

✔ **Giving up control:** When the founder (or organization) owns too much of a company, she can easily lower that percentage of ownership by selling a portion to new shareholders by way of stock sale.

✔ **Expanding the shareholder base:** The more shareholders a company has, the better. In fact, many of the major stock exchanges require that companies listing with them have a minimum number of unique shareholders. By issuing new shares into the market, the shareholder base expands as new owners purchase shares.

- ✔ **Paying executives and key employees:** Companies regularly pay their key employees, or lure top talent, via shares or stock options. Penny stock companies are particularly fond of this maneuver because they may not have much cash to compensate executives but are able to offer shares that have potential to increase in value.

- ✔ **Cashing in options and convertible debentures:** Sometimes new shares are created by using complex financial instruments. For example, a convertible debenture is like a loan in which the creditor could be paid back the amount owed or could convert that value into new shares of the company instead. Options also become shares of the company if and when they are exercised, or cashed in.

Issuing new shares can help a publicly traded company by giving it the greatest flexibility to take advantage of opportunities as it implements its business plan. The benefits can be great, as long as the company is cautious of the potential for causing shareholder dilution.

How dilution affects investors

Dilution can have a detrimental impact on penny stocks. Any time a company issues new shares, the share of ownership of each stock is reduced. Your job as an investor is to ascertain whether a company's dilutive financing is beneficial or detrimental to current shareholders. You want to avoid companies that don't produce gains for their stockholders.

For a company with 10 million shares outstanding, each share represents ownership of $\frac{1}{10},000,000$th of that company. If it doubles the number of shares available, each one should be worth half as much.

Dilution can also hold share prices down even when the company's value grows. Picture a company that trades at one dollar per share, while the number of outstanding shares doubles. If the shares are still at one dollar, but there are twice as many of them, that means the market capitalization (or total company value) has doubled. In this example, shareholders own stock in a company that has grown in size but may not see any increase in the stock price because there are so many more shares available.

Less-experienced investors often don't see the potentially detrimental effect that newly issued shares can cause. They may be proud of the 20 percent gain their stock has returned so far, not realizing that this occurred during a time when the company significantly diluted its holdings. Without that dilution, the investors'

returns may have been significantly higher, but this lost opportunity will never show up in any quantifiable way.

If you're a shareholder in a company, you don't want it to dilute your investment by issuing more shares. If you are not yet a shareholder in a company that you're considering investing in, you don't need to worry about dilution from the company, because it will simply make the shares you're thinking about investing in both less expensive and more available.

Companies can also select the price at which they issue new shares or at which their options may be exercised. For example, they may announce a deal to sell shares at $2.25 to a specific buyer or that the IPO price will be $2.25.

Setting a share price can be beneficial for shareholders if the price is higher than the current share price. Issuing new stock at prices lower than current share prices can have a negative impact on the stock. In addition, current shareholders can also feel like they overpaid, or that management is giving away portions of the company at unfair levels.

The impact of dilution on shares isn't instantaneous; instead, it has a gradual effect over time. However, because dilution implies lower shares prices, when a company announces that it will be issuing more shares, investors may react immediately by selling their shares.

When new share issues are a good thing

Dilution isn't always a bad thing. Sometimes it can actually be very beneficial for the company. In such circumstances, the shares can rise much higher, not in spite of dilution, but rather due to the benefits of issuing new shares.

Dilution can be effective when used properly or conducted for the right reasons, such as . . .

- ✔ **Legal battles:** Smaller companies often find themselves in costly legal battles with much bigger players. For example, many tech companies must go to court to enforce patents rights. To pay legal fees, companies may issue shares for general working capital purposes. When the company is on the right side of a legal battle, it can be beneficial for them and shareholders to dilute in order to litigate.

- ✔ **Accretive acquisitions:** When a company plans to acquire another company, a factory, or a brand that will immediately increase the penny stock's revenues (and possibly earnings), it makes sense to acquire them. While sometimes expensive, if the acquisition makes the corporation stronger, investors should look beyond the dilution to the greater gains.

✔ **Attracting key personnel:** Having the right people leading the company and in other key roles is of monumental importance. Issuing new shares to attract and retain the right personnel may be an acceptable practice.

✔ **Bridging:** Short-term, or bridge, financing can sometimes take a company to profitability, or the next level, or put them on a higher playing field. When dilution generates a bridge or temporary financing, it is often acceptable, especially when that bridge leads to something even better for the corporation.

The negative impact of dilution on the share price is generally limited when spread out in small chunks over longer time frames, as opposed to issuing huge amounts of new shares all at once. For example, one million new shares sold into the market at four times throughout a year will have less negative effect on the stock price than issuing all one million of those shares at once.

Almost all penny stocks will take dilutive actions. As an investor, you want to focus on the companies that do so in a responsible way — a way that helps the company and its share price in the long run.

Unfortunately, many penny stocks companies issue new shares in a less responsible way, which can negatively impact the shares' abilities to make long-term gains.

When new share issues are a not-so-good thing

Many penny stocks find it easy to raise money on the stock market but, unfortunately, they don't always use those funds wisely. When a company makes poor decisions with the money it can result in a slow (or possibly not-so-slow) decrease in the value of the stock and your investment.

Watch dilutive actions closely, especially for financings that don't do much to benefit the corporation. You should be very cautious when you see shares issued in certain circumstances, such as to . . .

✔ **Keep the company afloat.** Many penny stocks companies would be long bankrupt if not for a few financings. Some of them raise more money from diluting shareholders than they do from generating revenues. Each time they seem to be running low on cash, they simply go back to the markets for more. Investors eventually spot companies that use this tactic, and when the investors disappear . . . often so does the stock.

✔ **Overpay top executives when the company is languishing.** Using dilutive practices to overcompensate top executives is even more troublesome when the individuals receiving the huge bonuses and salaries are the ones who voted for them in the first place. While not common, you will see key personnel from time to time who take disproportionate payments, even when the underlying shares are languishing.

✔ **Generate easy money.** Many companies find it easier to generate the funds they need just by issuing shares on the market rather than controlling costs and running their business well. It typically takes less work to raise ten million dollars on the stock market than to earn ten million dollars through operations of the company. When a corporation is too quick to take this easy road, they could be diluting shareholders into the ground.

Stock Buybacks

A *stock buyback* takes place when a company buys back its shares on the open market and subsequently cancels, or eliminates, those shares. Any stock acquired in this fashion is thereby removed from the pool of available shares. Buybacks have a positive effect on the stock price.

In most cases, companies use buybacks (in addition to other methods) to increase their share price. Buybacks are typically implemented by companies that see themselves as undervalued and that also have plenty of cash in their coffers.

While buybacks aren't common among penny stocks companies, which use all their funds for research and development or to drive and pay for growth, you may come across a share buyback from time to time.

Having fewer shares available benefits current shareholders. Here are some of the ways that a buy back can help the price of a stock:

✔ **Displays confidence:** When a company buys back its own stock on the open market, it demonstrates that executives (who authorized the buyback) believe in their company's future and feel that the shares are at undervalued prices.

✔ **Best use of funds:** Often a buyback will come with a statement from management that this approach represents "the best use of funds." In other words, the company has excess cash and doesn't see as much value in any of the other channels for the funds. The fact that the company has money to spend demonstrates the success of its business, and by using those funds to reduce the amount of outstanding shares should increase the value of the stock.

✔ **Reverses dilution:** The fewer shares available, the greater portion of ownership in the company each of the remaining stock will have. Pay attention to what percentage of shares the penny stock intends to buy back because that should give you a direct understanding of how much the stock may rise in value. For example, if a company buys back 25 percent of its shares, theoretically the value of each remaining share should increase by 25 percent.

✔ **Increases demand:** Buying back shares on the open market is a big plus for thinly traded penny stocks. The buyback creates demand for the stock, which can motivate other buyers to increase their bid prices. At the same time, the supply of shares being sold decreases because some sellers will have their stock purchased.

Buybacks are almost always positive for the shares, and in some cases they have significantly beneficial effects.

Acquisitions and Takeovers

Other companies acquire penny stock companies quite often. Regardless of the effect this activity has on the share prices in the long run, the acquisition is usually detrimental to the stock of the buyer and beneficial to the stock of the "target" company being acquired.

Unlike mergers and amalgamations (discussed later in this chapter) whereby companies willingly combine themselves together and often change the combined company's name, much of its business activities, and management, *acquisitions* involve one company taking over another. In an acquisition, the buyer usually doesn't visibly change much (in terms of corporate name, business activities, management, and so on), but the company being bought may experience radical changes. Think of it as a big fish eating a smaller fish, or a big company eating a smaller one.

Takeovers are sometimes done against the will of the target company, in which case it is referred to as a *hostile takeover*. Takeovers differ from mergers, which are always agreed upon by both companies. With a takeover, the company being acquired usually sees its share price increase when the takeover becomes public knowledge. This increase is due to the premium price that the buyer is offering in order to buy shares. The buying company will see its share price drop when the announcement is made or its intention becomes public knowledge. This is because investors know that the purchasing company will need to . . .

- ✔ **Pay a premium for the target company's shares.** The acquirer needs to own a certain number of shares in the target company in order to make the transaction go through. It entices current shareholders by offering to buy the stock for much more — often as much as 40 percent or more above the current price — than the current trading price. The company also has the ability to raise that offer price even higher if it doesn't get the number of shares it needs.

- ✔ **Deal with acquisition growing pains.** Any time a company takes over another company, the acquiring will incur expenses in the process of bringing the two operations together. Even methods of lowering total costs through the acquisition will be expensive to implement at first. The acquiring company may take a year or more to fully absorb the target company and realize any financial or strategic benefits.

Sometimes the buyout makes sense to the management of the target company, at which point it will express its support for the acquisition, and generally the shareholders will agree and sell their shares at the offered level. Failing an agreeable board of directors, the goal of the buying company is to gain control of 90 percent of the total outstanding shares, at which point it can legally force the remaining shareholders to sell.

After a takeover has begun, your choices as a shareholder in the target company are to

- ✔ **Sell to the offer.** You will be sent information from your broker about how to sell your shares at the premium price. When a stock I am holding jumps up due to the price premium being offered by an acquiring company, I generally sell then and take my money.

- ✔ **Do nothing.** If the buyer is unable to gain 90 percent of the shares, you can keep your stock, but keep in mind if the takeover attempt fails and fades away, the shares generally fall back to the prices they were at in the first place. If the buyer does reach that 90 percent threshold, your broker will automatically provide your shares to the buyer and give you the requisite amount of money for them.

- ✔ **Sell on the open market.** You can always sell the shares as per usual on the market.

The road to survival is paved with mergers and acquisitions

Being acquired is often the best way for a corporation to survive over the long haul. The history of the auto industry in the United States bears out this example. Business historians estimate that from the year 1896 and beyond, more than 1,500 different automobile manufacturers opened their doors for business in the United States. The vast majority of those companies went out of business. Some of those that survived merged with other companies, and most of those merged companies also eventually went bankrupt or closed their doors. A few automakers, however, were acquired or taken over by other companies as the highly fragmented industry consolidated.

Penny stocks are acquisition targets more frequently than larger companies, and this can be positive for shareholders. In the short term, acquiring companies will see their share price pulled down. The takeover target will enjoy a significant and almost instantaneous jump in its stock, based on the premium being offered from the buyer.

Why penny stock companies are frequently bought

Penny stock companies are generally easier targets to be taken over by other players in the same industry. Unlike multibillion-dollar corporations, penny stocks are more suitable for acquisition for the following specific reasons:

✔ **Small size:** Smaller companies are proportionately easier to acquire. Based on the lower market capitalization of many penny stocks, they represent bite-sized acquisition targets for bigger companies.

✔ **Niche-specific:** Penny stock companies may have very specific assets — certain customers, employees, or intellectual property — that a larger corporation can grab through takeover without having to fight too hard for them.

✔ **Fragmented Industry:** Penny stocks are often found in newer industries, which typically start off or become very fragmented in their early phases. As the industry consolidates (and they all do), many of the players will be acquired as the bigger companies jostle for market share and the sales lead.

Given the benefits that acquiring a certain penny stock may offer a larger company, takeovers among lower-priced shares make good business sense. But sometimes, especially during times of consolidation for an industry, the penny stock companies may be the ones doing the buying.

Resisting a takeover

Acquiring the right penny stock can be very beneficial to the buyer, although the smaller company may not always be looking to be absorbed or bought out. While staving off a suitor that is several times larger may be difficult, companies can employ a common tactic known as a *shareholder rights plan* (also called as a poison pill) to possibly prevent any unwanted, or hostile, acquisition.

With a shareholder rights plan, additional shares will be automatically issued to current investors in the event of a hostile takeover. The shareholders then have a larger investment, and the purchaser will need to pay them for their original shares as well as the new shares.

While a shareholder rights plan will make acquisition of the company more expensive, it does not prevent another corporation from buying the shares if it is willing to pay the additional price.

As a penny stock investor, I try to invest in shares that are poised for very significant growth. If I know that the company is fundamentally solid and growing rapidly, my biggest concern becomes a takeover. After spotting a company that is going to multiply in size (and share price), the benefits to the shareholders can be curtailed if a larger corporation picks up all the shares, even if it does so at a significant premium in price. Picture a $10 million company that I expect to grow four times over. If a billion dollar corporation scoops it up for $15 million, I've only gained 50 percent on my money. If the penny stock did grow four times over, the gain on the shares would have been much more than the 50 percent I realized.

Understanding which companies are takeover targets

Not all penny stocks are appropriate takeover targets. When a corporation is assessing specific companies for potential acquisition, it considers several factors.

Although predicting any potential takeover can be a crapshoot, you can increase your odds of benefiting from it by considering the factors that could make a company attractive to another, larger corporation. By being aware of what makes a superior acquisition target, you can look for opportunities to purchase shares in potential target companies and then reap the profits when those shares are purchased in a takeover. Even without an eventual takeover, the specter or rumors of the possibility can sometimes lift share prices higher.

The following sections describe factors that increase the likelihood of a penny stock company being taken over by a larger company.

When bigger fish are swimming in the pond

When a company is small, yet surrounded by much larger ones, a buyout is possible. But when that company is too tiny or new, or the bigger fish are too large, then that actually lowers the odds of a takeover. The penny stock in question needs to be large enough to be noticed.

When the industry is trending toward consolidation

Takeovers instigate other takeovers. When a very fragmented industry suddenly starts consolidating, numerous companies may be bought out. Larger players in the industry don't want to be left out of the action while their peers get stronger, and any that were thinking about a potential acquisition may now be motivated to act. Consolidation trends come and go, but getting positioned in front of one while it passes through an industry can be very profitable for investors.

When the penny stock shows financial strength

Growing revenues attract the attention of larger companies. If the penny stock is profitable, that's even more compelling. The bigger corporation may enjoy economies of scale and, as such, be able to increase the profitability of the smaller business's sales. Any time a small company can be acquired and its financial results will instantly be accretive to the bigger corporation's financial statements, it has a high likelihood of being part of a takeover.

When acquisition is cheaper than production

In some cases, it is less expensive for a company to acquire another than to build up the business on its own. For example, it is often easier for a gold mining company to buy a smaller producing mine than to explore for the resource, get the necessary permits, build the mine, and start extracting and selling the gold. Never mind the time that would be saved by buying the smaller and already operational company!

To acquire the employees, clients, or intellectual property

When the value of the assets and alliances — such as the employees, clients, or intellectual property — of a company are great, perhaps even greater than the entire value of the company itself, they are often acquired through takeover. Larger companies may acquire penny stock companies because they want their employees, customers, intellectual property, or clients.

To eliminate competition

When an upstart or tiny company becomes a thorn in the side of a bigger player, or it would become even more expensive for the larger company to compete with the smaller company than buy it, the larger company may instigate an acquisition.

When the companies have similar corporate cultures

Although simply having matching corporate cultures isn't a reason for one company to take over another one, the presence of matching corporate cultures does increase the likelihood of a takeover if other factors also suggest that the merger would be beneficial. For example, an upstart Internet company that lets its employees bring their kids to work, make their own hours, and provides free donuts every day may mesh well with organizations with similar cultures. Similarly, when the corporate cultures don't match, that fact could negate an acquisition, even when all other factors indicate that it would be a good idea. In our same example, a 200-year-old conventional 9-to-5 business would be unlikely to acquire the upstart with the easygoing culture.

Being the buyer

Although penny stock companies are usually the targets of acquisition attempts, they sometimes do the acquiring. Penny stocks tend to target companies that are even smaller than themselves.

All the reasons a penny stock makes a good acquisition target apply when that company is looking to advance its strategy by buying other businesses.

One thing you will notice more frequently with penny stocks is that their acquisition targets are often very small, and not publicly traded, businesses. They may pick up a company for $2 million dollars because they want the underlying sales force, and then maybe they buy out another company for $10 million to capture its customer base.

Whether a penny stock is acquiring a publicly traded company or a mom-and-pop shop, what really matters is that the purchase advances the penny stock's plans and that the company doesn't pay more than it should.

As an investor, you should ask if an acquisition makes sense. Some businesses buy out other companies for the sake of trying to grow, but if those moves are poorly conceived or executed, they will be very detrimental to the company in the long run.

Mergers and Amalgamations

Companies can merge together, or "amalgamate," which simply involves becoming one entity. They may combine employees, facilities, executives, and products, and potentially benefit from the increase in capabilities, product offerings, and financings.

Mergers are unlike acquisitions (see "Acquisitions and Takeovers," earlier in this chapter) because mergers involve two businesses voluntarily combining. The merging companies are not being swallowed up against their will, but rather are coming together to benefit from improved capabilities, enhanced economies of scale, and an increased skill set. While a takeover typically results in the target company losing its identity and becoming a part of the buyer, companies that merge tend to maintain most of their presence and operations.

Penny stocks can reap many benefits from merging with another penny stock or even with a larger company. Assuming the amalgamation makes strategic sense, the benefits can include . . .

✔ **Economies of scale:** If the merger increases the number of products produced, or total revenues generated, a company can decrease expenses on a per-item or per-dollar basis. The right merger can also significantly decrease fulfillment costs, which are the expenses required to provide products or services.

✔ **Increased takeover defense:** Larger companies are harder to take over. By growing through mergers, a penny stock becomes that much bigger, and as such, that much more difficult to be bought out.

✔ **Consolidating operations:** Whether bringing all the administrative functions under one roof, or running the sales and production in a single location, there can be significant advantages to both companies by consolidating their operations.

✔ **Expanded offerings:** Often two companies in a similar industry but with different specialties can come together to provide a more complete solution for their customers. For example, a printing company that is also able to offer design services becomes more attractive to its prospects.

✔ **Accretive revenues and earnings:** When a business is already generating earnings, or bringing in revenues, those earnings and revenues go to the postmerger company.

Through amalgamation, penny stocks can become larger and more relevant. They can make their operations more efficient and attract more customers. By merging with the right companies, a penny stock can advance its operations and strategy.

Stock splits and reverse splits

Sometimes a company can decide to *split* its shares, which simply involves turning the existing shares into a greater number, based on any multiple it chooses. For example, a two-for-one split would turn every share into two shares, while a four-for-one split would turn every share into four.

A split results in a greater total number of shares available, while each share is then traded at a lower price. Consider a company with 10 million shares outstanding, trading at $50 each. After a 2-for-1 split, there would be 20 million shares, with each being worth half as much, or $25 in our example.

Companies split their shares to keep the prices lower, usually after a long-term and significant price increase. The split makes the stock more attainable by smaller investors and may bring the share price more in line with competitors and other companies in the peer group. Splits also widen the shareholder base by increasing the total number of shares available to investors.

Without splits, many of the most successful companies on the stock market would be trading at tens of thousands of dollars per share. Thanks to numerous splits over the years, you can purchase shares in those companies for $20.

Often after a split, the shares continue to rise in price. The stock has already been doing very well, and the split signals that success to investors.

Share splits are very rare among penny stocks, because most lower-priced shares are not interested in trading at even lower prices. With penny stocks, the exact opposite of the split, called a *reverse split* or *share consolidation,* is quite common.

Reverse splits combine the existing shares together by whatever ratio the company decides. A $1 stock with 50 million shares outstanding could conduct a 1-for-5 consolidation, which would result in that company having 10 million shares trading at $5 each.

Reverse splits are used to increase the price of the shares, which can give a company the impression of legitimacy or help it maintain a stock market listing by meeting the minimum share price requirements.

Typically, after a reverse split, the shares continue to fall in price. Although the shares are, relatively speaking, higher in price (such as a three-for-one reverse making each share worth three times as much), they generally continue to slide to lower relative prices. For example, shares may consolidate on a one-for-five basis, bringing their price up to six dollars, but they will start trading lower, perhaps toward five dollars or even lower. The slide takes place because companies having experienced falling stock prices usually conduct reverse splits, and the consolidation signals that fact to investors.

Why you don't see splits in low-priced shares

Penny stocks don't split their shares because there are usually too many shares out already and the price is already too low.

Let me do the math to show you why splits don't make sense for penny stocks: A typical penny stock company may be trading at 30¢ per share, with 200 million shares outstanding. If it were to split 3 for 1, the share price would lower to 10¢ and the number of outstanding shares would increase to 600 million. The end result would be a very low share price and an excessive amount of shares available, both of which make the company less compelling to investors. The fewer the number of shares, and the higher the price of those shares, the greater the implied value.

Companies want to seem more legitimate, and higher share prices create that appearance. They also want to keep their outstanding shares under control, which means that they don't want to be splitting and multiplying them on the market.

Why reverse splits are common in penny stocks

Penny stock companies consolidate their shares more frequently than any other size of investment. They may take this step to achieve any of the following goals:

✔ **Maintain or gain a stock market listing.** If a company needs a minimum share price to be listed on their exchange but fall below that threshold, it could do a reverse split to bring the share price higher. For example, a 25¢ stock could consolidate 1 for 10, bringing the theoretical price to $2.50 and reducing the number of outstanding shares to one-tenth of the original amount.

✔ **Increase perceived legitimacy.** Higher-priced stocks typically imply higher quality companies. Although share price really has nothing to do with the success or prospects of the business, a higher prices does look better to investors and clients.

✔ **Decrease outstanding shares.** Many penny stocks have far too many shares available because of their tendency to continually issue new stock to raise money. One way to quickly reduce the outstanding shares is to consolidate.

Although the vast majority of penny stocks don't undertake reverse splits, stock consolidation is a more common practice among penny stocks than it is among larger corporations. Generally the consolidations have a negative effect on the company's value, even when they are enacted for positive reasons.

Bankruptcies

When a company goes bankrupt, its shares typically are eventually cancelled and become worthless. Any remaining assets are sold to pay back the banks and other creditors. But after the bankruptcy announcement, stocks may continue to trade on the stock market for weeks or months, and traders can still buy and sell the shares, which can cause problems for uninformed investors.

During this time, most investors who have not already done so will try to sell their shares. The price of the stock usually falls to a few pennies per share.

Many investors who don't understand bankruptcy proceedings think that they are getting a good deal when they buy a household name for pennies. They think that when the company emerges from bankruptcy the shares will regain value. What they don't understand is that the company will cancel its bankrupt shares and issue new stock, which is where any future value will be generated.

Not realizing the guaranteed downside, investors actually buy the bankrupt shares and think that they will do well with them. Sometimes they even come to me and ask about the company. My response is always the same: "You will lose all that you invest in a bankrupt company."

Bankrupt companies are indicated by most stock exchanges with a "Q" on the end of their ticker symbol.

Chapter 4

Avoiding Promotions, Scams, and Bribes

*P*enny stocks are prominent targets for manipulation and misleading information. As an investor, you need to protect yourself from these negative influences, which anyone entering the world of low-priced shares will certainly encounter.

The good news is that you can easily avoid the common pitfalls.

In this Chapter, I introduce you to the negative impacts of promotions and scams. I also discuss why penny stocks are prime targets for price manipulation, and how that can be very costly for you. Next, I describe features of poor-quality companies so that you can identify them, and talk about some of the events that can completely derail a small corporation.

Why Penny Stocks Are Perfect for Price Manipulation

Penny stocks are a perfect vehicle for any number of traders, scam artists, or promoters to profit by artificially moving the price of shares. The majority of victims of these activities are ill-informed investors who don't understand what is really going on with their penny stocks, and who may be a little too trusting.

Their naiveté doesn't make them any less of victims, but rather illustrates the degree to which shady characters are willing to take advantage of others. As a penny stock investor, you need to protect yourself from these events, which is quite easy to do with even the smallest amount of knowledge.

Penny stocks become common targets for unethical behavior, because they are

- **Priced low:** Some even trade for fractions of a penny. If a promoter can push the shares from one-tenth of a cent to two-tenths, they theoretically have doubled their money.

- **Thinly traded:** The fewer shares that trade hands, the easier for a big wave of buying to move the price. When very few shares are being sold, any significant purchase may push the stock to much higher levels.

- **Appear legitimate:** Because penny stocks have a listing on a stock market, many investors assume that they must be legitimate and high-quality companies. The truth is that shady characters often target companies close to bankruptcy, or those on the market only due to some legitimate operations in the past that have long ceased.

- **Plentiful:** With thousands of penny stocks to choose from, dishonest players can move their efforts frequently and choose which type of company or story they want to push.

- **Anonymous:** Most of these unethical players want to stay anonymous. They can potentially scam people out of millions through penny stocks, but never poke their heads out of the window in their mom's basement.

- **Vulnerable:** Shady characters don't need the permission of management or anyone else to run a promotion of any publicly traded company. Just like you, they can trade any shares on any market, and they very often run scams without the executives of the company having any knowledge of it whatsoever.

For anyone who is fine with taking the money of trusting people, and doesn't mind seriously bending their morals, penny stocks probably seem like the perfect vehicle. Despite the odd arrest or charges laid by regulatory bodies, the shady players in the world of penny stocks will continue to mislead investors until the investors stop falling for their tricks.

Some of the dishonest tricks that you may encounter include

- **Misleading information:** Whether through a free e-mail newsletter, press releases, or a comment on a message board, these shady promoters know that they don't need to trick everyone . . . just a few unwary investors is enough. They may stretch the truth, or flat out lie, to make a penny stocks company look extremely compelling.

✔ **Focusing on (ridiculous) potential:** Instead of talking about how a company is almost bankrupt, or generates no revenues, the promoters focus on how its product — an engine that runs on gravity, a cure for that major disease — could change the world (even if it borders on the ridiculous). Inexperienced investors may fall for the promotion and think that the shares are a great investment.

✔ **Pump-and-dump schemes:** A very common practice with penny stocks, *pump-and-dump schemes* involve dishonest promoters who buy massive amounts of very inexpensive shares in nearly nonoperational companies. The promoters then talk up the shares (usually to lists of investors who signed up for their free newsletter) and generate buying interest in the stock. That demand can drive the prices higher, until the characters behind the scheme sell all their shares, take their profits, and stop promoting the stock with false and misleading claims. Without the promotion, the stock collapses back toward the real value, which is usually near zero. Investors misled into buying shares lose very significantly.

✔ **Coordinated price drives:** This trick is different from pump-and-dump schemes because the investors in the stock are well aware that the underlying company is awful. They hope to profit from increases in the share price of the near-bankrupt company and know that the only reason the stock would move at all is because of actions by buyers like themselves. The investors know they are playing a game of hot potato. They hope to ride the shares higher and jump ship before the promotion ends. Most of these investors may make a few dollars once or twice but, in the long run, they lose. That's why you've never met anyone who got rich this way.

✔ **Scalping:** *Scalping* is the process of an investment advisor or stock picker suggesting that investors purchase a certain stock while at the same time, they are selling those exact same shares. In other words, they are taking the exact opposite action that they suggest you take yourself. The practice of scalping is illegal, but financial professionals and stock pickers do it anyway. Sometimes the regulatory bodies catch them, but not often enough to fully end the dishonest practice.

The biggest problem with these tactics is that investors sometimes fall for them. Instead of asking why a free newsletter cares what they invest in or why it's telling them about some stock, investors sometimes follow the dishonest information and purchase shares.

Generally, these individuals get burned and never come near penny stocks again.

The Securities and Exchange Commission (SEC), and other regulatory and enforcement bodies, take action against the worst scams from time to time. But because they they're underfunded, these organizations have a hard time combating the dramatically rising wave of penny stock promotions.

While regulatory bodies catch only a fraction of the troublemakers, their ability to do so discourages many others from taking the same path. My hope is that the SEC eventually gets the resources they need to go after the majority of con artists.

Free penny stock picks are the single biggest method of scamming investors. With misleading information, unethical promoters push their latest stock on people through repeated spam. If only a very small fraction of recipients buy shares in the thinly traded stock, the price will go up. The promoter then sells his shares at the inflated price that he has unethically generated and walks away with a big profit — while the trusting investors watch the price of their shares collapse.

While the pitfalls abound, you can easily avoid penny stock scams and promotions if you take these steps:

- ✔ **Choose companies on better markets.** Only trade penny stocks found on the NYSE, AMEX, NASDAQ, and OTC-BB. Better markets attract more legitimate companies, while almost all scams occur with shares traded on the very low quality stock exchanges. Check out Chapter 3 for details on all these exchanges.

- ✔ **Avoid free picks.** Whether offered free of charge from a free e-mail newsletter, an unsolicited fax, or an Internet message board, free picks almost always have hidden motivations behind them.

- ✔ **Do proper due diligence.** Even if you get a pick from a trusted source, you should put it through your own rigorous due diligence, as I describe in Chapter 6. Make sure that you feel good about anything you invest in and always take responsibility for your own trading decisions.

- ✔ **Discern the source.** You may hear about companies from a friend at work, or stranger45338 on some message board. Either way, even if they have good intentions, maybe they don't have a clue about what makes a good investment. Don't follow what they tell you just because they're excited or adamant about the company's prospects.

- ✔ **Build trust.** When someone demonstrates a strong track record, or leads you to some winners, you should gradually (but cautiously) put more faith in them.

My (best) huge mistake

I was 14 years old when I made my first trade. I earned and saved up $3,600. I was determined to turn that into something more.

I invested all of it (mistake #1) into Siberian Pacific Resources, a company which I knew nothing about (mistake #2), but which was on the stock market so I figured was legitimate (mistake #3).

The shares were at 14¢. They dropped in one week to 13¢, but I didn't sell (mistake #4). I figured if they dropped to 12¢, I could sell {mistake #5} and learn my lesson.

The next week, they were "halted." I had never heard the term (mistake #6), so called the company and the stock exchange. Turns out, the company didn't want to pay the listing fees any more and decided instead to wind down its operations.

All my money from my first trade was gone in two weeks! After some contemplation and mourning, I realized that if the market could take that much money that quickly, it could also create that much just as quickly.

I started to paper trade while I read every stock market book I could get my hands on. I developed and refined Leeds Analysis. And most important, I only blamed myself for my mistakes and used them to motivate me as I learned. I was finally doing things the right way!

Investors who are aware of the potential scams and promotions in penny stocks inoculate themselves from these sorts of shady deals. By easily sidestepping the pitfalls, you will open up the potential to find really excellent investments that will be very profitable for you.

My team members and I have made several reports to the SEC over the years, and to other regulators when we see major promotions or scams. It is in our best interest to help keep the penny stock markets free from manipulation and dishonesty. If most of these detrimental promoters were stopped, it would be a lot easier for us to run our legitimate penny stock newsletter and help people find out about the proper way to invest in the highest-quality companies.

Who Is Moving the Price?

The share price of a company should change based on the expectations shareholders and potential investors have for the operational results. Unfortunately, with lower-priced, thinly traded penny stocks, other players are often at work.

As a penny stock investor, you need to understand the individuals who may be influencing the price of a stock. By knowing who is pushing the share prices, you gain a clear idea of how much to trust their influence and have a good idea of how long their promotion or pump-and-dump scheme is going to last.

Promoters

Individuals who profit by artificially manipulating the prices of penny stocks are known as *promoters*. They employ numerous unethical tactics, such as misleading information or aggressive spam campaigns, to push thinly traded shares into higher prices, and they profit as they sell millions of shares of the near-worthless company to all the naive buyers.

The activity of promoting a penny stock and then selling shares just before the promotion ends, is know as a *pump and dump*. Promoters drive stock in near-bankrupt corporations to foolish valuations and then sell their shares. The promotion ends, the stock collapses, costing everyone except the promoter.

Promoters are the main cause of penny stocks getting a bad name, and their activities are very costly to their victims. Because the very act of promoting a very low quality penny stock is devoid of integrity, there are few limits to the degree to which they will take the pump and dump.

Investor or public relations

Individuals or firms involved in investor relations (IR) can have a legitimate place in the world of penny stocks. In order to get noticed, many companies hire an IR firm to help spread their message in hopes of enticing shareholders, which should potentially increase the share price.

Mainly through press releases, but also via industry conferences, online information, or one-on-one discussions, IR or public relations folks explain all the good things about a company and talk about how it will grow and expand.

Keep in mind that a company hires an IR firm to cast the penny stock in the best light possible, and it usually measures success by the increase in the stock's price. So although IR firms are more professional and honest than promoters, they still have an interest in presenting the most optimistic case.

There are many degrees of IR firms, and while some are very straightforward and honest, others can be very aggressive in talking up a company.

Take a look at other stocks an IR firm has represented in the past, and peruse the press releases they published about those companies, to get an idea of their balance between honesty and professionalism.

Many investors question the value of companies hiring investor relations firms to help drive up share prices. While stocks do sometimes rise during a period when companies are covered by an IR firm, there are just as many instances of the exact opposite result. Considering the cost associated with retaining professional IR assistance, its value is debatable for penny stock companies already short on cash.

The touter

A *touter* is anyone who talks up or recommends a penny stock. They could be bloggers, write a stock-picking newsletter, or just be folks who talk about their investments at the office water cooler.

Usually they have good intentions but know just enough to get themselves and anyone who follows their opinion into trouble. Touters are very often wrong in their picks or opinions, so they increase the appearance of being correct by speaking louder, touting more often, or citing specifics, which they believe will support their position.

For every touter who thinks shares in a specific company are going higher, there's another touter who thinks they are going lower. So should you ignore or discount these opinions? I think you should. Stick to reliable and professional sources that earn your trust over time, rather than follow the assertions of some touter just because they sound convincing.

The advisor

Investment advisors and full service stockbrokers often suggest specific stocks to their clients. Although they tend to shy away from penny stocks in general, sometimes they may suggest specific penny stocks for purchase.

If the customer is interested in increasing the risk and reward portion of his portfolio, the advisor may suggest certain low-priced shares. In addition, if a financial professional has a very optimistic outlook for a specific penny stock, he may want to share that company with his clientele.

The impact of financial advisors on the price of penny stocks is usually insignificant because they rarely suggest the shares to their network. However, because the purchasing power of their clientele is often very high, when brokers do recommend a penny stock, the influence on the share price of penny stock can be significant.

Rooting Out Poor Quality Companies

With lower-priced shares, the proportion of lower-quality companies is greater than compared to high-priced and blue-chip stocks. And although the winners among penny stocks could produce gains dramatically higher than anything you would ever see among large cap companies, you first need to be able to identify and eliminate the types of companies that may be lackluster investments.

 Typically, about 95 percent of shares trading below five dollars are financially weak, have questionable or unproven management, are not seeing market share growth, or hold important intellectual property. However, 5 percent of those low-cost shares do meet higher standards, and those stocks are much more likely to increase in value than the rest.

As a wise investor, you want to avoid several common business situations. If you come across any of the situations described in the following sections, the best move from an investment standpoint is to steer clear or move on.

A good story

A very compelling and exciting story motivates traders to buy shares in a company, with no thought to financial strength or appropriate stock price valuation. These good stories are the main reasons investors lose their money.

Companies that ride their stories to ridiculous share prices, no matter how unbelievable those stories are, almost always cost their shareholders close to 100 percent of their investment.

Examples of tall tales I've seen in penny stocks, all of which cost their investors 100 percent of their investment within months, include

- A car engine that runs on gravity
- A water box that converts salt water to fresh water.
- Drugs or treatments that may come close to curing some major disease

✔ The world's largest gold find

✔ A beneficiary of legalized marijuana

✔ An all-natural, healthy energy drink

✔ Just about any business story behind the latest pump-and-dump stock promotion

The old phrase, "if it seems too good to be true, it probably is," couldn't be more applicable here. The really low quality companies absolutely need an unbelievable story just to trick investors — and to stay in business.

Whenever you find yourself very excited by the story of a specific penny stock, remember that there are probably thousands of investors who are also just as motivated to buy in. In such a case, it is not uncommon for a stock worth one-tenth of a cent to trade for several dollars per share . . . until it returns to the appropriate valuation once again.

Financially broken

People often ask for my opinion about a certain penny stock. They seem surprised when I tell them the company has $20 thousand dollars, $47 million in debt, and losses of more than $2 million per month.

I can only assume that most investors don't look at a company's financial position. Perhaps they don't understand how to do so. If they take a quick minute to check, they can save themselves (and me) the time.

In penny stocks, it is very common for the companies to be financially broken. Beyond simply "not performing well," they are crushed beneath debt loads so large that they can't even possibly pay the interest expenses, let alone the principal. They are often bleeding cash, with losses of millions of dollars more than they ever can hope to make in revenues, even if everything went right for them for the next five years.

I have mentioned that 95 percent of penny stocks don't pass my minimum criteria for investing. Of those, a significant proportion are financially broken companies, with no prospects or strategy to ever turn things around.

As soon as a company is financially broken, it makes significantly more sense for it to go bankrupt or close down operations than to try to resurrect the lost cause. Even if the business concept still has some merit and there are individuals committed to making it work, their first step should be to let the current corporation go under while they start up with a new entity that isn't yet saddled by debt.

Weak business model

Some business ideas may make logical sense but in actual application are doomed to fail. No matter how great your marketing, or how popular your service, you can never make a business out of selling bags of dog food online. Nor would it work to offer over-the-phone surgery tips, or to provide security-monitoring responses by e-mail.

When the underlying business model of a company is questionable, it is doomed to failure. This is most true when a company incurs greater losses the more sales it achieves. In the online dog food example, if a $9 bag of kibble weighs 25 pounds, the shipping costs will exceed the product value itself!

 Companies with weak business models will continually post losses and will very often change direction or focus in ongoing attempts to make their concept work. It never will. Don't invest in any company whose business model doesn't stand on its own.

Swimming against the trend

A company on the wrong side of a social trend may be destined for failure. Companies selling cigarettes have been under dramatic pressure as smoking has been falling out of favor, especially compared to many years ago. The bigger players in the industry are only able to survive by branching out to alternative revenue channels and spending millions on advertising.

Picture instant cameras, which were completely wiped out by the rise in digital photography. Companies that specialize in fur coats can't grow their businesses, no matter how aggressively or wisely they spend advertising dollars.

Be aware of social and industry trends that may affect a company, whether that impact will be beneficial or detrimental. Smaller companies can benefit when trends go in their favor, but when shifts move against the company, the negative impact can often be serious. Penny stocks may try to adapt or sidestep any negative trend shifts, but they are often the victims when forces beyond their control change for the worse.

The 2-pound gorilla

You've heard the old joke. "Where does a 500-pound gorilla sit?" "Wherever it wants."

Penny stocks can be worth a few million dollars, but their direct competitors may be worth billions — with a *b*. When a small penny stock is trying to function in an industry with much larger players, they need to be very careful.

As an investor you may want to avoid tiny companies that are at risk due to . . .

- ✔ **Rising competition:** Whether the threat of new competition is in the form of brand-new companies entering the same space or massive corporations deciding to take over a new area, any time there is the potential for increased competition, smaller companies are put under major pressure. This becomes more of a problem when the barriers to entry to their particular markets are low.

- ✔ **Surrounded by direct competitors:** Even if the competition is not new, the fact that there are currently many businesses fighting for market share means that all the players in that space face low profit margins, high advertising requirements, and constant customer attrition.

- ✔ **Specific workforce skill set:** Any time companies rely on their employees for specific skills, competition for those employees can be fierce. Smaller companies in this type of situation are at a major disadvantage.

- ✔ **Legal and intellectual property (IP) maintenance:** Larger corporations may spend only 5 percent of their revenues on legal fees or IP. Considering that the costs are set but that small companies have much lower revenue levels, the legal and IP costs are proportionately much higher. When legal fees, for example, are running at 35 percent of sales, it is much more difficult for that penny stock company to pursue the legal channels in disputes, even when it may be in the right.

- ✔ **Perception:** Recognized names generally have an easier time attracting executives, staff, and customers. When a penny stock is new, or small, that lack of familiarity causes people to trust it less than they would a recognized name, which can put pressure on the company from numerous angles.

If the penny stock shows any progress, or gains any market share, larger companies can easily harness their resources to squash it.

Obstacles That Even High-Quality Companies Face

Even if a penny stock you're interested in is in the top 5 percent in terms of quality, it may still face difficulties simply due to its size. Several factors can easily derail smaller businesses, and anyone investing in low-priced shares should be aware of, and prepare for, some of these common situations.

Besides the fact that they're smaller, and potentially have lower sales and proportionally higher debt, other reasons why penny stock companies have difficulty with many events are as follows:

- ✔ **Employee resources:** Small companies are less likely to have dedicated employees for specific tasks, increasing the likelihood of the employees having numerous responsibilities rather than specializing in any one, specific duty. This can cause responsibility confusion and will very often create situations that are taxing for the employees. Meanwhile, the company may not have the funds to hire anyone to address unique needs as they arise.

- ✔ **Time resources:** With fewer employees to deal with situations as they arise, and with a broader array of duties falling upon each team member, smaller companies very often run into time constraints that hamper their ability to run their businesses smoothly.

- ✔ **Knowledge and expertise:** With fewer employees, smaller companies have less brainpower. When a company only has one technology officer, she will not be able to run concepts past others who speak the same language. When getting opinions on the latest advertisement idea, a marketing manager may not be able to generate as many, or any, valid options.

- ✔ **The respect factor:** Other corporations, corporate customers, and even potential employees generally have less respect for small companies. For example, a lawsuit from an unknown, less-expensive firm hired by a cash-strapped penny stock, won't strike fear into the hearts of its billion-dollar competitors.

- ✔ **Logistical chokepoints:** With smaller businesses, employees and executives are responsible for everything. Sometimes one small or seemingly trivial issue, such as getting the CEO's signature on a check, can delay numerous aspects of the corporation.

- ✔ **Lack of clear strategy:** Smaller companies are notorious for operating on the fly, piecing together what eventually becomes their idea of a plan or strategy. Operating in this way increases the likelihood that the company will make decisions and take actions that don't adhere to the specific (albeit theoretical) goals. In some cases, one executive will work directly counter to another, and neither can point to any specific strategy to clarify for them which path would prove best.

Ideally, small penny stock companies will grow their way out of most of these problems. While growth can be the cure for a low share price and diminished operational flexibility, growth can also add stability to the corporation and help it achieve a more solid business footing.

When my corporation was smaller, there were days when I hired an employee, gave several media interviews, worked on a new book, and then took out the trash and set mousetraps! In small, and even medium-sized, businesses, executives are responsible for everything, at least until they hire the right people for the right roles. Of course, hiring and training then becomes another responsibility as well. Keep this in mind when looking into your investments. They may have shares trading on the stock market but are often still in the small-business phase of their life cycle. In other words, they may be developing a new technology that can change the world, but someone still needs to take out the garbage. Ask yourself, how does that reality play into a company I like?

Lawsuits

Beyond any legal merits, businesses use lawsuits to distract or interfere with their competitors. Even frivolous legal actions need to be defended, which can involve costs of tens of thousands of dollars, even at the low end. Dealing with legal actions also puts a great deal of strain on the executives and keeps them from using their time more productively.

While larger companies can easily spend the thousands or even hundreds of thousands of dollars that they pay to disrupt a smaller company's operations, that smaller company will certainly feel the expense.

The sad fact is that large corporations do target penny stock companies for lawsuits. They do so in part because the original strategies and technologies of the newer companies often test preexisting patents and trademarks. For example, a brand-new technology may be similar to a pre-existing patented process, and while both sides have different opinions as to whether the patent is being violated, the situation ends up in court.

Penny stock companies also take legal actions against other companies of similar size. While these actions tend to be based on legitimate legal issues, rather than used as a strategy to distract the competitor from acquiring more business or to create a financial strain, the expenses are no less significant.

Large companies will survive a significant legal battle whether or not they eventually win. Smaller corporations may be completely wiped out by the distraction and litigation fees of any lawsuit, regardless of whether they emerge victorious in the end. The same isn't true of penny stock companies.

Keep in mind that with lawsuits, the impacts on a stock can be numerous and include

- ✔ **Shadow on shares:** The uncertainty of a lawsuit, regardless of whether the company is suing or being sued, will hold the share prices down until the suit is resolved.

- ✔ **Resource distraction:** Take it from me: I've been on both sides of legal conflicts, and whether you win (as I always have) or not, the process is a major distraction!

- ✔ **Exaggerated damages:** The suing party will always shoot for the moon in the hopes of getting a better settlement. That's why you see lawsuits for $50 million, when neither party involved has ever made more than $1 million.

- ✔ **Usually instigates a countersuit:** When one body launches a lawsuit, the first response by the target's lawyer, beyond proclaiming that the action is "frivolous and will be vigorously defended," is typically to launch an equally large countersuit. Again, this is regardless of merit of that counter argument.

Few legal battles actually go into the most expensive stage, where lawyers battle in court. The vast majority are dropped or settled, and when that occurs, the negative impact of the uncertain outcome is lifted from the shares. Penny stock prices usually respond well when outstanding litigation is concluded or removed from the picture.

You won't always see lawsuits among small companies. You will, however, see them more commonly than would be present for large cap companies. Keep these considerations in mind when a company you're considering investing in is facing litigation. Legal battles can be extremely detrimental to penny stocks in their early phases.

Lost customers

Penny stocks typically will have a lower customer count, not only because the companies are small, but because they are newer and still working to introduce themselves to prospects and potentially convert those prospects for the first time.

When a company has fewer customers, those customers are each more meaningful. For example, losing one client from a base of 500 will have far less impact than losing one of three customers. With even the smallest fluctuations in customer numbers, the small company can find it very difficult to survive, let alone grow.

Every company starts with zero clients or customers. In the early days, every new addition is not only meaningful but also possibly even monumental.

Some penny stock companies have characteristics that insulate themselves from the impact of lost customers. These characteristics include

- ✔ **High customer loyalty:** Some products (automobiles) have higher customer loyalty than others (shampoo). You want to invest in penny stocks where the customers care about the product they buy and become loyal to that brand or specific offering.

- ✔ **Low customer attrition:** The fewer customers a company loses, the more resources it can focus on acquiring new clients rather than keeping the current ones happy. A good (meaning low) attrition rate also demonstrates satisfaction among the users of the product or service.

- ✔ **Returning orders:** When customers return for more, in terms of both frequency and size of their order, that penny stock is insulated from the potential downside of losing any individual clients.

- ✔ **A broad client base:** When a penny stock has a broad client base, it is less likely to be affected by the loss of any individual customer. A client base can be broad in terms of the total number of customers or be based on any other factors, such as region or type of customer. For example, a company with customers in 20 different countries isn't as vulnerable to events that negatively impact any one of those specific nations, such as a civil war, while any business with all their clients in only that one nation would be very negatively impacted.

Penny stock companies will always be proportionately more vulnerable to losing clients, especially when those losses stem from a smaller initial base. By being cautious of the downside to lost clients, the likelihood of those losses, and the potential impact each may have, you will be able to position yourself into penny stocks that will experience less detrimental effects from fluctuations in their customer base.

The 500-pound gorilla

Sometimes success can be the kiss of death for penny stocks. That's because as soon it starts succeeding, the competition starts taking notice. And when one company is so much larger than another, if the smaller one starts stealing clients or demonstrates success in its operations, the larger one may find it worth its while to stomp out the little guy. The big guy has a number of tactics at his disposal:

- ✔ **Acquisition:** The competition's response may come by way of buyout or acquisition, which may be good for shareholders in the short term. However, it will curtail any long-term potential that penny stock had because it is absorbed by a much larger entity.

- ✔ **Head-to-head competition:** The attack could also come by way of massive directed competition, from which the smaller company can't hope to emerge. When a multibillion-dollar company directs its cash reserves at a penny stock's customer space, that may be enough to crush the penny stock company.

- ✔ **Poaching:.** The larger corporation may also decide to poach all the best industry-specific minds straight from the ranks of the penny stock, until the brain drain leaves the smaller company unable to operate.

Whether through brain drain, direct competition, buyout, or otherwise, it is very often less expensive for a much larger corporation to stomp out a smaller one than to let it continue operating. This becomes even more true as the penny stock demonstrates any degree of success.

Even the Good Can Die Young

Even after you become an excellent penny stock investor and you continually uncover the best low-priced shares in the greatest up-and-coming companies, you will encounter an investment from time to time that performs very poorly for reasons that you can't readily identify. Despite fundamental strength, rock-solid financial position, rampant sales growth, and an incredible management team, the shares don't seem to gain any traction.

Flagging performance may be due to an overall market slide. However, sometimes even when the markets are performing well and no amount of research reveals any cause for concern, the stock remains lackluster. In such cases, investors are treating the stock unfairly; in other words, by failing to recognize the underlying value in the shares, they're trading them for much lower prices than the company's situation merits.

Besides the loss in the value of your investment, the real tragedy is that your investment may be declining despite having so much potential for growth.

Fortunately, you can still come out on top if you observe a few simple techniques:

- ✔ **Observe loss limits.** *Loss limits* are a way to automatically sell your shares when they slip a certain percentage. You can use this tactic to limit your downside; it will insulate you against even the highest quality companies going south for no reason. Check out Chapter 8 for details on loss limits.

- ✔ **Never fall in love.** Well, fall in love, but never with an investment. Often, people get too attached to their shares, whether because they invested too much money into the stock or they simply have too much belief in what the company could do. In any event, investors who fall in love with a particular stock are more likely to hold their shares as the prices nose-dive instead of selling at the first sign of trouble.

- ✔ **Recognize a buying opportunity.** If the penny stock is indeed as good as you think, but the share price keeps sliding lower, it may represent an excellent buying opportunity. Just triple-check to make sure that you're not overlooking some material issue. If the company is getting stronger, and the shares are going lower, this may be a tremendous value from an investment standpoint. The trick is to figure out where the price will bottom and reverse, which the concepts I disclose in Chapter 12 can help you ascertain.

My hope is that you never encounter shares of an excellent penny stock that fall for no reason. However, even when your due diligence is stellar, it does happen from time to time, and the more active you are trading penny stocks, the greater likelihood of just such an event.

If you accept the possibility and prepare for it accordingly, you can turn just such an occurrence into an opportunity.

Part II
Research and Investment Strategies

Five Ways to Dramatically Improve Your Penny Stock Trading Results

- ✔ Trade risk-free on paper before you start using real money.
- ✔ Call the company and speak directly with its investment representative(s). Prepare the list of questions you want to ask in advance of the call.
- ✔ At all costs, avoid free stock pick sites and tips from friends.
- ✔ Stick to the best markets for trading penny stocks, and steer clear of the low-quality exchanges.
- ✔ After choosing an investment, give yourself time to consider it by waiting a day before you actually buy it.

Find a list of questions to ask a company's investor relations representative online at www.dummies.com/extras/pennystocks.

In this part . . .

- Find out what you need to make your first trade.
- See why effective due diligence makes all the difference.
- Learn how to identify trends and risks that affect your investment success.
- Discover how to make winning investments.
- Harness the power of stock screeners to improve your results while narrowing down your investment choices.

Chapter 5

Developing a Strategy

· ·

In This Chapter

▶ Practicing trades without using real money

▶ Getting everything you need to make your first trade

▶ Finding a broker who handles penny trades

▶ Placing market, limit, and other specialty orders

▶ Understanding the difference between investing and trading

· ·

*T*rading penny stocks is almost always about making money, and a big part of turning a profit comes down to having a superior investment strategy. In this chapter, I show you how to develop an effective penny stock trading strategy. By adopting a few simple, yet highly effective, strategies at the outset of your trading adventure, you can mitigate your risks and increase your profits.

You already know that anything worth doing well requires practice. So you're probably not surprised that I recommend practicing investing in penny stocks before using real money. Fortunately, when it comes to trading penny stocks, you have an easy means to practice without risking any of your hard-earned dollars.

You also need to get set up with a reliable broker — someone well versed in the nuances of penny stocks and who charges fair commissions or fees. I walk you through the process of selecting a broker that best meets your needs.

Finally, I introduce you to the most popular types of trade orders and share a few characteristics of consistently successful investors. After reading this chapter, you'll be well on your way to making profits from low-priced shares.

Trading Risk Free without Using Real Money

Before jumping into penny stocks with both feet — and all your cash — I encourage you to spend some time practicing with imaginary money. *Paper trading* simulates the trading process without you having to spend a single penny. This type of virtual investing gives you the opportunity to learn the ropes: You get to see how your penny stock trades would have done without risking any capital.

Even if you "lose" money in your practice trades, you can still profit from the experience without suffering any financial harm. If you consistently turn a "profit" in your virtual trades, then you're on the right track and may be ready to start investing real money.

Many newer investors paper trade until their strategies prove consistently reliable. Only after their paper trades turn a consistent profit do they substitute funny money with serious cash.

The beauty of paper trading is that you have an endless supply of money to invest. This bottomless virtual bank account means that you can make lots of paper trades in many different penny stocks and, therefore, significantly shift the learning curve in your favor. You have many more opportunities to gain experience and benefit from your mistakes with a $100,000 paper portfolio rather than with a real-life $1,000 portfolio.

Keeping it simple: What you need to get started

To get started paper trading all you need is an Internet connection to track the prices of penny stocks (I tell you where to find penny stock pricing info on the Web in Chapter 6), a pen, and a piece of paper — hence the name *paper trade* — to record your virtual investments. That's it!

You don't need any fancy software or a complicated spreadsheet. The simpler you make paper trading, the fewer mistakes you'll make — and the easier it will be for you to develop a superior trading strategy.

Decide on an amount of imaginary money to start. You can invest $10,000 or $50,000 or more — that's the beauty of imaginary money. Just choose a nice even number, so that when you calculate your progress you can see at a glance if your paper trading strategy is working. For example, if you start with $100,000, and your stocks are worth $105,000 or $85,000, you can immediately tell that you are up $5,000 or down $15,000.

Setting your paper trading parameters

Because you're not dealing with real money, you can experiment with various techniques and strategies without fear of hurting your investments. However, you can still benefit from establishing a few parameters from the outset. Think of these parameters as guidelines that you can tweak as you gain experience trading in penny stocks:

✔ **Source(s) for information on penny stocks:** I list a variety of sources in Chapter 6.

✔ **Research and analysis tools, such as stock screeners and trading charts:** Flip to Chapter 6 for a detailed description of the kinds of analytical tools you can use.

✔ **Amount you will pay for imaginary broker commissions per trade:** I give you the lowdown on commissions and fees later in this chapter.

✔ **The duration of the trading period:** You can paper trade for weeks, months, or even years. See if you have different results depending on the duration of the exercise.

✔ **The types of penny stocks you want to invest in:** Choose specific industry groups (such as technology or healthcare), and certain sectors (such as biotech and restaurants). See if you have better results with certain kinds of penny stocks than others.

✔ **The method to track results over time:** Record trades and profits/losses in a place and with the method that's easiest for you. Keep detailed notes that you can review. Figure 5-1 illustrates a chart you can use to monitor your paper trades.

You don't need to know all the details of paper trading yet. Just remember that part of the process is to help you establish paper trading parameters, which you can apply after you begin trading real money. For example, you may start out using sources A, B, and C for leads on potential investments, but through investing imaginary money you discover that sources A and B aren't nearly as reliable as source C for generating profitable investments. You can now refine your parameters by removing sources A and B from your source list and using source C with more confidence.

Establish ahead of time the purpose for your trading exercise. Do you simply want to learn the ropes, or are you trying to establish a rock-solid, no-fail investment technique that will make you a millionaire? Are you trying to decide on the best sources of stock picks, or do you want to establish the most lucrative sectors from which your investment ideas will come? Your answers to these and similar questions help determine your methodology.

Start Date: 04/23			Starting Cash: $100,000		
Date:	Company:	Market:	Action:	Share Price:	Result:
04/25	Gatlan Tech.	OTC-BB	Buy 10,000	$2.58	Cost $25,800
05/20	FTTX	OTC-BB	Buy 5,000	$1.40	Cost $7,000
06/01	BRMM	AMEX	Buy 2,000	$3.70	Cost $7,400
06/29	Gatlan	OTC-BB	Sell 5,000	$3.20	$16,000 Proceeds
08/14	Gatlan	OTC-BB	Sell 5,000	$4.25	$21,250 Proceeds
10/13	JDK World X	AMEX	Buy 12,000	$1.50	Cost $18,000

Review Date: 11/30	Total Portfolio Value: $121,500	Change: Gain of 21.5%

Figure 5-1: A template you can use for tracking paper trading investments and progress.

Some paper trading considerations

You can increase your odds of success when you paper trade if you follow a few basic rules. Strict adherence to the following guidelines will also serve you well when you make the jump from paper trading to investing real money:

- ✔ **You don't have to invest all your money at once.** Keep some in imaginary cash in case new opportunities arise later on during your designated trading period.

- ✔ **Buy or follow several penny stocks at once.** Following several stocks allows you to see how different types of investments behave. Also, the more investments you watch, the more buy-and-sell opportunities you will have.

- ✔ **Don't have unrealistic goals just because it's "play" money.** If you don't take the process seriously because you're using imaginary money, you won't gain any insights to apply when you advance to using real cash.

- ✔ **Choose penny stocks from the same sectors or sources you plan to use when you invest real money.** If you want to eventually invest in biotech and pharmaceutical penny stocks, practice trading in those industries.

> ✔ **Adjust all aspects of your strategy regularly, based on what you discover.** The best paper trading strategies are the ones that evolve over time. Adjust what and how you trade from one week to the next, with the goal of continually improving your results.

Tracking the success (or failure) of your paper trades

Check in on your paper trading results daily. Take note of how each penny stock performed that day, that week, and since you originally picked it. If you don't see a lot of activity, consider doubling the number of penny stocks you're watching.

You may want to identify your best and worst trades each week or month. Was there something that was causing the big losses? The big gains? Use the answers to these types of questions to guide you in your future trades.

Compare the results of your penny trades with the overall performance of the stock market. If almost all shares are crashing by 50 percent, your 4 percent loss in your paper trade penny stocks may not be so bad after all. If the shares you paper trade are only up 10 percent at a time when the rest of the shares on the stock market jumped up 35 percent, you may need to rethink your trading strategy.

You should also get a feel for what types of investments are most appealing to you. Are you more comfortable with high-risk, high-reward penny stocks? Or are solid, slow-growth investments more your speed? Also consider which types of investments were most profitable and try to decipher the reasons for that success.

Treat your paper trading strategy as a work in progress. As you study your results, adjust and fine-tune your strategy. No paper trading methodology is going to be perfect right out of the starting blocks, but by making tweaks here and there, you can use your strategy to build a very profitable investing career.

Many successful paper traders wind up being not so successful after they make the jump to real money. Perhaps they didn't factor in the costs of brokerage commissions when they were playing with imaginary money. Maybe they have an entirely different mind-set when it comes to actual cash. Or perhaps they just suffer some bad luck and unfortunate timing.

Are you risking less with penny stocks?

A lot of investors think that because penny stocks cost so much less than blue-chip stocks, they risk a lot less money investing in low-priced shares. They also believe there is less downside to penny stocks because the prices are already so low. Unfortunately, these investors are misguided. Trading penny stocks doesn't reduce your downside risk at all; the practice poses just as much risk to your investment dollars as trading blue-chip stocks.

Any time you buy any stock — whether it trades at $99 or 25¢ — you're risking 100 percent of your investment. All the money that you invest is on the line. Any stock — no matter its original price — can lose all its value.

To help avoid a rocky transition from practice to the real thing, always treat your paper trading as if it's the real deal. Factor in all broker commissions, buy and sell the exact same penny stocks whether you're using real or imaginary dollars, and use the same information sources for generating your investment ideas. The closer to reality you can get with your paper trading, the less of a difference you will see when you move to actual trades.

What You Need Before Your First Trade

Before you can buy your first penny stock, you need to take care of a few details:

- ✓ **Make sure that you have a secure, reliable Internet connection to make your trades.** Remember to take proper security precautions when using the Internet for financial transactions, such as using a strong password, avoiding public connections, and logging off properly.

- ✓ **Set up an account with an online broker.** Make sure that your broker is "penny stock friendly." Find out if he tacks on extra fees or imposes minimum deposits for penny stock trades. I offer specific tips on working with a broker in the following section.

- ✓ **Deposit the funds you intend to invest into the brokerage account.** Deposit the money several days before you need it because there is often a delay of anywhere from a day to a week between when you deposit the money and when you can use it for stock purchases.

The delay in using money sent to your broker isn't the same as the three-day settlement period for stock market trades. The three-day settlement period applies to all trades, whether you buy or sell. This means that the brokers have up to three days to provide you the shares you purchased or the funds from a sale. Although brokers are legally obligated to act within three days, the good news is that almost every broker will generally process the transaction within minutes, if not instantaneously, which means that you won't be affected by a settlement period of several days.

Choosing a Great Broker

Before the Internet dramatically changed the investment landscape, almost all stockbrokers were considered *full-service brokers*. An investor called the broker on the phone whenever she wanted to make a trade, and the broker charged a hefty commission — sometimes hundreds of dollars! — for his efforts. Fortunately, the Internet has changed all that.

Today, almost all brokers are considered *discount brokers*. Their commissions are very low — anywhere from $5 to $19.95 per trade, generally — and they have online tools and account platforms for researching and trading stocks. When you want to trade stock though a discount broker, you generally enter your buy or sell details through the Internet instead of placing them over the phone. If you do call to make a trade over the phone, the broker will charge you a much higher commission, often as much as double the regular fee. With discount brokers, you don't get the personal service of a full-service broker, of course, but that's not a top priority for most penny stock investors — especially not for $200 per trade.

The characteristics you want in a stockbroker depend on your personal goals and strategies. For example, if you only plan to invest a few hundred dollars, you probably want a broker with no minimum balance requirements to open an account (meaning that you don't have to have a certain amount of money in your account to get started). If you plan to be a very active trader, making 20 buys and sells per week, low per-trade commissions may be more important to you. If you have lot of penny stocks in your account, you want a broker who doesn't add fees or apply penalties for low-priced shares.

Some of the criteria that you may look for in a broker may include, but aren't necessarily limited to, these:

✔ Minimum amount to open an account

✔ Penalties for low account balances

✔ Commission fees per trade

✔ Special commission rates for lower-priced shares

✔ Ability to trade (or not trade) on certain markets

✔ Ease of use for online account, and trading interface

✔ Customer service (both phone and e-mail)

✔ Research and analysis tools

✔ Speed of trade executions

✔ Size of the client base

By deciding which criteria are most important for you, and then doing a little research on potential brokers, you can choose a discount broker who best meets your needs.

Penny-stock-friendly brokers

The criteria you use for choosing a broker depends on the type of trades you plan to do. An ideal broker for larger, blue-chip shares may not be so ideal for trading penny stocks.

For trading penny stocks, find a firm that doesn't have minimum balance requirements to open an account and that charges low commissions.

Ask potential brokers for their *commission schedule.* This information is available online or by e-mail and indicates how much the broker charges per trade. The commission schedule should also spell out any restrictions or extra fees for trading low-priced shares, and may even explain if any specific markets or sizes of stocks are restricted or come with additional fees.

If you're relatively new to investing, I encourage you to find a broker who provides clients with helpful, easy-to-use online tools, such as price alerts and interactive charts. Of course, if you're planning to do most of your research through sources other than your discount broker, what tools they offer is a less significant factor.

Just about every discount broker has research and analysis tools you can use after you have set up an account. However, to use their more advanced tools you may be required to pay additional fees. Although these cost-based services can be very good, the free options can leave much to be desired (depending of course on who you ask, and which broker you're talking about). Due to this situation, the majority of penny stock traders rely on free online tools to do their research rather than those provided by their discount brokers. For example, you can use high-quality charting websites, get price quotes, set up price alerts, and review financial information all at no cost, and from reliable sources. Flip to Chapter 6 for some great sources for researching penny stocks.

When to upgrade your broker

Don't be afraid to change brokers if your current one isn't meeting your needs. A lot of fish are swimming around in the broker sea, and most of them want your business.

Yes, changing brokers can be a hassle, and your original broker may not make the transition easy for you. However, going to the effort of changing brokers is worth the trouble if your current broker isn't meeting your trading needs.

 You don't have to do all your trades with a single broker. Many investors have multiple brokerage accounts. You may choose to have one account just for the tools it offers, another account for making penny stock trades, and yet another for trading larger equities.

Types of Trading Orders

To understand types of trading orders and how to use them, you need to know how stocks are bought and sold. Later in this chapter I explain bid and ask prices, and what you need to understand about price spreads. Then you will be ready to use the various types of trading orders.

When you buy or sell shares of any type of stock, you choose between two main types of orders:

- Limit orders
- Market orders

Understanding the two types of orders is important for trading any type of equity, but the distinction is particularly significant when it comes to penny stocks. Because low-priced shares are more thinly traded (meaning that fewer shares generally trade hands than with larger stocks), and are more volatile by their nature, using the wrong order type can prove very costly. I describe the differences between market and limit orders in the following sections and list the pros and cons of using them for trading penny stocks.

Bids, asks, and spreads

Stocks trade hands when buyers and sellers agree on a price. Buyers "bid" what they're willing to pay for shares, while current shareholders who are looking to sell "ask" for the price they want.

Markets give priority to buy and sell orders based on price. Higher bids move to the front of the line, ahead of investors who aren't willing to pay as much. The market gives the same priority to sellers, with the lowest asking price taking priority.

For example, if the highest bid is 45¢, and the lowest ask is 60¢, no trade will take place. If the buyer raises her bid to 60¢, or the seller lowers his ask to 45¢, the shares will trade hands.

The difference between the bid price and the ask price is the called *the spread.* In the preceding example, the spread is 15¢. Although 15¢ may not sound like much, from a percentage basis, such a spread can be quite large. Consider Ironclad Performance Wear (ICPW), whose bid and ask prices are 25¢ and 30¢, respectively. That tight spread is only 5¢ but represents a difference of almost 17 percent. Generally with fewer buyers and sellers, as is the case with most smaller stocks, the bigger difference you will see between the bids and asks.

Limit orders

When you place a *limit order,* you set the price you're willing to pay for the shares you want to buy. For example, you can place a limit order for 200 shares of a stock at 65¢ per share. You will get as many shares as are available at 65¢; if shares happen to be selling for less than 65¢, you will get them for the lower price. However, if the shares have an asking price of 66¢ or higher, your trade order will not take place at all. That is, of course, unless one of the sellers lowers his asking price down to your limit price. You will never pay a penny more than your stated price.

You pay a full commission to your broker for each day that you execute a portion of your trade order. For example, if you use a limit order to purchase 10,000 shares of ABC stock, and you get 4,000 shares on day one and 6,000 shares on day two, you will be charged two separate trading commissions, one for each day. However, you won't be charged a commission for those days in which your open order doesn't result in any shares trading hands. For example, if you have an order to sell 3,000 shares, but none end up selling at the price you specified, you won't be charged a commission because you didn't sell any of the stock.

Due to penny stocks' price volatility, the small size of the underlying companies, and the limited trading activity in the shares, I highly recommend that you use limit orders when buying and selling penny stocks.

You should be aware of some potential drawbacks when using limit orders to trade penny stocks:

- **Low availability at your limit price:** Penny stocks generally have much lower trading activity than blue-chip or large stocks, so you may only get part (or none) of your order filled.

- **Multiple commission charges:** Because limit orders are often only partially filled, the orders are subject to commission charges from your broker for each day your order results in shares changing hands.

- **Wide spread between bid and ask prices:** Placing a limit order (or knowing what price to buy or sell shares at) is an additional step for penny stock traders. If a penny stock is bid at 45¢ and the ask is 70¢, that leaves a large price spread of 25¢ between what buyers want to pay and what sellers are willing to take in exchange for their shares. You need to decide a price at which to trade shares. You may want to use the current bid and ask as a guide, but you may even want to go outside of those ranges if your analysis tells you to do so.

Limit orders aren't generally the default among brokers, so you need to make a point of selecting limit prices (or instructing your broker appropriately) when you want to enter a limit order. Often this involves entering a price you're willing to buy or sell shares at when you place your order through your online broker. However, instructions can differ from one online broker to the next, so make sure that you understand the type of trades you're entering.

Market orders

When you place a *market order* you agree to pay the best available price for a stock. For example, if a penny stock has an asking price of 65¢, when you place a market order you agree to pay 65¢ for that stock.

Market orders are the default for your broker. Unless you specifically choose to trade with a limit order, you're making a market order.

The downside of placing market order is that you can't control how much you pay for the shares. The upside to market orders is that you get all the shares you try to buy. A market order is simply saying that you will buy at the best available price. Because there is always a best available price, you get all the shares you want. You just may end up paying much more for them than you expected.

I don't recommend using market orders to trade penny stocks. Here are the reasons why:

- **Low availability at the asking price:** Penny stocks generally have far fewer buyers and sellers, and much lower dollar amounts in total daily trading, so there may not be a lot of shares available for purchase. If you buy more shares than are for sale at the lowest asking price, your purchase order keeps going up to the next lowest asking price, which can be much higher than the previous price. For example, if you order 200 shares at 65¢, but there are only 100 shares available at that price, you may be stuck paying 70¢, 95¢, or even more for the remaining 100 shares.

- **Low trading volume:** Many penny stocks are prone to very low trading activity per day. This means that any significant buy (or sell) order may be enough to push the prices up (or down).

- **Wide spread between bid and ask prices:** Even if the last trading price was 45¢, you end up paying the lowest available asking price. That price may be 45¢, or due to the generally large spreads between bid and ask prices in most penny stocks, it may be something much higher.

Other types of orders

Market orders and limit orders are by far the most popular types of orders, but you can use other order types in conjunction with the previous two, or on their own. These order types include good-until-close, all or none, stop-loss, and trailing stops. The usefulness of each of these types of orders depends on the specific underlying stock and your own trading strategy.

Good until close

By default and unless otherwise specified, all orders are *good until close,* meaning that they are good until the end of the current trading day. If the market has already closed for the day at the time you submit your order, or if an order is entered on the weekend or a holiday, then it expires at the close of the market for the upcoming trading day.

Whether you enter an order on Saturday, Sunday, or Monday at 2 p.m., it will expire with the close of the market on Monday afternoon.

If you want to keep your trade order open for longer, you can specify how long the trade will stay active. You can keep your buy or sell active for days or even weeks. Setting an expiration date that is farther in the future allows limit orders more time to fill all the shares that you intended to trade. It also keeps your position in line at that price, because when your order expires and you re-enter it, you go to the back of the line at that price. For example, if you're the fifth investor out of eight to place an order for shares of a particular stock at 40¢, you're in line behind the first four and ahead of the other three. If you cancel your order and then reenter it at the same price, you become the eighth order in line.

With market orders, your order is immediately filled, so you never need to set the expiration date when placing market orders. Choosing dates that are farther in the future, however, can be a very valuable tool when used with limit orders.

All or none

Most brokers allow you to choose an *all or none* option. This means that you won't accept a partial fill, but rather will only trade shares if you buy or sell the complete amount that you want with your order.

For example, suppose that you want to buy 40,000 shares at $0.25. With an all or none order, you stipulate that you will trade none of them until 40,000 are available at your price (or a price that is even better for you).

Placing an all or none order helps you avoid multiple commissions. Such orders also help you avoid ending up with small positions of shares that may come with partial fills, meaning that you get only a fraction of the total you wanted.

The downside is that it decreases your chance of getting the shares at all, because investors who want to trade at the same price or better, and who don't have an all or none order, will generally take precedence.

Specialty trading orders

Other specialty trading orders you may have heard of include stop-loss orders and trailing stops.

Stop-loss orders are trades that happen automatically based on the price activity of the shares. For example, you can set up a stop-loss order at $1.50 for a stock you hold and if the shares decrease to that price, the sell order is automatically entered. You can limit your downside (in this case, to $1.50 per share) by using stop-loss orders.

Trailing stop orders are a version of stop-loss orders in which you keep increasing the stop price as the shares rise in price. If you have a stop-loss order at $1.20, but shares are trading toward $2, you may want to increase your stop-loss price to $1.60. This action locks in more of a gain. If the shares go even higher, toward $2.75, you may want to raise the stop-loss price to $2.50. You are "trailing" the rising price and locking in more gains, hence the name.

Some brokers won't allow investors to use of these types of more advanced orders with penny stocks. Due to the price volatility common in penny stocks, I don't generally recommend using them for trading low-priced shares. However, there are times when such specialty orders can come in handy, such as to minimize downside risk in certain situations (see Chapter 8 for details).

Consider Investor A and Investor B. Investor A buys too small of a position, and uses a market order through an expensive broker. Meanwhile, Investor B buys an appropriate position size, using a limit order through a low-commission broker. Investor A will almost always perform better over time, thanks to a superior trading strategy.

Characteristics of a Successful Penny Stock Trader

Penny stocks differ from larger equities or blue-chip stocks. To achieve success with these low-priced shares, you need a special mind-set. Effective penny traders tend to have many of the following characteristics:

✔ **Realistic expectations:** Some penny stock traders think that they can turn their $100 investment into $10,000 overnight. Individuals with these unrealistic expectations generally lose money and they generally do so quickly. Realistic traders who understand what they can potentially accomplish through each investment move generally do a lot better, by making the right decisions at the right time.

✔ **High tolerance for risk:** Trading penny stocks can come with great rewards, but because the investments are smaller and more volatile, they also come with greater risk. Fortune may favor the brave, but when it comes to penny stocks, fortune also favors those who can accept a high degree of risk.

✔ **Not married to the companies:** Successful penny stock investors think of their shares as vehicles to profits — period. They are quick to cut losing positions and they don't pin all their hopes on any specific penny stock, despite the upside potential of any of them. Their investment focus is less about trust in any one company, and more about balanced understanding of the potential of the underlying shares.

✔ **Patience:** The biggest gains in penny stocks usually come over longer time periods, as the underlying companies get discovered, move up to trade on larger stock exchanges, or produce improved quarterly results. This process can take years, but it's often worth the wait. Most penny stocks aren't widely followed, so it's only natural that they take a lot longer to get discovered by mainstream investors.

✔ **Ability to monitor companies on an ongoing basis and adjust accordingly:** Penny stocks can make big percentage moves and they often make these moves very quickly. The best investors can adjust and adapt rapidly.

✔ **Understanding of volatility:** A great penny stock on its way to higher prices can still suffer massive downward moves due to the nature of the volatility inherent in low-priced shares, just as shares heading lower can suddenly leap dramatically higher. The best penny stock investors know when the volatility is just that, and not a reflection of events in the underlying company. Successful investors are able to discern the difference between the two types of volatility and know when to ignore it and when to make a quick entry or exit.

✔ **Ability to make decisions based on research and not impulsiveness:** penny stocks can move faster, and by bigger percentages, than larger equities and other types of investments. This potential for significant gains tends to attract impatient and impulsive investors; however, they generally don't do as well as people who base their trades on research and measured decisions.

✔ **Willingness to do due diligence, and then some:** The most successful penny stock investors are the ones who do more than online research. They call the companies, they try the products, and they speak to employees and competitors. In fact, driving by the company's headquarters, or even doing an unannounced drop-in, tells you more about your investment than just about anything else you can do. This type of research can make massive differences in your results.

Although many of the preceding characteristics benefit any type of investor, they are almost always found among the more successful penny stock investors.

Investing Versus Trading

I use the terms *investing* and *trading* interchangeably throughout this book. However, you should be aware that the two terms do describe two different types of approaches. With penny stocks, the two approaches and likely their results, can be very different.

In fact, trading may be appropriate for certain types of people but not for others, while investing may prove quite profitable for some, but be not as effective for others. Think of it like trying to win a baseball game with numerous singles and bunts (trading), versus shooting for the home runs and grand slams (investing).

Investing in penny stocks

Investing generally involves looking over a longer term and getting involved with specific penny stocks because you believe in their business and their fundamentals, or you expect strong financial results to appear over time, which may help the share price go higher.

Investing is much less work, generally, than trading. Of course, investment research can be a seemingly endless task, but overall it should generally take up less time than trading. Investing involves researching a penny stock company (or companies) at your own pace, and on your own timeline, and then investing with the hope that the companies grow.

With investing, profits can be massive, as shareholders can often keep shares for the longer term and allow the prices to rise many times over, rather than cashing out for returns at the first 10 percent or 30 percent gain. Investing is a more appropriate approach for the majority of those getting involved with penny stocks.

I recommend that you treat your penny stocks as investments (rather than trades) if you're a newer and less-experienced investor. But many experienced individuals also embrace the investment approach. With investing, you can get involved with small companies before or as they get discovered and ride the share prices dramatically higher for gains of 2 times, 5 times, or even 20 times your money. A trader generally takes her profits at much lower levels, perhaps cashing out for a 20 percent gain, only to watch shares drive significantly higher.

How long until I see a profit?

The time it takes to make a profit depends on the underlying penny stock. The time frame also depends on the timing of your investment, because most price moves for penny stocks occur during brief periods of the overall trading time. I have statistics to back up this claim: Approximately 80 percent (or more) of any price move takes place during about 20 percent of a penny stock's total trading time. In other words, shares trade within a narrow price range for the majority of the time, only to explode or collapse in price during brief spurts. Such moves are generally — but not always — based on underlying events, such as lawsuits, new contracts, or FDA approvals.

More incremental gains or losses, typically anywhere from 5 to 20 percent, happen more frequently. However, such moves reverse in the majority of cases and so are usually temporary.

The biggest returns — those that increase in value 1,000 percent or more — often accumulate over a period of years. The rise in share price is frequently based on the underlying penny stock company slowly and methodically expanding its market share, picking up new contracts, or just generally producing better and better financial results over time.

Trading in penny stocks

Trading generally involves looking for short-term gains. Traders tend to ignore the fundamentals of the underlying companies and instead make buy and sell decisions based on technical indicators on the trading charts.

Trading generally requires more work, especially during the hours when the stock market is open. Traders attempt to make frequent, smaller gains, and to achieve these goals that make multiple buys and sells during the trading day.

A profitable trading strategy generally involves more trades than a profitable investment strategy. Due to the high volume and quick turnaround, trading enables shareholders to realize profits and losses more quickly. Some people find trading to be more exciting than investing. However, because trading requires more advanced analysis and trading tools, it is generally more appropriate for individuals with high levels of stock market experience. If you're new to penny stocks or the stock market in general, I recommend adopting an investing, rather than a trading, approach.

Chapter 6

Doing Your Research

· ·

In This Chapter

▶ Doing research you can rely on

▶ Asking the company effective questions

▶ Understanding analyst expectations and corporate guidance

▶ Profiting by anticipating trends

· ·

*B*efore you buy any penny stock, you need to know exactly what you're investing in. Specifically, you need to know:

✔ What the company does to make money

✔ What you expect to get out of the shares (and by when)

✔ What factors to watch to ensure that it's on the right track (or if it has fallen off the rails)

You can fill in all these details by spending some time researching the company.

Doing proper research is the most important step in successfully trading penny stocks. Research is your ally in tracking down the highest quality investments and avoiding the many duds. Researching penny stocks is less difficult than people expect and when you know how to do it well, it is very rewarding.

Also known as "doing your due diligence," researching penny stocks will help you find the best investment opportunities, recognize which options to avoid, understand what shareholders expect from the company's results, and anticipate how current trends will affect the company's business.

In this chapter I also explain the differences between company-specific and market-specific risk, and I help you understand exactly how many investors are betting against any particular stock by looking at the short interest. With this added knowledge of the tides of the stock market, you will be able to better anticipate and profit from price changes in your shares.

Ticker symbols

Ticker symbols are unique identifiers, expressed by letters, for each stock trading on the markets. For example, AAPL is the ticker for Apple Computers, while WMT represents Wal-Mart. Anheuser-Busch goes with the symbol BUD, which represents its bestselling beer. No two companies have the same ticker symbol. Using unique ticker symbols reduces the chances of investors accidentally trading in the wrong stock.

In some rare cases, such as a merger or corporate name change, companies may request that the stock market change its ticker symbol.

In the case of a bankruptcy, the stock will have a "Q" added to the end of their ticker symbol. Companies that are delinquent in filing their financial results will have an "E" added to the end of their ticker symbol.

Doing Your Due Diligence

Due diligence involves assessing timely and reliable information about a company in order to make judgments about the potential future share price — from which you hope to profit. It stands to reason that the more effective your research, the greater your trading successes should be.

Although research is valuable with any type of investment, it is of paramount importance with penny stocks. That's because the underlying companies are much smaller and so can be more easily derailed by a lost contract, a single customer leaving them, or a lawsuit, just to name a few of many possible events. The upside of such sensitivity to events is, of course, that penny stocks can also multiply quickly in price thanks to a single contract win, or by gaining a new customer, or settling a lawsuit.

You won't find nearly as much information about low-priced shares than you will about higher-valued stocks, and a greater portion of the information you do find will be less reliable or even misleading. Don't worry, though — that's why I'm here. In this chapter I steer you to information sources you can trust — and tell you which ones to avoid — so that you can invest in penny stocks with your eyes open.

Skimming the surface

All stocks are identified by unique *ticker symbols,* which are sets of letters used to identify individual companies. You can trade any stock just by knowing its ticker symbol, which is even more important to your broker than the company's name. Tickers generally range in length from one to five letters, depending on the exchange. For example, Ford, General Motors, and Exxon Mobile have tickers of F, GM, and XOM, respectively.

Tens of thousands of stocks trade on the various markets, and many of those stocks have similar ticker symbols. Always double-check the symbol to make sure that you buy or sell the shares that you want — and not those with a similar symbol. For example, if you want to buy shares in Ford Motor Company (F), make sure that you don't accidentally bid on shares of Forward Industries (FORD). You also don't want to confuse Wolverine World Wide (WWW) with World Wrestling Entertainment (WWE).

I never suggest that anyone trade any penny stock without knowing the specific company inside and out. However, in order to buy or sell a stock, all you actually need to know are . . .

- **The name of the company:** You certainly should know this if you're thinking about investing!

- **The ticker symbol of the stock:** This unique identifier is the most important piece of information your broker will need from you if you want to trade shares in a company.

- **The price per share:** You find this by getting a stock quote from your broker or from one of the thousands of free online services. Most quotes are delayed by as much as 15 minutes unless you pay a service or your broker extra to get "real time" quotes. Generally, you only need real-time quotes if you're an active day trader with a significant portfolio.

Digging a little (or a lot) deeper

To invest *successfully* in penny stocks, you need to know a lot more than the name, ticker, and price. By digging a little deeper into the company, you can gain a clear picture of the operational strength of a business, understand its branding and marketing strategies, and find and profit from patterns in its trading charts (more on these a little later in this chapter). This more in-depth research generally falls into three distinct categories:

- ✔ **Fundamental analysis:** As its name suggests, *fundamental analysis* considers a company's fundamentals, which include everything from knowing the management team, to looking at the financial results, to reviewing press releases, and to anticipating how these items will play out given the outlook for the company's industry. Flip to Chapter 9 for the nitty-gritty details on the fundamental review, and check out Chapter 10 for a discussion of the financial ratios used in this type of analysis.

- ✔ **Abstract review:** An *abstract review* is a more advanced version of fundamental analysis, which considers the strength of a company's marketing, branding, and customer loyalty. Few analysts understand or conduct abstract reviews, a surprising fact considering that a company's success often hinges on the features analyzed by this type of review. I walk you through the process of doing this aspect of due diligence in Chapter 11.

- ✔ **Technical analysis:** *Technical analysis* involves studying a stock's price movement and trading volume over time in order to predict future share price activity. I discuss the most (and least) effective technical analysis techniques in Chapter 12.

The Where's and How's of Research

The amount of time you spend researching penny stocks depends very much on your investment personality. While one investor may be satisfied — and successful — performing due diligence for only a couple of hours per penny stock, others may need days of review and weeks of watching in order to find acceptable investments.

Success is generally directly proportional to effort, but also remember that you could spend 100 years researching a penny stock only to have the same results as if you had spent 2 hours.

Several sources of information provide useful information on penny stocks, enabling you to make profitable trading decisions. Each source has its strengths and weaknesses, but by using them in combination with one another you can gain a great deal of clarity. The "right" combination differs from one investor to the next. You will find which combo works best for you as you find out more about each of the sources of information.

In the following sections I describe the various sources for getting the skinny on the penny stocks you're interested in.

Stock quotes

Stock quotes tell you at what price the shares most recently traded. More important than knowing the latest price is to keep an eye on changes in price by tracking stock quotes over time. For example, a stock quote of 50¢ per share only tells you the price at which the stock most recently traded. But if you also know that it traded at 25¢ the day before, you know that the shares have doubled in a short time. And if the stock was trading at 70¢ an hour ago, you can see that the shares are now on their way down.

Penny stocks can change quickly and dramatically in price, so you want to keep an eye on the company by getting frequent quotes. The more active and volatile the penny stock, the more frequently you should check the price.

The general rule is that you never want to be surprised by the activity of a penny stock. Checking a stock quote and finding that shares haven't changed in value won't hurt you, so check them as frequently as necessary to know exactly where the shares are and where they appear to be headed.

Keep in mind that sometimes a penny stock plays possum, or lulls you to sleep, by trading for years within a tight price range with very little movement, only to suddenly triple or collapse in value. To be prepared for events like this, you can set price alerts with your broker or one of many free quoting services. A *price alert* warns you (by e-mail, instant message, or some other method) when the underlying shares trade at whatever price trigger you set. You can also set alerts for a stock's total trading volume.

You can get stock quotes from thousands of places, and the majority of them are free and online. Your brokers can provide you with quotes, as do financial websites such as www.CNBC.com, www.Quote.com, www.Finance.Yahoo.com, and many others.

Remember that in most cases, free stock quotes are delayed by 15 to 20 minutes. If you want real-time quotes, which have no delay at all, you usually have to pay for that service.

Trading charts

In penny stocks, a picture is worth a thousand words. *Trading charts* display a penny stock's price — and usually trading volume, too — over time, in chart format. You can choose the duration of time and see how the price performed over a day, week, months, a year, or even longer.

You can view trading charts for free from your broker and on numerous websites, including www.BigCharts.com, www.CNBC.com, www.Quote.com, and www.Finance.Yahoo.com.

What you'll find on a typical trading chart

Here's a rundown of what you'll find on most trading charts and what you can do with that information:

- ✔ **Price trends:** A *price trend* can appear in the price of the stock for a particular duration of time. By observing the trading activity in the price of the shares you can spot, well, trends. Based on this information, you can determine whether the penny stock seems to be moving in the right direction. You can also see big price movements and, by looking at the date, cross-reference the change in the penny stock with an event, financial release, or news item. For example, if a penny stock doubled in price on a single day two months ago, you may find that it happened in direct response to a major FDA approval announced that same day.

- ✔ **Trading volume trends:** *Trading volume* is the number of shares that trade hands; the more shares that change hands, the greater the trading volume. A bar on the bottom of the chart tracks trading volume for the time frame (day, hour, or week) you select. The more shares trading hands, the greater the volume bar will be for that time period. If the trading volume is noticeably greater over a certain period, you know that the buying and selling activity was that much more active during that span. Trading volume gives investors clues as to increases or decreases in activity over time.

You can use trading charts to apply more advanced analysis to the penny stock. For example, by examining trading activity combined with price activity, you may find that the shares are highly likely to go up in the short term. This is referred to as technical analysis (TA), and I discuss applying TA to trading charts in Chapter 12. However, even without TA, the charts are very useful.

Types of trading charts

The three main types of trading charts, each with its pros and cons, are as follows:

- ✔ **Bar charts:** Perfect for investing in penny stocks, bar charts display just the right amount of information investors need. They show:

  - • The high and low price each day, indicated by the height of the bar

  - • What price the shares opened and closed at, represented by a dash to the left or right of the bar, respectively.

✔ **Line charts:** These simple charts only show a penny stock's closing prices over time, represented by a single line.

✔ **Candlestick charts:** These complex charts use a system of color codes to display whether a stock closed up or down for the day. For example, gains may be shaded black and losses shaded red.

Stock screeners

Stock screeners are online tools that allow you to set certain search parameters, such as price per share or market capitalization, and only return results of stocks that meet the criteria you selected. Screeners are important for conducting research into penny stocks. They allow you to set certain parameters, such as price per share, company size, industry group, stock exchange, and more, and only return results that meet those criteria. You can read an in-depth discussion on stock screeners in Chapter 7.

Company financials

The purpose of a business is to make money. The *corporate financials* tell you exactly how much money a particular penny stock is, or isn't, making. They also show you many other important things, such as how much debt a company has, its asset levels, and the sales growth of its various divisions.

Assuming that a penny stock you're interested in trades on a respectable exchange, the company must regularly and honestly report its financial results. (For more about the various stock exchanges, head over to Chapter 3.)

Companies release their financial results by quarter (three-month period), and the four quarters make up the year's annual results. If a company has a fiscal year ending on April 30, then the quarterly results will include results of operations as follows; the first quarter (usually referred to as Q1) is May to July; Q2 is August to October; Q3 is November to January; Q4 is February to April. As soon as a company has its Q4 results, it can also release its annual report for the full fiscal year.

Stock exchanges impose a reporting deadline for quarterly and annual results, and the listed companies must adhere to this timely reporting requirement for their stock to remain in good standing. Financial results are generally released about two months after the end of each quarter. This delay gives companies time to compile and review their results, provide official versions to the stock exchange, and publicly release the details.

Reported financial results become public data, and as such you can access the information as soon as it is released. The information is available directly from the companies, as well. as many free online sources, such as `www.Finance.Yahoo.com` and `www.MarketWatch.com`.

I provide a full discussion of what to look for in financial results and tell you how to interpret them in Chapter 9. I continue the discussion in Chapter 10, where I talk about financial ratios, which are derived from the details in the financial reports and provide a deeper level of analysis.

Press releases

Press releases can come from various sources, but generally the companies themselves issue them. You can glean a great deal of information from the press releases that a company puts out, but like everything from a biased source, take what you read with a grain of salt.

In general rule, companies issue press releases to announce positive events that are time sensitive or newsworthy. For example, a company may announce a new CEO, new contract win, gaining a listing on a better stock exchange, or the award of a new patent.

Consider adding your e-mail to a company's mailing list or setting automatic alerts to be notified any time a certain penny stock has news. That way you get the latest press releases right when they come out. Getting the information as soon as it is available — and before many other investors — increases its value tremendously.

Keep an eye on how frequently a penny stock company puts out press releases and what kind of effect the releases tend to have on the stock price. Some penny stocks announce "news" every week while others go for months without putting out a word. Some penny stocks spike at the slightest hint of optimism in a press release, while others don't budge in price no matter how glowing an announcement happens to be.

By getting an idea of a company's press release strategy and knowing what kind of reaction you should expect from investors, you will have a much better understanding of how to trade and profit from the underlying penny stock.

Media outlets

Pay attention to as many media outlets as you can as you perform your research. Often you can find reliable articles discussing the specific penny stock you're interested in, while other times you'll find information that gives you a better understanding of the underlying industry, the company's competitors, or important shifts in social trends.

For example, if you're watching a penny stock involved in the photography market, read trade publications about the photography industry and look for mentions of the company's name, products, or stock. Check out local publications (where the business is based) as well as major mainstream and financial media.

Because penny stocks are such tiny companies, getting the right kind of media coverage can drive their prices dramatically higher. If a major news network highlights a penny stock company's product, for example, sales can quintuple overnight, while a feature on home security systems or spas for pets, for example, can lift all stocks in the sector higher — including that obscure little penny stock that you've been watching.

Keep in mind that media generally has much less impact than many people think. Being interviewed by a big newspaper, or having a six-minute segment on a popular morning show, doesn't translate into a winning penny stock pick. While it certainly can help, it is usually not enough on its own to drive a company forward.

When it comes to penny stocks, not all media coverage is a good thing. Poor product reviews, a glowing highlight of the competition, or even a major (yet completely unrelated) event that takes over most of the media's focus and coverage can negatively impact a stock's value.

Media coverage can be one of the most important avenues for finding and researching potential. Combine what you glean from media outlets with the rest of your due diligence practices for the greatest effect.

Paid analysts

In some cases, a penny stock company will pay an analyst to produce detailed reports about it. While these reports can often be very professional and thorough, the fact remains that the company is paying the analyst for the review, which automatically casts a shadow of doubt on the value of the information.

The purpose of these paid analyst reports is to push the share prices higher, but instead of trying to pump up a stock through manipulation, these reports make an argument for why the shares should trade higher and that argument often has a great level of detail. As such, these reports can sometimes be useful when doing your due diligence simply because of the detailed nature of the review.

Like free newsletters, the job of paid analysis isn't to help you invest well but rather to move the price of the penny stock higher. Remember that they will paint the company in the absolute best light and omit or ignore the downside concerns. But if you approach these paid reports with these cautions in mind, you may be able to derive some good, albeit one-sided, information from them.

Investor relations (IR)

Most publicly traded companies are mandated by their stock exchange to have an investor relations (IR) representative. IR reps help attract prospective investors, and more investors generally translates into higher stock prices and a broader investor base.

One of the responsibilities of IR reps is to answer any questions that shareholders have about the company. The IR can be a very valuable resource when doing your due diligence, although very few investors ever take the time to contact them. In the section "Questions to ask management or IR," later in this chapter, I suggest some questions you can ask a company's IR representative in order to assess the merits of the underlying investment.

Like paid analysts, investor relations representatives are beholden to whichever company they represent. However, you will find that they tend to be less about sales pitch and more about facts. IR representatives are also used to speaking with management personnel and media, so they need to convey accurate, detailed information.

Penny stock newsletters

Penny stock newsletters can be a great way to get ideas and guidance on low-priced shares. These resources are almost always provided online, whether through e-mail alerts or a website, although a few send out printed newsletters or faxes.

In most cases, the service or website simply asks for your e-mail address, and then they start bombarding you with frequent "hot tips" about penny stocks they claim are going to explode in value. Unfortunately, the free newsletters usually have hidden motivations, and the majority of their selections seem to fare very poorly.

Paid newsletters, on the other hand, have a responsibility to provide sound investment opinions and maintain their subscriber base by making legitimate and profitable selections for their readers.

I've never done an official count, but it sure seems as though there are more newsletters specifically about penny stocks than any other type of investment. The number of newsletters available means that you have a great deal to choose from, but you should also recognize the equally significant risks.

Don't follow the advice of any penny stock newsletter until you understand the difference between the two types you may encounter; free and fee based. The difference between the two types is significant.

Free newsletters

Free penny stock newsletters make up the vast majority of publications about low-priced shares. As the name implies, you can access them at no cost; instead, all you need to do to receive their free alerts about stocks they claim will explode in price is to provide them with your e-mail address.

Generally, free newsletters and stock-alert promoters run websites to drive pump-and-dump schemes. In such schemes, price manipulators buy millions of shares in the company for pennies, tell their subscribers that this company is the next big thing, and then sell their holdings as foolish investors buy the stock for hundreds of times more than it is worth. As soon as the promoter unloads his shares on the market, the share price collapses far below what his subscribers paid. (I talk more about these manipulative schemes in Chapter 4.) Most investors who get burned by these pump and dumps never took the time to ask why these free websites brought the penny stocks to their attention in the first place. Even though not technically illegal (as long as the pump-and-dump artist mentions his ownership of the shares deep into a fine print disclaimer), pump-and-dump practices are highly immoral and very damaging to unsuspecting investors.

Subscription newsletters

To gain access to subscription-based newsletters, you must pay a fee. In exchange for that fee, however, you generally get much more reliable and effective guidance from a service that's in the business of profiling high-quality penny stocks. Because fee-based newsletters earn their revenue from subscriptions rather than manipulative pricing schemes, they're motivated to do proper analysis and uncover picks that perform well.

If you follow a penny stock newsletter, wait to see if its picks are going up in price before you give it your full trust. Treat its suggestions only as ideas, to which you can then apply your own due diligence. Always proceed with the knowledge that every buy and sell decision you make is fully your choice and responsibility.

Be wary of paid promotions in any newsletter — whether free or subscription. Many subscription newsletters receive compensation from the penny stocks they profile, and what appears to be a legitimate newsletter is actually little more than a cleverly disguised paid advertisement. Read the disclaimer that comes with any report, even if it is located in fine print and seven paragraphs deep on another page. Paid promoters are very good at hiding the fact that they receive money to cast the penny stock in the best light. The majority of publications have significant vested interests, and therefore you should not trust what they tell you.

I own a company that publishes *Peter Leeds Penny Stocks,* the most popular penny stock newsletter available. Keep in mind that my comments about fee-based penny stock newsletters may be biased.

Message boards

Message boards, or *chat rooms,* are forums where anyone (and I do mean anyone) can add their own comments to the discussions. For example, you could visit a message board where participants are having a discussion about a particular stock and jump right in with a bunch of made-up facts for everyone to see, and potentially believe. Message boards are often full of misinformation and blatant lies. Many investors use them to attempt to push up the prices of their favorite stock rather than as a forum to discuss meaningful data. I almost never go on message boards, but you should decide for yourself if they're beneficial to you. You can have a complete and healthy career trading penny stocks even if you never lay your eyes on a message board.

One of the concerns with Internet forums about penny stocks is that you may be inclined to act upon information that will eventually turn out to be misleading. Message boards are also a popular place for promoters to drive their pump-and-dump schemes and make comments with the intention of controlling how you and other investors act.

If you decide to visit message boards about specific penny stocks, enter at your own risk and don't believe anything you read.

Calling the Penny Stock Company

Every publicly listed company has an IR contact (or contacts) who can tell you about the corporation and answer any questions you may have. Many penny stocks make the CEO or other top management available for investors as well. Contacting one of these company representatives is the absolute best way to find out more (and more quickly) about a specific company and supercharge your investment results. Oddly enough, few investors take advantage of this opportunity.

The contact information for the IR representatives is usually on the company's website, in the investor relations section. Additionally, the IR name and phone number is generally included at the bottom of every press release. In the event that you're unable to locate the information for the dedicated IR contact, just call the company's main line and ask with whom you can speak.

If you only do this one thing — call the company — you will very likely be a much more successful investor. You will understand where the company is heading and how they expect to get there. You will even know what obstacles they're facing and how they anticipate overcoming them. And besides all this, the call is free (not including any long-distance charges), doesn't take long, and gives you information that most other investors don't have.

Be prepared before you dial

You will get a lot more out of your call if you know what to ask ahead of time. You don't want to ask a bunch of questions that you can find the answer to just by reading the website. And you don't want to waste anybody's time with queries about the latest financial report if you haven't read it.

Before I call a company, I know exactly what I am going to ask, I have notes and plenty of blank paper in front of me, and I even have expectations of the kinds of answers I hope to hear. This way the IR contact is able to relay the greatest volume of information in the shortest time.

Keep track of the name of the person you speak to and his contact information. That way, the next time you call, you can say, "we spoke about two months ago, and I just wanted to check in on progress . . . "

Keep in mind that even though talking to you is part of this individual's job description, he's still doing you somewhat of a favor. Therefore, respect his time, and don't call too frequently. A quick phone conversation once every few months, or after a major event like the release of the company's quarterly financial results, should enable you to get the information you need to make a smart investment.

IR personnel will appreciate your interest in their company. Don't be afraid to tell them that you're a newer investor. If you're a shareholder already, or just a prospective investor, tell them. If they use a term that you don't understand, don't be afraid to ask for clarification. Many people don't make the call because they don't know what to ask or they're afraid that they may sound foolish. Don't be afraid to make that first call and don't be afraid to make that tenth call! Follow the advice of the Chinese proverb: "He who asks is a fool for five minutes, but he who does not ask remains a fool forever!"

Questions to ask management or IR

You will get the best results from your phone call if you ask the best questions. Avoid dead-end and vague queries, and instead ask focused questions that require the contact to answer with specific, detailed answers.

Here are some examples of great questions that you should ask management or IR personnel include:

- ✔ **What is the current headcount at your company?** Follow up with "What was it two years ago?" "Where do you expect headcount to be in a year?" "How does this compare to your main competitors?"

  You will get an idea of whether the total number of employees is increasing or decreasing. If you see any significant trend, probe deeper. "Why is the headcount increasing so quickly?" "Are you able to get enough skilled workers that quickly?" "Is this rapid growth changing the culture of the company?" "What is your company's employee turnover rate?" "How does this compare to the industry's turnover rate?" "Why is your company's turnover so much higher/lower?"

- ✔ **On the quarterly financials, you cite $3 million in revenues. What percentage of this is from sales overseas compared to here at home?** Follow up with, "Do you expect this breakdown to change, and how?"

  You want to understand where the growth in revenues is primarily coming from and where the company is expecting the majority of its future sales increases to be generated.

- ✔ **Who do you consider to be your main direct competitors? Your main indirect competitors?** The answers might surprise you. A fitness gym may have a direct competitor in the form of a gym down the road, but its indirect competition may be weight-loss pills and weight-loss surgery.

You need to hear this from them, so that you can assess if they really understand what they're up against.

✔ **How many of the employees have been with this company for less than two years?** This will give you insights into company growth, employee loyalty, and turnover. It also tells you how many of the workers have extensive experience with that particular company.

✔ **Where did you work before, and how long ago was that? Why did you leave?** Getting a good sense of key personnel's experience will tell you volumes about how effective they were in previous roles.

✔ **How would your competitors describe your product? How would your customers describe your products?** Management is often blind to their own weaknesses, making it harder for you to discover the negatives. When you pose the questions like those above, you will often get a more accurate and substantive answer.

✔ **What do you feel will be the sales drivers for this company?** They can't tell you where they expect the share price to trade (it's against the law), but they can tell you where the company's growth will come from. From this, you should be able to understand if the shares are likely to move higher.

✔ **What is your attrition rate, meaning what percentage of customers stop using your service, and why?** Companies that have high customer turnover are in a constant struggle to find new ones. Companies that retain current customers benefit from predictable and recurring revenues.

✔ **How many years can your mine/well produce at the current rate before the resource runs out? (Also known as the reserve life index, or RLI)** Some resource extraction companies have great financial results and strength for now, but their wells are close to running dry or their mine is almost tapped out, meaning that they won't be producing strong results for much longer. Never invest in resource penny stocks unless you know how many years of reserves they have.

✔ **Will you need to raise more money to keep operations going? Please outline how much, when, and the potential sources.** Penny stocks that are constantly in need of more money can dilute shareholders by dumping more shares onto the market (see Chapter 3 for a detailed discussion of dilution). You will want an understanding of how much investment a penny stock anticipates it will need, and how the company plans to go about securing those funds.

✔ **The growth rate for your industry is 6 percent, which is double what your company reported on the last quarterly financials. How will you close this gap, and what is the exact growth target?** Questions comparing a company to industry trends are fair game, and such questions are certainly very important. You want to find those penny stocks that are out-performing their peers or that at least have a plan to do that.

Dead-end questions to avoid

Now that you know what types of questions you should ask, here are a few examples of dead-end questions that you shouldn't waste your breath on:

✔ **Is your company going to do good?** This is way too vague and provides no definition of what you mean by "good." The answer to this query will undoubtedly be, "yeah, we sure are." No knowledge has been gained here.

✔ **Is your product the best on the market?** Anyone you ask at the company will say yes. So will each of its competitors when you ask them about their product. This question is subjective and the answer has no bearing on whether or not the stock increases in price.

✔ **Is the stock's price going to go up?** A company can't legally talk about what its stock price might do or give you specific numbers of where the shares will trade at. Questions like this waste your time and theirs.

You will not really gain any knowledge or clarity by asking dead-end questions. You may also appear like you are a newbie, and the answers may be quite lackluster.

How to interpret IR responses

Your contact at the company will usually (but not always) be very optimistic for the company's prospects. Take her hopes and expectations with a grain of salt. Instead of trusting everything she tells you, try to delve into her answers to tease out what they're really saying.

If she says that the penny stock company is growing rapidly, but also says that the headcount is half what it was a year ago, then something does not make sense. Ask for clarification.

If she tells you that the company is expecting to sign a huge, new contract, don't believe it until the contract is signed and announced to the general public. IR contacts are notorious for explaining what they *hope* will happen as if it were assured. In my experience, their hopes turn into reality only about half of the time.

More important than the actual details and numbers that the IR contact tells you is her morale. Great penny stock companies on the rise have employees who love what they do, are hyperexcited about what's to come, and thoroughly enjoy telling you every detail of the company's story.

Getting to the point where you can spot the difference between genuine excitement compared to simply responding to your questions takes a lot of patience and more than a single phone conversation or two. The good news is that you start to find how to interpret management and IR comments with your first few phone calls and improve even further with each subsequent conversation. Your conversations will soon become an effective and profitable research technique.

Corporate and Analyst Guidance

Guidance numbers are simply projections of the range of expected financial results, such as sales between $1.2 to $1.4 million for Q3.

The most popular guidance numbers involve earnings per share, total revenues, and/or operating margins. They also sometimes may include additional or alternative financial data, such as debt load, cash levels, or whichever metrics they best expect will tell their company's story. (Flip to Chapter 10 for more about financial numbers.)

Companies are not legally required to calculate and publish guidance numbers, and a minority of penny stock companies actually does this. Sometimes professional stock market analysts generate their own guidance numbers for penny stock companies based on their own reviews. Additionally, because issuing guidance numbers is optional, companies also get to choose which financial details to provide.

Guidance can have positive or negative effects on the price of the company's shares, based mainly on whether the anticipated numbers are higher or lower than what the market was already expecting. If the company surprises the market by announcing an expectation that revenues will be doubled, this will generally (and almost instantly) drive prices higher. The same effect can hold true in reverse.

If the company or an analyst issues guidance, watch to see if the actual numbers come close to what was predicted. Some companies or analysts regularly issue guidance and just as regularly hit the expectations, which means you can have a higher degree of trust in their predictions. Other companies or analysts seem to have difficulty hitting the mark, continually missing what they had anticipated, whether to the upside or the downside, and in that case you should be more wary of their guidance numbers.

The type of company also impacts the accuracy with which they are able to provide guidance. A volatile penny stock engaged in an unpredictable industry, such as a movie production company, may not provide any expectations at all, and if it does, their numbers may be wildly off from one quarter to the next. A penny stock that has a set number of subscribers on a recurring billing plan should be able to come out with very accurate guidance.

Management and IR of any publicly traded company have an obligation to speak and report honestly, to the best of their knowledge. Doing so will keep them in good standing with the stock exchange and keep them out of trouble with regulatory bodies. If the CEO indicates that profitability is expected by Q2, or a financial officer mentions that his company is debt free, they had better be right or at least believe that the information they're disseminating is correct. For events they're not certain about, they generally won't say anything to avoid the risk of being held accountable for mistakes. This is one of the reasons many companies on the stock exchange prefer to not issue guidance.

Should you trust guidance issued by the company?

Following corporate guidance is a reliable method of knowing what to expect from a company. While corporate guidance is much less common among penny stocks than among blue-chip stocks, you should definitely take advantage of it when available.

The combination of a penny stock having access to its own ongoing financial numbers on a day-to-day basis and the legal requirement for materially important statements by management to be relatively accurate, means that guidance issued by a company is generally close to correct.

If a penny stock says that it expects sales for Q4 to fall between $3 and $4.5 million and earnings generated from operations to equal 1¢ to 2¢ per share, they will usually have final results that fall within those indicated ranges.

As events take place that lead management to believe that the company will exceed or fall short of its previously issued guidance, the company can adjust its expectations (usually disseminated to the public by way of a press release). Using the example numbers I mention above, the company may report that it now expects sales to fall between $4 to $5 million with earnings of 1.5¢ to 2.5¢ per share.

If the company doesn't want to provide new ranges or quantifiable data, it may issue a press release that sales (or earnings, or profit margins, and so on) are expected to come in at the high (or low) end of the previously issued guidance.

Following analyst guidance

Professional analysts often follow specific companies and generate guidance about those companies based on their calculations. Such analyst guidance is generally rare among smaller or penny stock companies, but in the instances where professional analysts do provide guidance, you should take their outlook into consideration.

The analysts work for brokerage firms and investment banks, and part of their job is to generate an opinion on the underlying stock in order to determine whether to buy, sell, or hold. They, and their parent companies, have reputations to maintain, and so it stands to reason that the analysts are providing an honest assessment of a stock when they issue an opinion.

Because analysts generally don't have access to information that the companies haven't made public, they are only able to provide educated guesses. Some analysts are better at generating guidance than others, but overall the figures that they calculate are not reliable, and very often wrong. This is why you may see very different numbers from multiple analysts who cover the same company.

Use analyst expectations as a guide in your own research, but don't rely on the information until they have proven themselves to you through a history of making accurate guesses. Also, put more stake in more opinions — that is, if ten analysts agree that earnings will hit a certain level, you can rely on this information to a greater degree than if it were only one analyst's opinion.

Generating your own guidance data

When you do research on a penny stock, you should be able to come up with your own expectations for future results. Generating your own guidance data is one of the best ways to position yourself to profit from low-priced shares, but doing so takes a significant amount of work.

If you know how many units of a product a company sold, what its growth rate in product sales is, and how much of each sale becomes profit, then you can calculate your own estimates. For example, picture fictitious FFFF company. If it sold 1 million units last quarter and sales have been growing by 5 percent per quarter, you can postulate that it will sell about 1,050,000 units this next quarter.

If you know that the company makes a profit of $2 per unit, its total profit will be up from $2 million to $2.1 million. If it has 10 million shares outstanding, then its earnings will be up from 10¢ last quarter to 11¢ this quarter.

I've simplified this example for explanation purposes, but the concept can be a very powerful tool. Calculate your own guidance expectations to get to know the ins and outs of a penny stock's operations much better and to find opportunities that may not be reflected in a company's share price.

When you calculate guidance, you want to focus on total revenues, profit margins, earnings per share, and debt load. You can head over to Chapter 9 to find out more about these numbers and how you can use them for guidance.

How Expectations Drive Prices: Getting Baked in the Pie

Companies grow as they increase their sales and profits; when a company grows, its stock price will often increase. But the relationship between a company's growth and rising stock prices isn't a direct one. Instead, the rise in value of the stock is based in large part on investors' expectations of higher future results based on those latest numbers.

In most cases, investors anticipate what they expect a company to do, and the shares reflect that expectation more than actual results that were attained previously. In other words, investors are forward looking, and a stock's value is based on what it may do, rather than what is has already done.

When information becomes publicly available and investors adjust their expectations based on that information, the shares of the stock in question will change. As traders absorb and react to this new information, those of us in the industry think of it as being factored in — or baked into the pie, so to speak.

Expectations are more important than results

Investors who profit the most from penny stocks generally have a solid understanding of a company's expectations and actual results and know how the two relate to each other.

The shares of most larger companies are based primarily on results, with only a small amount of their value coming from expectations. Penny stock markets, on the other hand, react more to expectations than results. The difference between the two markets leads to confusion for investors familiar with larger markets but new to penny stocks: These investors are often surprised when a penny stock that has just reported a doubling of its sales doesn't see an increase in its share price.

If a company doubles its sales, this result will only have a positive impact on the underlying shares if the market was expecting less than that. If investors had been anticipating a quadrupling of sales, the announcement of doubled sales may result in the share price collapsing.

 Investing well has a tremendous amount to do with spotting the companies that are exceeding expectations rather than finding those that are simply growing. This strategy is especially important with penny stocks because their prices have more of a basis in speculation and they are prone to rapid and dramatic price moves when expectations and real results divert.

Besides finding those penny stocks that may beat expectations, it is also important to avoid those stocks whose expectations may fall short. Penny stocks that don't meet or exceed what the stock market expected may see their shares heading lower, whether or not their companies are enjoying operational growth.

Expectations are more important in penny stocks than in larger companies for the following reasons:

- ✔ **The fog of war.** Penny stocks have fewer (if any) analysts following them, and the companies issue guidance much less frequently (if at all). This lack of information leaves a lot more mystery surrounding the potential financial results, and so when the actual numbers come to light, there can sometimes be a major reality check (and ensuing price change) for investors.

- ✔ **One-trick ponies.** Penny stocks usually have very few business lines or products and very often they have only one. When expectations for sales, or customer adoption and retention, don't match up with actual results, that disconnect will have significant implications on the viability and acceptance of the company's product or service. When investors realize that everyone is buying, or that no one is, the share prices will immediately react to the new reality.

✔ **Speculation has more uncertainty.** Penny stocks are traded more on speculation than results — on what a company could do compared to what it has done. You could say that investors rely more on hope than quantifiable results. Speculation by its nature gives penny stocks wider price spreads, and there is often a lot more room for correction when those expectations are compared with a company's real results.

✔ **These companies are babies.** Penny stocks usually inhabit an early phase of their corporate life cycle. Investors are still trying to figure out exactly what they have here, while many others are just hearing about the company for the first time. Many of these penny stocks don't have revenues, earnings, or even a history of results for comparisons or to gauge growth against. The price of these shares may be based entirely on expectation, and so whether the shares do well or poorly may be based primarily on changes in forward-looking speculation.

Beating estimates

When a stock beats estimates by releasing financial results that are better than the company and most analysts predicted, the shares tend to go higher. The degree of the upside move depends on the amount by which the company beat the estimates.

If only one or two analysts made predictions on the operational results of the company, beating their estimates may not have a significant effect on the share prices. If several analysts made the same prediction, or the estimates of the company itself were beaten, then there may be a significant upside response among shareholders.

Missing guidance numbers

When a company's reported financial results fall short of investor expectations, this is called "a miss," or "missing estimates." When a penny stock doesn't deliver what investors were anticipating, the shares usually decrease in price as a response. For example, when a company is expected to earn $2 per share, but their final results fall short with earnings of only $1.75, that company is said to have *missed estimates.*

Companies that miss estimates have an instant negative reaction in their share price. Investors anticipated that the results would be stronger, and the stock reflected that expectation; as soon as the financial numbers fall short, the share price drops lower to account for the weaker-than-expected performance.

The weak numbers may indicate growing problems with the company, a trend of decreasing acceptance of the products or services, problems with the company's distribution network, or some other significant issue. As a result, estimates going forward will need to be lowered, unless the company has a legitimate reason why there was weakness in the reported quarter that they expect to rectify, such as a worker's strike, machinery malfunction, or any other one-time event.

In penny stocks, watch misses in guidance very closely. They can be one of your earliest warning signs that not everything is going well with a company and may serve as a valuable indicator that you should sell your holdings before things get worse.

Penny Stocks Are Affected by Trends

The market is filled with trends, which are swirling all around you right now. These trends come in all shapes and sizes — you can find trends in social choices, consumer behaviors, and even within industry groups and sectors. For example, consumers buy more of such and such product, or they stop eating at restaurants that use Styrofoam for takeout, or they begin taking staycations (close to home) rather than vacations.

Trends also come with different speeds. Long-term trends take years to play out, while fads and short-term trends can come instantly and sometimes go within days. Consider the difference between a slow trend, like the declining popularity of smoking, and a fast trend, such as the September 11, 2001, terrorist attacks, which changed the focus and priorities of most of the world nearly instantly.

Whatever form they take, these trends affect how your penny stocks perform, serve as a warning to stay away from certain types of investments, and tip you off to which shares you should be loading up on. You can benefit by anticipating these trends and reacting accordingly.

What sector is your industry in?

Many investors confuse the terms *industry* and *sector* with one another. *Sectors* are very broad, while *industries* have a more specific focus. For example, the basic materials sector includes copper mining, specialty chemicals, aluminum, synthetics, oil and gas, and many other industries. The main sectors include basic materials, conglomerates, consumer goods, financial, healthcare, industrial goods, services, technology, and utilities. Within each of these sectors are several hundred industries, which include everything from the data storage device companies to water utilities, and from insurance brokers to meat product corporations.

You can be an excellent penny stock investor without understanding trends or knowing how to anticipate or react to them. But if you're able to get a handle on the social shifts in society or the industry a company operates in, you'll have a better understanding of obstacles and opportunities affecting the penny stocks you analyze.

Sector and industry trends

When an entire industry or sector (if you don't know the difference between the two categories, check out the nearby sidebar, "What sector is your industry in?") is affected by a trend, it will create both profit opportunities and risk. Some famous trends that have changed sectors and industries involved the move away from smoking and fur coats, the development and growth of the Internet, and the move toward greater security measures after the attacks on the World Trade Center and Pentagon on September 11, 2001.

A trend of rising oil prices will affect penny stocks in the oil production industry. Oil companies will be pumping and selling a more valuable commodity, so their share price should benefit. This trend would also affect other energy sources, such as those in the renewable energy, nuclear, and coal industries, because these industries may become proportionally less costly in comparison and so see demand rise.

Stay in tune with trends affecting various industry groups by keeping the following considerations in mind:

✔ **Be on the lookout.** By simply paying attention to trends in the first place, you will find that you start to notice them. The more you notice, the more you will begin to understand how they may affect the penny stocks you're watching.

✔ **Follow the media.** The news media both creates and follows trends. By paying attention to what trends the media is focused on, you have a pretty good handle on what's trending in society. For example, as media coverage of the Occupy Wall Street dropped off rapidly, you would have been able to surmise that the popularity of the movement would diminish.

✔ **Read industry and trade publications.** By reading newspapers, magazines, and blogs that are specific to certain types of industries, you will be able to pick up on trends that may affect certain penny stocks. Importantly, because these are niche publications and not as widely followed, you will have a trading advantage over traders who only look to the mass market for their information. For example, if you read medical publications and find out that the government is considering changing its regulation of stem cell research, you may find opportunities by getting ahead of the curve with your related investments.

✔ **Ask the companies you're following.** The penny stocks you're following already know what trends are likely to impact their operations. Call the company and ask them straight up. (I give you tips for calling companies earlier in this chapter.)

If you anticipate a sector or industry trend and position yourself accordingly with your penny stock investments, you stand to benefit a lot more than traders who didn't see it coming. Many of the bigger trends can last for years and transform entire business landscapes — and the portfolio values of many investors along with it.

Trends in the overall market

Most trends that affect the stock market occur due to the herd mentality of investors. Certain types of shares can be affected all at once, or certain price ranges of stocks, or even groups of investments based on the nation they are from, or the product they sell, or the age of the management team.

For example, investors may decide that companies based in China are the next hot thing, and shares of every penny stock from Beijing almost instantly doubles in price. Or perhaps companies in the biotech space make a lot of news with a major discovery, and investors get motivated to pile into any similar shares. If rumors start spreading about a few gold production companies falsifying their exploration results, you may see a sell-off across all the shares in that industry.

Stock market trends can be even bigger than simply affecting just a single sector. The entire market may be hurt or helped by an overall positive or negative feeling about trading stocks in general. During the dot-com bubble, days before it popped, investors were throwing money at the stock market and driving the prices of shares higher. This trend then reversed sharply, shares collapsed across the board, and it seemed like no one wanted anything to do with investing anymore.

Trends can affect the entire hunger (or revulsion) for stocks. Ride the trend when it is moving in the right direction but be aware that it may change course any time.

Trends in consumer and social behavior

Sales of products and services are the result of choices made by consumers. When you decide to eat at Burger King or get a new iPod and buy it at Wal-Mart, those are choices. Companies then react to the similar actions of you and millions (or hundreds, or dozens . . .) of other people by changing prices, or producing more, or expanding/contracting their market.

These adjustments by the companies are called *market-driven* adjustments, because they are facilitated or curtailed by the actions of the customers in the marketplace. A company can't raise prices if no one is buying and it generally only produces as much as it expects its customers to purchase.

Trends affect consumer choices. Those choices affect the market-driven aspects of companies producing the products and services that they make available to consumers. If the popular trends are to wear track pants and eat healthy, you may see demand at yoga clothing stores increase and the lines at McDonald's getting shorter.

As a result, you'll see yoga stores offering more products, charging more, hiring more employees, and staying open longer. You will also see McDonald's roll out a new, healthy menu.

You can see social trends and consumer behavior all around you if you know what to look for. Here are some questions to get you started:

- ✔ Which restaurant is suddenly popping up on every street?
- ✔ Which stores at the mall have the longest lines of customers?
- ✔ Which product are your friends suddenly talking about?
- ✔ Where is everyone's new favorite vacation spot?
- ✔ Which regions are your colleagues suddenly avoiding?

Profiting from trends

Not long ago it seemed that the world was going crazy for the stock market. Even your grandma might have been calling you with the next hot stock pick. This was the time of the dot-com bubble, and shares had been flying high for months. Everyone was making money buying just about any shares in just about any company, and those who weren't getting involved were missing out while their friends gloated.

During the bubble, I profited over 100 percent on an investment simply by watching the overall trend. Despite the fact that I had just written an article warning that the frenzy was ridiculous and that the Nasdaq market was due to collapse, I put some money into an obscure penny stock. I didn't know anything about the company, but I invested knowing that the majority of new investors into this penny stock wouldn't know either, and that they would be buying based on the trend rather than the company's fundamentals. In fact, during the dot-com bubble, fundamentals didn't matter to investors at all. I invested a bunch, let the trend do all the work, and took out twice that amount a couple of days later. This isn't a smart way to invest but, at the time, simply by being aware of the trend, I was able to take advantage of a great profit opportunity.

Spotting social and consumer trends is fun and easy. Now that you're aware of the concept and how it may lead to opportunities in penny stock investing, you'll have to go out of your way to *not* notice them.

Market and Company Risk

The two primary types of risk for your investments are market specific risks and company-specific risks, also called systemic risk and nonsystemic risk (the "system" in the name refers to the stock market).

Market specific risk, or systemic risk, relates to factors that can bring the overall stock market, sector, or industry down to lower prices even though there may be nothing inherently wrong with each of the underlying stocks. If the stock market crashes, that is risk related to the system, or systemic risk. If a single sector or specific industry group is likely to sell off, that is also systemic risk. When shares of many companies drop in price in unison, investors say that they are "trading in sympathy.

Company-specific, or nonsystemic, risk relates to a company directly. If a penny stock you're holding gets hit with a huge lawsuit, the downside risk is focused only on that company. If the entire management team of a certain low-priced investment you hold suddenly vacates their positions, the probable decline in the share prices is risk you face that is specific to that penny stock rather than its industry or sector.

Knowing which type of risk you are experiencing, or may experience, will go a long way in providing clarity for your trading moves. You may not need to worry if your shares are lower along with the overall market. However, if a specific penny stock you own is trading lower while the industry and overall market are on the rise, you need to know exactly why.

Let the rising tide lift your boat

When the stock market is on the upswing, even poor quality penny stocks can rise along with it. This holds true in reverse, as the best penny stocks can sink when everything around them is also going lower. This makes trading penny stocks very forgiving when you go along with the currents in the stock market and very punitive if you go against it.

One of the most profitable times to invest is when stocks are moving higher in general and the markets are making upward progress. As the positive tide rolls in, most stocks should benefit simply because they're on the improving market. They are in the right place at the right time, and their shareholders are as well.

Investors are encouraged by rising stock markets. The upward move affirms the beliefs of investors who are betting on higher prices and makes those who don't get involved feel like they're missing out on profits. The end result: buying, which creates more buying, which in turn creates even more buying.

Investing against the current

Every penny stock investor will face times when the markets are pushing against him. You may be holding a great, well-run, and up-and-coming penny stock, but the stock market is crashing all around you.

In cases like this, no matter how much you believe in that particular penny stock, or how great the company's technology or solution is, the value of the shares may be sliding lower. In times like this, even great news or glowing press releases may do little to bump the shares at all.

When deciding how to proceed, ask yourself if the worst of the drop is already over. If you think so, selling in reaction to the downward slide could be a major mistake because the shares may pop back up to former values pretty quickly.

If you feel that there is a lot more downside, even from the current depressed prices, consider selling and buying back at even lower prices as the downward trend plays out. Even if you've already lost 10 percent, it may get a lot worse. You can either go down with the ship or step onto the lifeboat with the intention of getting back onboard later.

If you are looking to buy certain penny stocks, a down market may be a great time to do so because bargains will abound. And considering that a lot of the weakness is market specific and not necessarily company specific, this could be a good time to start picking up all the shares you've had your eye on.

When the entire stock market is facing weakness, many investors sell various holdings to raise money to cover other parts of their portfolio. For example, if a speculator is hurt by market weakness which results in him owing his broker $30,000 within a few days, he may sell all sorts of assets, penny stocks included. This may affect or exacerbate the downside of certain penny stocks, even though the downward shift is unjustified in terms of the underlying quality of the penny stocks.

Reacting to nonsystemic (company-specific) risk

When a share suffers a downside move, you need to recognize whether this weakness is based on an issue with the company itself or is due to a downward slide across the entire industry or market. Compare the company's trading direction against the overall industry. Your reaction should be different depending on whether or not the negative move is an issue with the specific company.

Take nonsystemic risk events very seriously. Depending on the severity of the issue, it may be time to sell your shares, especially if you expect things to get even worse or if there will be a very long time before the company will be able to resolve the concern.

If a penny stock is hit with a significant lawsuit, loses one of its few clients, or has a new billion-dollar competitor enter its space, these company-specific events will change the company's outlook and weigh on shares for an extended period. If a stock you're holding runs into major detrimental events, you may want to consider selling your shares.

Keep in mind that penny stocks can sometimes do well despite major company-specific risk events. Every penny stock and situation is different, so don't run for the exits each time a negative event occurs.

Assess each situation and decide every trade on a case-by-case basis. Give the penny stock a fundamental and technical review (as detailed in chapters 9 and 12, respectively) to decide what action to take.

Sometimes you will want to hold the course, other times you should dump your shares as fast as your computer can send in the trade. The better you get at knowing how to react, the greater success you will have with your penny stock trading.

Reacting to systemic (market) risk

Failure to understand the difference between market risk and company risk is a major source of trading mistakes for penny stock investors. In fact, when all stocks trade down in sympathy to overall market weakness, the shareholders who panic and sell individual stocks very often regret their decision within days or weeks.

Don't react to market risk in the same way as company-specific risk. Weakness that affects entire segments of the stock market (systemic risk) isn't necessarily indicative of problems with operations of specific companies that just happen to be caught up in the downward current. Making a decision to sell based on price weakness that is completely unrelated to that specific penny stock is often a mistake.

If a news story about deadly bacteria in some of fictitious FFFF's vegetables spooks investors, they may sell off all food and farming stocks. As the problem is addressed within a couple days, is related only to FFFF corporation, or even turns out to be false altogether, those same food and farming stock shares will return to former levels.

The investors who lose are the ones who sold their stock in the companies (other than FFFF) in reaction to the nonsystemic event. They cashed out at lower prices and missed out as those same stocks returned (and pretty quickly) to former levels.

Taking advantage of market panics

Market panics and reactions to systemic risk are a great way to pick up penny stocks at discount prices. When an event pushes an entire sector down, but specific penny stocks you've been watching remain strong — they're still growing their market share, increasing their revenues, and shrinking their loss every quarter — it's a great time to pick up shares at discounted prices.

Managing long-term systemic risk

Some market risk events result in long and significant weakness in entire industry groups, and you shouldn't expect that shares will recover any time soon.

Although systemic risk usually isn't a reason to sell, there are times when selling is appropriate. For example, consider a nuclear meltdown that is front and center in the media, spooking investors, and driving shares of uranium mining stocks down sharply. All companies related to nuclear power will take a hit, and that systemic risk may remain (or get worse) for months or years; the smart move may be to sell your shares.

Buying What You Understand: The Free and Instant Advantage

Buying what you know is a great way to increase your odds of success. You will feel more comfortable with investments that you understand, and will almost certainly make better decisions.

If you know a lot about a certain industry or type of business, you will have an advantage over most other investors. A computer programmer has a better chance of understanding Internet companies, while a doctor may be a good judge of healthcare stocks.

Besides understanding the industry's lingo, you may even have used the company's products, read the trade publications, know someone from the management team, or attend the trade shows. In addition, you may be familiar with or use the specific company's products or services, or that of their competitors.

In some cases, you may work at a company that is a publicly traded penny stock. This will give you a major and firsthand advantage if you decide to invest in the shares. Just keep in mind that you need to maintain some objectivity — the fact that you enjoy working for the company doesn't necessarily mean that it's a good investment.

Keep an eye on short interest

You can see how many investors are expecting a specific penny stock to drop in share price by checking the number of people short selling the stock.

A certain portion of shares are held by investors who use a risky method known as *short selling,* whereby they sell shares first and try to buy them back later at lower prices. The *short interest* is the number of shares that are currently sold short relative to the total number of shares of the company. Short interest is usually expressed as a percentage (such as short interest of 8.3 percent), and can be a very useful analysis tool because it demonstrates what proportion of investors are betting against a company or expecting it to decline in share price.

You can see the short interest (or what percentage of outstanding shares have been sold short) via many of the top stock market websites, such as Yahoo! Finance (`www.yahoo.finance.com`) or MarketWatch (`www.marketwatch.com`).

Chapter 7

Picking a Winner

. . . .

. . . .

Success in penny stocks comes down to investing in the right small companies and then profiting as their shares grow and multiply. With hundreds of investment strategies out there, numerous pitfalls, and so many small investments competing for your attention, choosing a winner can be both difficult and intimidating.

Because you've shown an interest in penny stocks, you recognize what the upside can be like if you become adept at choosing the right shares: fairly quick and significant returns on your money.

In this chapter, I offer numerous strategies for narrowing down the thousands of penny stocks out there so that you end up with a manageable lost of options you can research in detail.

I explain certain selection parameters and criteria that will dramatically reduce your total number of choices, while improving your odds of success. This chapter focuses on what many penny stock investors consider the most important aspect of trading low-priced shares: profiting by picking the right ones!

Narrowing Your Choices

If you were to count all the penny stocks trading on various exchanges around the world today, they would number in the thousands. Penny stocks are so numerous because many of the exchanges they trade on have very lax listing requirements, making it possible for even the tiniest and most financially broken companies to join the ranks of penny stocks. Choosing from among this glut of low-priced shares the world over can be daunting.

The Peter Leeds approach

For the Peter Leeds newsletter, we start our analysis with the full universe of penny stocks and then eliminate huge chunks of them very quickly by imposing the following strict parameters:

- ✔ We only consider American penny stocks.
- ✔ We don't choose those companies trading on the Pink Sheets and other inferior exchanges.
- ✔ We avoid companies involved in certain industries.

This first level of screening is actually quite simple and not at all time intensive. My team then screens the remaining stocks to determine whether they warrant a full Leeds Analysis review. Only stocks that pass our full review are profiled for our subscribers.

Consider a similar approach for your own investments, when you want to bring the full universe of penny stocks down to a handful of potentially rewarding and high-quality investments.

You may not think so at first, but the fact that the vast majority of penny stocks are very poor investments is a good thing for you. By identifying the types of low-priced shares that you should avoid without a second thought, you're immediately able to eliminate the bulk of them and, potentially, enjoy superior odds by choosing among smaller, theoretically higher-quality groups of shares. I tell you how to do just that in the following sections.

Eenie-Meenie-Miney-Mo: Your Elimination Criteria

By applying some strict elimination criteria, you can make the number of available penny stock investments much more manageable. And in addition to shrinking the total universe of choices, you'll ideally also be left with penny stocks that are somewhat more likely to represent high-quality investments.

You can make the number of potential investment choices dramatically more manageable by eliminating significant subsets of penny stocks based on the following characteristics:

> ✔ **Market:** Avoid shares that trade on many of the lower-quality stock markets, as I describe in Chapter 3. This is the easiest

elimination approach and will do a great deal for your final investment results.

✔ **Industry:** Refining your potential investments to certain industry groups is a quick and easy way to shrink the universe of penny stocks. An added benefit is that, by keeping a close watch on a specific industry, you'll have greater clarity about corporate players and the overall trends within the industry — knowledge that may help steer your trading choices. You may have an added advantage by focusing on a specific industry you're familiar with.

✔ **Share price:** This is an easy technique to quickly limit the potential investments. Focusing on shares priced at 50¢ or above, for example, will also help you control the caliber of companies, as the higher the price of the shares, typically the better quality the investment.

✔ **Company size:** You may want to focus only on companies with a certain market capitalization. By only considering penny stocks worth more than $100 million, or less than $5 million, you eliminate all the shares that don't meet your criteria.

✔ **Trading activity:** You may want to avoid stocks that haven't traded in the last day or two or that are too volatile. I show you how to do this in the section "Stock Screeners," later in this chapter.

Always adjust your choices of groups over time, based on the results you achieve. For example, you may find that your investing returns are awful when you focus on shares with market capitalizations of between $10 and $20 million, so you may decide to change that parameter to higher levels.

Who Do You Trust?

Most penny stock investors begin the process of choosing stocks by getting leads from third parties, such as newspaper articles, financial newsletters, and stock screeners. These and others sources can be a great jumping-off point for your own due diligence, but the source of the information matters tremendously. Not all individuals making a penny stock pick have your best interests in mind, and the quality of any potential leads varies significantly from one source to the next, or even from one pick to the next.

In my opinion, the best way to approach penny stock investing is to get picks from a reliable, unbiased source with a great track record, and then apply your own due diligence to those shares. I've found that the most successful investors combine their own common sense and hard work with high-quality information sourced from a third party with an excellent track record.

An important part of this approach involves getting the best picks in the first place. This is a skill you will refine over time, as you are able to assess the quality of the information by seeing how the picks actually perform on the market.

Your number one ally: You

The first and most important step to being an effective penny stock investor is to trust yourself. Use common sense, and believe in the power of your own instincts.

You can't rely exclusively on the opinion of others, even when they have your best interest in mind and have a good track record. The common denominator in any choice or penny stock trade should always be you, and you alone.

You are far and away the best person to trust in your trades, because you

- ✔ **Remain constant.** You can switch the analyst you trust, you can upgrade the newsletter providing you with picks, and you can adjust your stock screening parameters, but you can never change you. As the common denominator, ongoing losses will all involve you, as will any gains.

- ✔ **Will improve.** A newsletter or analyst will often remain the same, but you have the ability to continually improve over time. In fact, you may find that you discover more — and more quickly — from your errors than you do from you victories.

- ✔ **Won't trick yourself.** You truly can trust yourself. No hidden motivations will ever convince you to be dishonest with yourself.

- ✔ **Have your own best interest at heart.** You know what's best for you. Anyone else may want you to fail, not really care about how things work out, or may have other priorities. You, however, know your goals and are the most ambitious about achieving them.

At the end of the day, you should take full responsibility for any and all trades you make. Never blame anyone except yourself for losses and use those mistakes as opportunities to become better rather than as reasons for regret.

Considering the motives of others

Any time someone introduces you to a potential penny stock investment, you first want to figure out his true motivations. Often numerous motivational influences are at play.

Among the reasons that an individual or organization may the shares of a specific company in front of you and other investors are

- ✔ **They want to be on TV.** Just like winning the Super Bowl is the pinnacle of football, getting on certain shows is the peak of the investment world for many people. Many individuals measure their success only by the media yardstick. Somewhere in all their attention-grabbing efforts, the true and valuable stock market analysis may have fallen to the back burner.

- ✔ **They're contrarian.** A certain portion of the population likes the visiting team just because they're not the home team. They go against widely held beliefs only to stand out or shock people. Of course, sometimes contrarians are right, but you want to avoid people who take a contrarian position merely for the sake of standing out from the crowd.

- ✔ **They want to be right, no matter what the facts say.** People love to be right. This applies to guests on the most popular stock market shows as much as it does to third graders. Remember that as much as anyone likes to be correct, and dislikes being incorrect, nobody can be right all the time.

- ✔ **Sticking to their guns.** Maybe an analyst or guest on a stock market show, or in an article, had made a comment or prediction previously. They often double-down on their prior comments, especially when that statement is proving to be incorrect. By saying the same thing, they often feel like it erases their earlier error and makes the current situation look that much more compelling.

- ✔ **They don't care.** Sometimes an analyst would rather be deep sea diving or golfing. Believe it or not, giving you a great stock pick isn't at the top of her priority list!

Try to identify the real reason behind people's recommendations. Look beyond the surface to find out what's really driving them and their opinions. Very often their true motivations will be far different than the superficial reasons.

Reviewing their track record

All stock market analysts and newsletters worth their salt provide a track record of their past selections. In other words, they tell you how their picks have performed over time.

Ideally, that track record will cover at least a full year, but of course longer time frames are even more revealing. While any stock picker may have a good year, if they can show consistency over several years, as well as through both up and down markets, then you may be able to increase your trust and reliance on their selections.

Before you put any faith or trust in any source, first make sure that they provide their track record for previous selections. If they offer one, you need to ask yourself why they are not promoting their success. And the answer may be that they don't have any.

But don't stop there. You next need to decide if you trust the track record. Especially in online formats, it's easy to post misleading or just plain inaccurate information.

A great way to ascertain the trustworthiness of a newsletter's track record is to follow along with its picks in real time. Watch to ensure that it includes each pick it makes in its data. Even though the newsletter's track record may not be updated for months after it make its picks, when it does recalculate its performance, watch to see if it includes all the selections you know that it made.

When you do find a source whose track record you trust, compare the results of the potential picks to other sources. Although past performance has little to do with future success, it can demonstrate an analyst's ability to routinely select winning penny stocks.

Paid advertisements: The wolf in sheep's clothing

Whether published by a promoter or professional investor relations firm, the moment the coverage is produced in exchange for compensation, it loses all credibility.

Whenever you read any comments about a publicly traded company and its prospects, before you actually put any stake in the information, take a moment to find out if any money exchanged hands. Stock promoters have a legal obligation to disclose any compensation they received for talking about a stock.

This information will usually show up in a disclaimer. Cleverly, the publisher will attempt to hide the fact that their opinion was "bought" by only mentioning it in small print on page two, surrounded by paragraphs of text.

Many paid promoters "bend" the law by not mentioning their interest in the company, or they only do the bare minimum to meet the requirements. In either case, the real problem is that their target audience is generally too trusting.

The SEC imposes very outdated and ineffective laws on stock promoters and paid corporate advertisements. Very few people actually bother to read the three-page disclaimer. They don't notice the fine print line, 23 paragraphs in, which reveals that the company paid them $30,000. What I would like to see is a standardized, upfront disclaimer that must accompany every paid advertisement. The SEC should regulate promoters to provide clear disclosure right at the top of any report so that investors know what they are reading. For example, "We were paid 1.5 million shares in exchange for producing this information."

Unreliable analysts

Sometimes even the most popular, highest paid analysts make the wrong calls. They may even hit cold streaks, where they make a series of bad calls in a row. You need to be able to distinguish good analysts having a bad streak with just plain bad analysts.

Unfortunately, many analysts consistently make poor suggestions. Even if the analysts are unbiased and work with a top firms or newsletters, they simply may not be good at selecting stocks. As an investor, if you choose to follow any analyst, your job is to determine the quality of the ongoing opinions that she or her firm provides, and do complete due diligence even on the highest-quality penny stocks.

Don't rely on the opinion or comment of any individual simply because financial television shows seek her out for interviews and advice. The so-called experts are often wrong, despite the size of the stage they are afforded to make their statements.

Stock Screeners

Stock screeners are automated online tools that find stocks that meet criteria that you set. Specifically, they refine the thousands of potential penny stock investments down to hundreds, or even a few dozen, or one, based on your search parameters. Stock screens are invaluable tools for any investor.

Screeners do all that work for you, and the results they spit out are quick and flawless. When you decide on a parameter, for example shares between two and three dollars, the screener eliminates every other stock and only produces those shares that meet your criteria.

You can access many free online stock screeners through the major financial websites such as Google Finance and Yahoo! Finance, and many stockbrokers provide them as well. If you don't mind paying a small fee, you can access stock screeners with even more advanced features, such as screening by technical analysis indicators or chart patterns; check out the stock picker tool on www.stockwatch.com and the screener provided through www.StockFetcher.com.

Stock screeners do have limitations, though. A screener can assess and sort only by data available about the shares of a company, such as the price, the market, and the industry group. Screeners can't sort or eliminate shares based on anything other than data directly related to the stock itself. Anything to do with the underlying companies, or their operations or prospects, is beyond the scope of the screener.

Given their great value yet significant shortcomings, think of stock screeners as wonderful tools to use in the first step of your analysis. To trade penny stocks well, you still need to properly analyze companies that your stock screener produces.

Choosing criteria to focus your search

You need to decide which criteria to screen for based on the options available on the particular tool you're using. Here's a rundown of the types of search criteria most screeners offer:

- ✔ **Price:** Stock price is the easiest method by which to screen companies.

- ✔ **Market:** Filtering out stocks based on the exchange they trade on is the best way to eliminate most low-quality penny stocks in one quick click. With this screen alone, you can dramatically improve your odds of finding winning companies.

- ✔ **Industry:** A great way to screen companies is by industry, especially if you know a lot about a particular market or have reason to be optimistic about it. Screening by industry will return far fewer results than if you base your parameters on price or market alone.

- ✔ **Price situation:** Some screeners allow you to select companies based on the situation or activity of their shares. For example, you could choose any stocks making a new year-high in price. Several other price criteria may prove useful:

  - • **Percentage of high or low:** You can focus on shares that are trading within a certain percentage of their year high or year low in price. An example of this is a screen for any stocks trading within 10 percent of their lowest share price for the previous 12 months.

- **Trading volume:** You may have success screening for stocks that are seeing major increases in the buying and selling activity in their shares. For example, you could set your screen to include every company that is showing triple the average trading volume.

- **Volatility:** Some screens can focus on stocks with certain levels of trading volatility in relation to the overall market. You may find success trading penny stocks that are twice as volatile as the overall market; or perhaps shares that are only one-fifth as volatile are more your speed.

- **Fundamentals:** You can set screeners to return results only for stocks that demonstrate certain fundamental criteria. For example, you may choose to only see screened results of stocks that have a price to earnings (P/E) ratio of 12 or lower (Head over to Chapter 10 to find out about P/E ratios.)

✔ **Company size:** Screening by market capitalization is a great way to single out companies based on size. By setting a minimum size, you can also eliminate those businesses that are too small, such as penny stock companies that may pass your other screening parameters but may be worth only $100,000 in total and thus not be a wise investment choice.

With any particular screening criteria, you will significantly pare down the number of options. However, by combining numerous parameters — such as price, industry, and market capitalization — you can achieve even more refined outputs.

Try combining a price restriction within a percentage of the year high in price. For example, you may want to screen for all stocks priced between two and three dollars and that are within 10 percent of their highest price for the year. This will return low-priced shares that are enjoying strong price momentum and so, by extension, may enjoy solid stock growth to come.

Don't be afraid to experiment until you feel satisfied with the results the tool produces. You can change your criteria or try numerous combinations.

Screening your screens: Getting even more focused

Even after using multiple search criteria you may sometimes end up with thousands of results. Usually this is due to your screening parameters being too broad. To generate a more manageable number of results, go back and make those criteria tighter, lower, or more demanding. You may need to refine your screens several times before you end up with a reasonable number of stocks.

As soon as you do start producing manageable lists of stocks that pass your screen, you may want to apply an additional parameter before you start looking at them any closer. Screens will always include companies that fall within your search parameters but that you know you'd never invest in. Take a few minutes to manually scan the list and remove companies based on your own criteria — criteria that aren't available as a screening tool option. For example, your screened list may include mining companies, but if you know you aren't interested in investing in such stocks, cross out or delete "Gold Mine Resources Incorporated."

You may be able to quickly pare down a list of a couple hundred companies to only a dozen or so by removing any stock that meets the following parameters:

- **Holding companies:** Holding companies have their own set of rules. They are typically indicated with the words "Holdings" or "Holding Company" in their name. If you are looking for holding companies specifically, or don't mind that they are more appropriate as legal-protection entities than as companies for investment, then by all means keep them in your results. Otherwise, remove them from the list.

- **Class of shares:** Companies can have different classes of shares, although this is much more common in larger stocks. The various classes of shares have unique rules and prices; for example, class A shares provide their shareholders with voting rights in the corporation and first rights to the corporation's assets in the event of a bankruptcy, while class B shares may not provide those same privileges. You may want to manually remove any special share classes, which are typically indicated by ".A" or ".B" after their ticker symbol.

- **Weak names:** I personally never invest in companies that have obviously weak or nonsensible names. A corporation known as "Industrial Production Company" has such a generic and uninspiring handle that I can only assume that its managers are questionable as well. And when I'm staring down a list of 200 other options, I don't have time to waste on what may be a middle-of-the-road investment option.

- **Specific industry groups:** Unless you set your screening results to come from a specific industry, you will get companies from all of them. Because an industry screen is often too specific, many investors don't set that as a screening criterion. You may not want to buy shares in any mining, or biotech, or industrial companies, but your other parameters will let these companies past. If you know that you're not interested in investing in them, you can manually eliminate them from your list of potential investments.

✔ **Specific nations:** You may decide to manually eliminate any stocks based on their country of origin. For example, when companies based in China but trading on the U.S. stock markets began widely reporting unreliable financial information, I eliminated any stocks from our screened list with names such as "China Dynasty," or "Technologies of China."

Screening previously screened results is the best way to refine the output. As soon as you get familiar with the process, you'll be able to pull in results of the better-quality companies and then quickly focus that down to a small collection of penny stocks, thereby increasing your chance of achieving excellent results.

What stock screeners won't tell you

As important and helpful as screeners are for refining your search, there are plenty of things they won't tell you. Some of these "omitted" or undiscovered facts are actually among the most important.

Stock screeners won't reveal to you several very significant factors, including (but not limited to) the following:

✔ **Management effectiveness:** Stock screeners have no way of assessing the quality of the executives. You, on the other hand, can speak with them, or see what they've done in the past, or watch as they apply and roll out their strategies.

✔ **Competitors:** Although you can include a penny stock's peers and competitors in your screen, the tool won't be able to predict or assess new competition that springs up or identify when a company or new technology moves into a new market segment. The screener also can't take into account barriers to entry or marketing and branding effectiveness.

✔ **Trends:** Stock screeners don't see trends. To spot trends, you need to rely on your common sense and observation skills.

✔ **Comparative values:** The more numbers and companies you want to compare and review, the more difficult and complicated the process becomes. Modern screeners can be useful, but you may be best served by using a limited number of criteria at first, and then delving deeper into those results the old-fashioned way: using your common sense and brain power.

✔ **Growth or decline of an industry:** Screeners can't factor an industry's growth into the results. Your best bet might be to know the average growth rate for an industry, for example, and then run a growth screen on companies within that space.

By combining your own knowledge with the results from a screener, you may improve your odds of finding higher quality investments.

✔ **Value of intangibles:** *Intangibles* include things like trademarks, patents, and copyrights. Because there is no quantifiable method to value such items, stock screeners can't filter for them.

✔ **Legal battles:** Screeners don't factor in lawsuits and their potential impact on companies.

Given their limitations, treat stock screeners as tools to help decrease your total number of investment options. Use them to kick off your analysis, but plan on performing further due diligence and analysis.

Choosing Penny Stocks Manually

Whether you first screen your penny stocks by using an automated screening tool or just hear about an interesting company on the news, you absolutely must perform manual due diligence on any potential investments. This means taking each individual company, one at a time, and reviewing it from head to toe.

Because this is the most time-consuming aspect of any research you'll perform, drop any company from your review as soon as you realize that you won't be investing in it for any reason. For example, perhaps most aspects of the company look great, but then you realize that that it's being sued. If you've decided to avoid any companies with litigation overhanging them, immediately cross that company off your list and move on to other stocks.

Investors often ask me, "How much due diligence is enough?" Because doing your own research and analysis is a truly bottomless duty, how would anyone know when to stop? A general rule of thumb is to keep doing your research until you get to the point where you would only blame yourself if the investment didn't do well. Even if you get picks from a source who was correct ten times in a row and is making you tons of money, if any part of you would be upset at that source if their next selection sank, then you need to keep doing more diligence. Do due diligence until you take responsibility for the trading choices.

Part III
Trading Penny Stocks

Five Indications That a Penny Stock Is Set to Multiply in Value

- ✔ Revenue growth is strong or accelerating without equivalent increases in advertising expenses

- ✔ Increasing market share is equivalent to losses in market share among the industry leaders

- ✔ The company currently operates in an industry with high and rising barriers to entry

- ✔ Customer attrition rate is low, and returning customers increase their average order size

- ✔ Sales are growing by more than 25 percent per year, while operational expenses are growing by 10 percent or less

Get advice for using trading windows to minimize your exposure to risk in the online article "Investing Using Trading Windows" at www.dummies.com/extras/pennystocks

In this part . . .

- ✔ Discover trading methodologies that preserve capital and maximize gains.

- ✔ Gain clarity through fundamental analysis.

- ✔ Directly contrast companies of different sizes with financial ratios.

- ✔ Benefit from the little-known abstract review.

- ✔ Find out how technical analysis reveals great trading prices and opportunities.

- ✔ Explore technical indicators that work best with penny stocks.

Chapter 8

Trading Strategies

· ·

In This Chapter

▶ Scaling in and out of penny stocks to improve results

▶ Averaging up rather than averaging down

▶ Protecting yourself by limiting your total investment downside

▶ Timing your trades using trading windows

▶ Knowing when to take profits and losses

· ·

*T*he way you trade can be as important — and sometimes even more important — than what you trade. By making the right investment moves in penny stocks, while at the same time protecting yourself from the downside risks, you increase the likelihood of achieving consistent profitability.

In this chapter I walk you through the process of moving in and out of positions in penny stocks and explain why you may want to make those trades in batches rather than all at once. I also talk about getting more involved in the penny stocks you already own, and help you see why paying more for shares is often a much better strategy than making up for mistakes by buying more shares on the downward slide.

I also give you tips for limiting your downside risk while locking in your profits. By combining these concepts with trading timing you will have the greatest success, while exposing your money to risk on the markets for the least amount of time.

Scaling In and Scaling Out

Too often investors, especially newer ones, think that they need to buy or sell their shares all at once. They want 10,000 shares, so they buy 10,000 shares in one fell swoop. Or perhaps they want to sell a penny stock investment worth $2,000, so they sell all $2,000 worth in a single trade.

Besides being a good way to incur the fewest broker commissions, there aren't a lot of advantages to buying or selling your shares in a company all at once. I'm a proponent of *scaling in and scaling out* of positions in penny stocks, which simply means buying and selling in portions rather than a single trade. For example, if you want buy $3,000 worth of a specific penny stock, you may want to spread the purchases out over three or four trading orders and enter them over the course of weeks or months.

The benefits to scaling in and out of positions are as follows:

- ✔ **You can more easily change your mind.** Rather than jump in with both feet and your entire bankroll, you can ease into the purchase. You minimize the energy, time, and cost of backing out of a position should you change your mind.

- ✔ **You gain consideration time.** You've heard the expression "sleep on it." Over time, you will gain more clarity, which may strengthen your decision and resolve or convince you to change your mind.

- ✔ **You have a chance to react to events.** Between the time when you make your first investment and when you commit more money to the stock, events may take place that affect the company's value. The company may issue press releases, or the industry may experience a significant event, or the shares may drop or double in price. If you're only partially committed, you have the luxury of reacting to events however you see fit.

- ✔ **You minimize potential losses and mistakes.** Sometimes you may just be plain wrong. You could buy a penny stock only to watch the shares slide toward new lows almost immediately. Investors who buy in with everything they have lose a lot more than those who scale in.

- ✔ **Dollar cost averaging.** Penny stocks can be very volatile and unpredictable. To avoid the major and short-term ups and downs in some penny stocks, investors can benefit by *dollar cost averaging (DCA),* which is the process of buying more of the shares at set intervals, regardless of the share price activity. Scaling in is very similar to DCA in concept. You will pay more of an average price for the shares over the time period you DCA.

- ✔ **You can lock in results.** After a major price run-up, you may not be able to tell whether the penny stock will maintain its huge gain, go even higher, or come crashing back down to earth. Investors in this fortunate situation sometimes opt to sell a portion of their holdings. In this way, they lock in some gains, while letting the rest ride so that they don't miss out on more gains.

✔ **You keep your options open.** New opportunities can arise at any time. You may start scaling in to one penny stock only to have another, more compelling, alternative surface. Or maybe your kid needs braces, or you decide to buy a hot tub, or you need the money for something else.

Scaling in has many benefits, and the better penny stock investors always trade in this fashion. However, the strategy of scaling in also two downsides:

✔ **You must pay broker commissions for each trade.** By buying or selling over three (or more) separate orders rather than one, you will have to pay three (or more) broker commissions rather than one.

✔ **You could potentially miss out on upside.** By not buying in all at once, you will miss out if the shares leap higher between when you purchase the first portion and before you buy the rest. My experience is that most investors fear just such an incident, but that it rarely happens.

The minimal and rare negatives to scaling in are outweighed by the positives. Trading penny stocks in this fashion is much more forgiving, and profits tend to increase.

Averaging Up . . . Not Down

You'll find more success — and a lot less downside — by investing in stocks on the upswing rather than throwing your hard-earned cash at stocks on a downward slide.

The many downsides of averaging down

Averaging down simply means buying more shares of a stock that you already own and that has fallen in price in order to lower your average cost per share.

The thinking with this sort of strategy goes like this: If you bought $1,000 worth of a penny stock at 90¢, why not buy another $1,000 worth now that it's at 30¢? You would then have an average cost per share of 45¢, with a total investment of $2,000 into what is currently a 30¢ penny stock. This type of reasoning can get you into a lot of trouble, though, and the general sentiment on the markets is that averaging down is simply throwing good money after bad.

Averaging down can be one of the most costly mistakes for investors. When a penny stock heads much lower, or even to zero, the traders who average down lose a lot more money than their original investment because they keep sinking more cash into the failing stock.

If the shares go back up after you average down, you may look pretty smart. However, the fact remains that you got the investment wrong in the first place, and a strategy of cleaning up your mistakes by averaging down will eventually catch up with you.

Typically, investors average down for the wrong reasons, among them the following:

- **To minimize a mistake.** After buying originally, the shares fell. The investor doesn't like being down such a hefty percentage, so she purchases more shares at the current lower price. She is now down on the investment overall, but the price of the stock compared to the average price she paid per share isn't as great.

- **Because of misplaced faith in the company.** Sometimes an investor is passionate about a penny stock's prospects. She believes this company will change the world and make its shareholders millionaires. But if that were true, the stock probably wouldn't be heading down.

- **To get a bargain.** If an investor bought shares at higher prices, those shares seem like an even better bargain now. Penny stocks heading toward zero seem more and more compelling all the way down! Don't be fooled.

- **They mistakenly believe that a lower price means a lower risk.** Investors who believe that stocks become less risky as their price goes down are incorrect. With any purchase, even to average down, the investor risks 100 percent of what she puts into the company, whether the shares are at $20 or 2¢.

- **They're missing an important piece of the puzzle.** Even with proper due diligence, an investor may watch the shares slide. He doesn't see the real issue that's pulling the stock lower and so continues to trust in his findings — all the way down to lower prices.

The upsides of averaging up

Professional investors and successful traders don't average down — they *average up,* meaning that they buy more of a stock they already own when it is increasing in price. When shares begin to move higher after your initial purchase, it may be a sign that this penny stock is beginning to move in the right direction . . . just like you knew it would!

Averaging up is useful for the following reasons:

- **Your choice has been validated.** When the penny stock moves above your purchase price, the upward swing demonstrates that you're doing a great job of picking investments. Your research and analysis may be rock solid.

- **The penny stock is behaving.** Regardless of the reason, the shares are acting like you hoped they would. A stock in motion tends to remain in motion, and as long as the shares are trending higher, averaging up may make sense.

- **Increased visibility.** As penny stocks go up in price, they attract more attention from the positive gains. The size of the company also increases, expanding the shareholder base and the number of people invested in them. With this increased visibility, the penny stock may have a long upward run ahead of it.

Limiting Your Losses and Locking In Your Gains

Penny stocks can be risky, but winning investors apply certain strategies to lower the downside risk while taking profits off the table.

Stop-loss orders

If the most you could ever lose on a penny stock was 10 percent, but your upside gains could be limitless, you would probably do pretty well as a penny stock investor.

The scenario I just described is the idea behind *stop-loss orders,* which are preset sell orders (either at the time you purchase your shares or soon after) that are triggered if the stocks fall a certain percentage below your buy price. Stop-loss orders can protect you from shares that fall significantly, while keeping your investments open to huge upside.

Consider a scenario in which you buy shares of a penny stock at $2.15 and then immediately set a stop-loss 10 percent below that — at $1.94. If the shares slide to $1.94 or lower, you would sell the shares, no questions asked, no matter what. However, if the shares soared toward $10, you would benefit from the gains. And if those same shares topple to 6¢, you will have sold out long before and only suffer a minor loss.

Automatic versus mental stop-loss orders

Some brokers allow you to set up automatic stop-loss orders. If an automatic option isn't available, you'll need to do them manually. Here's the difference:

- ✔ **Automatic stop-loss orders:** Some brokers will let you set up automated stop-loss orders on some penny stocks, meaning that the stock is put up for sale as soon as it hits your stop price. If this option is available, take advantage of it. I prefer automatic stop-loss orders to mental stop-loss orders because they're more reliable.

- ✔ **Mental stop-loss orders:** With this type of stop-loss order, you have a trigger price in mind and sell when shares fall to that level. Make sure to set up a price alert at your mental stop level when you first buy the stock so that you don't get surprised if the shares start falling. And remember: Your mental stop-loss order only works if you stick to selling when your stop is hit.

When your shares hit a mental stop-loss level, selling those shares is one of the hardest things to do in investing. Some investors try to reason their way out of unloading the position, and others justify reasons to keep the investment. For stop-loss orders to be of any value as an investment strategy, you need to stick with the strategy, no questions, no excuses. Otherwise, you won't gain the benefits and may be putting yourself at financial risk.

Avoiding getting stopped out

One of the biggest risks with using stop-loss orders on penny stocks is the potential of getting *stopped out.* This refers to a downward price swing, whereby you hit your stop and subsequently sell, just to see the penny stock bounce right back up. Penny stocks are particularly vulnerable to being stopped out because of their volatility.

Here are some actions you can take to minimize the risk of being stopped out:

- ✔ **Set stop-losses on shares with higher trading volume.** Penny stocks with greater trading volume generally experience less price volatility. When the stock starts to fall, many investors on the sidelines may purchase at the lower prices and drive shares higher.

- ✔ **Use stop-losses on penny stocks with a history of lower volatility.** The more volatile a penny stock already is, the more volatile it will probably be going forward. Less volatility means less chance of getting stopped out on price swings.

✔ **Set stops for greater price declines.** Rather than setting your stop only 5 or 10 percent below your purchase price, consider dropping it to as much as 25 percent below your original buy. Although this lower stop puts you at risk for more downside, it also minimizes your risk of getting stopped out if shares fall temporarily.

✔ **Buy shares on price dips.** If you wait to buy shares after a price dip, they're more likely to have upside in the short term and less likely to fall much farther. The more often you buy penny stocks on price dips, the less likely you will be stopped out.

✔ **Use trailing stops, either mentally of through your broker.** *Trailing stops* refer to adjusting your stop-loss trigger price higher as the underlying shares move upward. For example if you have a stop-loss at 45¢ on shares that are approaching $1.20, you may want to adjust the stop price up toward $1. If the underlying penny stocks then increase to $1.65, you can increase your stop level to $1.35. As the price rises, trail it higher to lock in your profits, and sell as soon as the shares drop back to your trigger price.

Position sizing

Position sizing is one of the most powerful, yet misunderstood, methods for protecting your portfolio. This strategy involves limiting each individual purchase to a predetermined percentage of your portfolio. For example, if you have a $20,000 portfolio, you may decide to limit your largest purchase to $1,000, or 5 percent of your portfolio. This strategy limits your upside, but it also insulates you significantly from downside in any one investment.

The amount you want to invest per trade is up to you. Investors with larger portfolios may buy more at a time but still keep the total purchase to 5 percent. Others may be more aggressive and risk 20 percent per trade. Whatever amount you decide is best for you, the point is that you limit your total exposure per trade.

Smaller portfolios don't work as well with position sizing. If you only have $750 to invest, there is no point in dividing it up among eight penny stocks — the commissions alone would wipe you out.

However, a trader with $300,000 may benefit by maxing out her buys at $5,000, which theoretically would leave her with 60 different stocks and a total risk per investment of $5,000.

Combine position sizing strategies with stop-loss orders (see "Stop-loss orders," earlier in this chapter), and you will have a very secure portfolio. Add the scaling in and out concepts (see "Scaling In and Scaling Out," earlier in this chapter) to your overall approach, and you'll very likely be a successful penny stock trader!

Diversification

You've more than likely heard that diversification is an important aspect of investing. *Diversification* involves buying lower amounts of more stocks to protect yourself from the downside of any one of them. In other words, don't put all your eggs in one basket.

You can diversify your investments by

- ✔ Industry
- ✔ Company size
- ✔ Share price
- ✔ Region of the world or country
- ✔ Volatility
- ✔ Stock market or parent exchange
- ✔ Type (stocks, bonds, real estate, and so on)

Diversification is appropriate for many investors, but the strategy doesn't help you achieve dramatic returns. The more you diversify, the closer your returns will mirror the market average you will achieve.

I practice *pinpoint investing,* in which I buy six or seven penny stocks at most at one time rather than spread the risk and potential gains around. This way the increasing share prices represent more of a percentage gain, but the losses are also more severe on a percentage basis. Although pinpoint investing isn't appropriate for most investors, I'm very comfortable with my research and analysis skills, and therefore pinpoint investing is more appropriate for me.

Limit orders

Limit orders are the best way to control paying too much or selling too low in penny stocks. Every investor in speculative and low-priced shares should use them. Flip to Chapter 5 to read all about limit orders.

Using only the best markets

Not all stock markets are created equal. The better stock exchanges have stricter reporting requirements, listing fees, regulations for managers, and a higher degree of investor visibility. As a result, better penny stocks migrate toward these superior stock exchanges while the inferior companies tend to collect among the inferior markets.

By investing only in penny stocks on the best stock exchanges, you dramatically, easily, and instantly improve your odds. At the same time, you significantly insulate yourself from all the shady companies and thinly traded penny stock pump-and-dump investments. I recommend which exchanges to use and which to avoid in Chapter 3.

Trading Windows

When information is released publicly that materially affects a penny stock company's outlook, investors react very quickly. You will see the adjustment to the perceived value (the share price) in the eyes of investors change to new levels almost immediately.

The majority of price moves in stocks occur over the minority of time. Generally, 80 percent of any penny stock's increases or decreases happen over 20 percent of the trading days. In addition, 80 percent of price changes generally come during a single period of time instead of spreading out at different times throughout the months or years.

While not always the case, you will generally be able look at a penny stock's annual trading chart and see major rises or falls in share price taking place over a very short time frame. When a penny stock makes a move, it will get to its new price range quickly and then settle into a less volatile, or relatively neutral, trajectory.

While low-priced shares are known to be more volatile, they do have extended periods during they don't change very much in price. Considering and anticipating trading windows is a great way to build profits up quickly while avoiding tying up your money on boring or sideways-trading investments.

Most of the significant price moves in penny stocks happen as a direct result of events. Material occurrences — whether a new product launch or strong quarterly results — are what drive the prices.

By doing a little research you can find out the approximate release dates of a significant portion of these corporate events, whether it will involve results of a medical trial, financial reports, or the outcome of an industry presentation. If the details come out in the company's favor, the shares of the underlying penny stock could move strongly and quickly.

By playing trading windows, you don't have to hold the investment for very long, which limits your risk exposure while opening yourself up to the potential of strong short-term price moves.

Timing Trades: When to Hold 'Em and When to Fold 'Em

Whether you're up on your position or sitting on a loss, properly timing when to unload your shares is even more important than knowing which penny stocks to buy in the first place.

You may be selling shares to take profits from a winning penny stock or to unload a losing position at a loss. While most people don't see the difference in terms of approach, they are two very distinct situations, with different considerations.

Know when to take a profit

Although selling stocks to take a profit is much more enjoyable than taking a loss, you still need to know when (and why) to take profits. Among reasons for taking profits, consider these:

- ✓ **To lock in gains:** Any time that shares of your penny stock are trading much higher than your purchase price, you may want to sell them to lock in the gains. Whether you sell a portion by scaling out or unload all the shares at once, you convert that theoretical gain into actual dollars. In addition to the nice cash influx, by selling you remove the risk of the penny stock dropping in value.

- ✓ **To beat the profit-taking stampede:** When a penny stock goes up dramatically in price over a short time period, a number of investors usually sell their shares in order to take these new-found profits. This selling can drive shares right back down, and you may do well to get ahead of that price fall.

- ✓ **When the outlook for shares is bleak:** If your analysis shows trouble on the horizon, you'll do better to take profits now rather than to hang around until the trouble actually arrives.

✔ **When trading volume declines:** When shares trade much higher but then see a marked drop-off in trading volume, the penny stock may be about to take a fall. Most upside gains are fueled by, and can only exist with, a high degree of investor activity. When that buzz goes away, the share price often fails to maintain its lofty new price.

Know when to sell at a loss

Until you actually sell your losing shares, those losses are only on paper (or displayed digitally in your online brokerage account). The moment you actually unload the stock, that theoretical loss becomes real.

Selling at a loss is one of the hardest things for investors to do in the market. However, you'll be more profitable overall by strategically selling your losing shares. Due to the risky nature of penny stocks, having a good handle on this aspect of investing is one of the most important tools in your arsenal.

While selling at a loss is a tough decision to make, it can very often be the correct one. Even the best penny stock traders have good reasons to sell shares at a loss, including:

✔ **When the price hits a stop-loss:** Whether your trigger price is set in your head or connected to an automated sale through your broker, as soon as your stock hits the predetermined price, you need to sell in order to minimize your losses.

✔ **When trading volume increases while share prices fall:** If the daily trading volume increases significantly while the share price drops, that represents a stampede out of the penny stock, which is a very negative sign. Trading volume that decreases to a fraction of the three- or six-month average represents a drop-off in total investor interest and activity and is not a good indicator.

✔ **When technical analysis (TA) indicates a downturn:** TA patterns can demonstrate when a penny stock has a higher likelihood of going lower; when your TA forecasts a fall in price, selling shares may help you escape further downside. I tell you all about applying TA indicators to penny stocks in Chapter 12.

✔ **When an event has minimal impact:** If you were expecting a certain event to bolster shares and that boost didn't occur, you need to consider if there is anything else on the horizon that may help your losing position recover. If not, selling and moving on may be the best move.

✔ **When you anticipate further downside:** Regardless of the cause for downside, if you expect more of the same, selling before the shares drop farther is the correct decision. Just make sure to understand the implications of buying the rumor, which I talk about in Chapter 14.

Chapter 9

Fundamental Analysis

• •

• •

*U*ncovering the best penny stock investments begins with *fundamental analysis* (FA), which is an assessment of qualitative and quantitative factors that impact the operations of the company. Some of these factors include its financial health, the management team, the marketing strategy, economic factors, and just about anything that could affect the value of the shares. Done well, FA will give you an understanding of a company's financial position, who is in charge, and the strengths in the company's operations.

Because the majority of penny stocks are very small, new, or financially weak companies, FA is of paramount importance among these low-priced shares. In fact, before investing in any penny stock, you should give it a complete fundamental review. The great news is that when you do find a solid company trading for pennies, the upside can be dramatic.

By undertaking FA as I describe throughout this chapter, you can gain insights a company's situation and prospects. I explain how to interpret financial reports and the types of numbers you should be looking for. I also address ways to review the management team and methods for interpreting the information you find in press releases and the media. Finally, I help you consider how shifts in the outlook for a company's sector and industry may play into the fortunes of the underlying stocks.

Financial Reports

Every publicly traded stock has an obligation to provide reports of its operational results. Unless you're dealing with very unprofessional or low-quality markets (and you're not, are you?), the financials will be mandated by the exchange and be issues on a quarterly (three month) basis.

For example, if a penny stock's first quarter runs from January to March, it will report the total results for that period as its Q1 release. You can then compare those results to the prior quarterly report (Q4 — the period from October to December) or the past year's three-month period (Q1 — January to March Of the prior fiscal year).

Each quarter, companies release the following main financial reports:

✔ Income statement

✔ Balance sheet

✔ Cash flow statement

I talk about each of these reports in detail later in this chapter. But for now, all you need to know is that these reports identify everything you need to know about the financial strength and position of the company. By comparing quarterly results, you will also be able to spot trends as they develop and play out.

Financial reports intimidate most investors because they appear complicated or hard to understand. In truth, they're actually as easy to interpret as they are helpful to your understanding of the company.

If you're thinking about investing in a penny stock company, you should know exactly how much money its bringing in from sales, and how much debt it has, for example. The financial reports tell you all of this.

While financial statements are generally standardized from one company to the next, there can often be major differences. For example, what one company calls "sales" on its income statement, another company may call "revenues,' but the terms mean the same thing. And some terms — "legal expenses," "investment income," and "goodwill," for example — will vary depending on the underlying company's operations.

From top to bottom

In stock market lingo, you will hear people refer to a company's *top line* and *bottom line* results. *Top line* results are a company's sales, so-called because the value is the first item displayed at the top of the income statement. The *bottom line* is a company's net income (profit at the end of the day after all costs). This value is displayed on the very bottom slot on the statement.

The income statement

An *income statement* illustrates how much money a company has generated by selling its product or service. It also shows all the costs incurred to make those sales happen. By considering revenues from sales over the period and then subtracting expenses, the income statement displays whether the underlying company is operating at a profit or a loss. Figure 9-1 shows a sample income statement.

The income statement is generally divided into the following five main parts:

- ✓ **Sales (also called revenues):** This shows the total amount of money the company brought in by selling products and services. This is usually displayed on the first line of the statement.

- ✓ **Cost of sales (also called cost of goods sold):** To fulfill the sales or produce the wares to be sold, a company incurs costs. These costs are detailed on the lines immediately below the revenue value; they're subtracted from the total sales figure.

- ✓ **Gross profit:** This part shows how much profit is left after the costs of sales are subtracted from the total revenue. If a company spends $75 to produce a product and then sells $100 worth of product, it has a $25 gross profit.

- ✓ **Operating expenses (also called overhead):** These are the numerous other expenses a company pays besides those associated with cost of sales. Operating expenses may include utility bills, rent, advertising, research and development, and so on. These operating expenses are subtracted from gross profit to give you the net profit number.

- ✓ **Net profit:** After subtracting all costs to produce and sell the product and all expenses to run every facet of the business, a company is left with its net profit number.

Sample Income Statement

Revenues (sales)	2,450,900
Cost of goods sold	1,400,320
Gross profit	1,050,580
Research and development	56,200
Selling and administration	345,090
Advertising	320,300
Total operating expenses:	**721,590**
Net profit	328,990

Figure 9-1: An income statement highlighting the five main parts.

By reviewing the income statement, you can understand many important aspects of a company. For example, you will know how much money was generated, the costs incurred to create that revenue, and whether or not it made a profit.

Balance sheet

The balance sheet (see Figure 9-2) displays how much a company owns and how much it owes to others.

With penny stocks, the balance sheet is of paramount importance because it illustrates a company's ability — or inability — to pay its debts.

Everything on the balance sheet is broken down into the following two groups:

- ✔ **Assets:** This includes anything of value that the company owns, such as inventory, factories, machinery, computers, cash, and prepaid expenses. It also includes amounts owed to the company, such as outstanding invoices that have been sent to customers or incoming royalty payments.

- ✔ **Liabilities:** Any amount owed by the company to others is a liability. These can include debt, monthly rent, accounts payable, equipment leases, and so on.

Assets and liabilities are further divided based on their timeframe:

- ✔ **Short-term (current):** Any amounts owed or owing within the next year are classified as short term:

  - • **Short-term assets** include accounts payable to the company and monthly sales.

  - • **Short-term liabilities** may include monthly rental payments due, bills, and interest payments on credit.

✔ **Long-term:** Any amounts owed or owing, but not for at least one year, are considered long term:

- **Long-term assets** include items such as factories, bonds redeemable in several years, and real estate.

- **Long-term liabilities** include any amounts owing but not due for at least a year, such as mortgages, loans, or future royalty payment obligations.

When a company owns a building and pays monthly mortgage payments, that building is a long-term asset. The total mortgage payments for the coming 12 months are current liabilities, while the remaining amount owed on the mortgage after those payments is a long-term liability.

Sample Balance Sheet

Current assets	
Cash and cash equivalents	21,349,909
Short term investments	2,304,888
Net receivables	1,440,232
Inventory	12,305,000
Total current assets	**37,400,029**
Long term investments	300,000
Property, factory, and equipment	13,400,876
Intangible assets	740,830
Goodwill	3,205,800
Total long term assets	**17,647,506**
Total assets	**55,047,535**
Current liabilities	
Accounts payable	6,795,045
Royalty payment obligations	4,000
Short term debt	1,900,000
Total current liabilities	**8,699,045**
Long term debt	3,100,989
Future royalty payment obligations	3,404,320
Income tax payable	355,908
Total long term liabilities	**6,861,217**
Total liabilities	**15,560,262**

Figure 9-2: A balance sheet illustrating current and long-term assets and liabilities.

As shown in Figure 9-2, balance sheets are divided into the following sections, in order:

✔ **Current assets:** The balance sheet always starts by displaying the company's current assets. These are items — such as cash on hand, accounts receivable, inventories, and investments — that hold value in the short term because they can be easily sold or used to fund the company's operations.

✔ **Long-term assets:** The next section on the balance sheet is a breakdown of all the assets a company has besides those which were applied to the current assets portion of the report. Examples of long-term assets include company cars, factories, computers, the value of the brand name, and the value of any trademarks.

✔ **Total assets:** This section combines the current and long-term assets, to reveal the total value of all the company's assets.

✔ **Current liabilities:** Current liabilities include all amounts the company owes within the next 12 months. These current liabilities are generally made up of numerous items, mainly because most companies generally have numerous expenses.

✔ **Long-term liabilities:** Anything the company owes, but not for at least 12 months, is included in the long-term liabilities section of the balance sheet.

✔ **Total liabilities:** The sum of the current and long-term liabilities indicates the total liabilities, which represents all that the company owes.

When reviewing a penny stock, you want to make sure that its total assets cover its total liabilities, but you also want to verify that its current assets cover its current liabilities.

By reviewing a company's balance sheet, you can see how much it has or is likely to bring in compared to how much it owes or will be paying out. When a company covers its liabilities with its assets, it's generally in a healthy position, especially when compared to any company that owes a lot more than it has available.

The statement of cash flows

Companies keep track of the cash that they generate or spend, and they report the results on the *cash flow statement*. By reviewing all the movements of money into and out of a corporation, you can gain a clear understanding of its fiscal strength and operational viability.

If you think of the income statement as showing you the profit or loss of a company based on its operations, and the balance sheet as a snapshot of its financial position, then the statement of cash flows tells you all the other ways that the company is generating or spending money. For example, if a stock raises money by issuing new shares, that amount shows up in cash flow under the item "financing activities." Take a look at Figure 9-3 to see an example of what a cash flow statement looks like.

The cash flow statement is broken down into the following categories:

- **Operating activities:** The profit or loss as displayed on the income statement is included in cash flow as operating activities. If a company made a net profit of $100 on its income statement, that $100 will show up as a gain to cash flow from operations.

- **Investing activities:** The results of purchases and sales of long-term assets, such as factories, real estate, or equipment, are categorized as investing activities. The net results of any stock and bond investments a company makes are also included in this section of the cash flow statement.

- **Financing activities:** Dividend payments, and the issuance or repurchase of bonds or shares, factor into the statement of cash flows as financing activities.

- **Supplemental information:** Supplemental information includes the impact of income taxes, interest payments, and gains or losses on fluctuations in foreign currencies. In addition, significant noncash adjustments or "off the books" items are applied to cash flow as supplemental information. For example, if an item owned by the company decreases in potential value by $1 million, even though the corporation has no intention of selling the asset, it may take a $1 million noncash charge. It doesn't actually lose a million bucks, but the value of its asset is now recorded at what may be a more realistic value.

The best way to think about cash flow is to relate it to your day-to day life. If you leave for work with $50 in your pocket, buy lunch for $11, and find a $5 bill on the street, you end up with $44, or a total decrease of $6. Your cash flow for the day is -$6.

Numerous events impact cash flows, and many of those events are unique to each individual company. As a result, the specific items mentioned in the cash flow statement vary from one company to the next. For example, one company may need to list dividend payments, while another may mention foreign exchange losses and a gain on an increased value of its trademarks.

Sample Cash Flow Statement

Cash flow from operations:	
Revenues	5,560,908
Dividends received	303,786
Interest received (paid)	(320,900)*
Net cash flow from operations:	**5,543,794**
Cash flow from investing:	
Upgrades to equipment	(24,300)*
Replacement of equipment	(450,544)*
Proceeds from equipment sale	763,099
Net cash flow from investing	**288,255**
Cash flow from financing:	
Proceeds from loan	645,800
Payment of loan	(35,809)
Repurchase of stock	(455,877)
Proceeds from stock options	2,340,322
Proceeds from sale of shares	23,809,543
Net cash flow from financing:	**26,303,979**
Net increase (decrease) in cash	**32,136,028**
Cash at beginning of period	1,240,890
Cash at end of period	33,376,918

*Negative values are displayed in (parentheses)

Figure 9-3: A cash flow statement, illustrating changes in cash from operating, investing, and financing activities, as well as supplemental events.

Of the numerous items you may see listed on cash flow statements, some of the more common categories include

- Borrowings
- Dividends
- Stock offerings
- Adjustments for changes in foreign exchange rates
- Loan payments
- Depreciation
- Adjustments to goodwill
- Changes in accounts payable
- Taxes

Off balance sheet adjustments

Companies often make what are called *noncash* or *off balance sheet adjustments.* These are typically changes for bookkeeping purposes rather than reflections of actual profits or losses, and so they may have less of an impact on a company than they at first appear. For example, if a corporation decides that the value of its trademarks is worth $20 million and the value of its brand name is worth $10 million, it will have $30 million as assets on the books. The company may never sell either, and if it does, it may get even more or far less than is reflected on the financial reports.

Picture management deciding that the company brand name is more accurately valued at $4 million rather than $10 million. In this scenario, it would take a $6 million noncash charge as a loss on the books. That may put the company in a situation where it reports a massive loss for the quarter, which would scare investors and look pretty bad, despite the fact that it actually didn't cost a penny in real life.

When considered along with the income statement and balance sheet, the cash flow statement gives you a very clear and deep understanding of the direction and viability of any company. Especially with penny stocks, which tend to have much more reliance on sufficient cash flow, reviewing the relevant financial reports will help you find fundamentally solid companies that, by extension, are better investments.

Numbers to Look for in Penny Stocks

With an understanding of financial reports, you can uncover and assess the investment potential of any penny stock. You will also see warning signs and sources of concern more clearly, and as such be able to protect yourself from fundamentally weak investments.

The most important aspect of reviewing financial reports is to put the numbers into perspective; otherwise, they're just numbers with no meaning attached to them. For example, is $4 million too much debt for a company? That really depends on the overall situation.

Here are several ways you can use the numbers to understand the merits of the underlying investment:

 ✔ **Compared to previous periods:** You can significantly add to the value of your analysis by comparing the most recent numbers on the financials to the previous quarterly and annual periods. For example, if today's sales are double what they were a year ago, you know that the company is enjoying strong growth (at least in relation to the previous period in question). Similarly, if current liabilities tripled over the previous quarterly report, you need to find out why, especially if current assets didn't increase in kind.

✔ **Contrasted with competitors:** Comparing a company's financial with its competitors is by far the most important way to derive benefit from your financial analysis. By watching how the underlying company is performing in relation to its peers, you can gain numerous insights. For instance, if the penny stock you're watching is enjoying major sales growth while competitors in the industry are seeing drop-offs in their sales, you can assume that your penny stock is taking over market share from the competition, and is almost certainly a better investment from the group.

✔ **Contrasted with the industry or sector:** Comparing a company's numbers to other companies in the industry or sector is sometimes useful. The industry or sector usually includes companies that don't directly compete with your company but that can still provide increased insights. For example, if a penny stock you're analyzing is doing better than its direct competitors and also outperforming other companies in the same industry or sector, it may be an attractive investment.

✔ **Compared to other investments options and types:** Consider any potential penny stock investment in relation to any other investment types you may be considering. For example, is the best penny stock in a troubled and slow growth industry a better investment than an average company in a growing and up-and-coming sector? Or better than paying down your mortgage? Or buying precious metals or bonds? You're the only person who can answer these questions.

When comparing financials of penny stock companies, the first step is to make sure that they have enough fundamental strength to endure as a company and take advantage of growth opportunities as they arise. In other words, they need to have and make enough money to advance their operations.

The second step involves choosing among those stronger penny stocks, based on which companies are bringing in the best profits, have the most money in the bank, the lowest or declining debt loads, or whatever metrics upon which you decide to rely. I go into detail about the types of numbers you should look for in a company's financials in the following sections.

Good numbers on the financial statements

You want to know that a company is making money, has a viable business plan, isn't crushed beneath a mountain of debt, and will still be in business six months from now. You can find out all of this and more by reviewing the financial statements.

The more you look into the financial reports, the better you will get at it, and the more quickly you will be able to ascertain the fundamental strength of a stock. While you will have different expectations in financial results from one company to the next, certain questions apply to all of them:

- ✔ Are they making money?
- ✔ Can they pay their bills?
- ✔ Do they have too much debt?

You can get the answers to all these questions by doing a quick financial review.

What constitutes a good or strong number depends in large part on the type of company you're reviewing. For example, investors generally expect biotech companies and technology start-ups to operate at a loss, while investors typically look for base metals producers or utilities to generate profits.

Yet, investors have certain expectations regardless of what industry a company is operating within.

Strong numbers on the income statement

One of the most important aspects of any business is to generate revenue through the sale of products and services. Although observing the sales figures is helpful, it only tells part of the story. You also want to see how much of that income translates into profit after factoring in all corporate expenses, such as the costs to produce their wares. With the full view of the income and expense situation of a penny stock, you will be in a much better position to understand the success (or lack thereof) of its operations.

Assess the strength of a company's sales results within the following parts of the income statement:

- ✔ **Revenues (sales):** Without sales, a company is just an idea. Revenues are a marker that customers find value in the products or services of the underlying company, and so when a company reports sales, it demonstrates the viability of the company's business model. The higher the revenues, the greater the demand for its offerings.

✔ **Cost of revenues (cost of sales):** Also referred to as cost of goods sold or operating expenses. This should be a fraction of the total revenues. Consider a penny stock with $100 in sales. If its cost of revenue is $40, then it made a $60 profit from producing and providing its wares. If costs were more than $100, the company is operating at a loss, and if it is at $100, it is breaking even. You almost always want to be involved with companies that have a cost of revenue well below their total sales number; otherwise, they won't see any profit!

✔ **Gross income (gross profit):** Companies calculate gross income by subtracting costs of sales from total sales. *Gross income* (also called *gross profit*) is how much profit a company achieves by producing and selling its wares. The greater the gross income, the better.

✔ **Operating expenses:** *Operating expenses* include costs such as rent, advertising, administrative costs, unusual one-time expenses, and more. These costs are subtracted from the gross income. You want to see that the operating expenses don't eat up the total gross income and that there is some profit remaining after taking these costs into account.

✔ **Net income (earnings):** *Net income* is what's left after subtracting the costs of sales and operating expenses from the revenue. Any money left is earnings, or profit! When a company has a net income, it means that it's generating more money than it is spending.

Strong numbers on the balance sheet

The balance sheet is the first statement I look into when assessing a penny stock because it reveals the company's ability to survive and expand, while also showing which businesses are running into financial trouble. You can see the viability of a penny stock in both the short term and long term by looking at its balance sheet. Scrutinizing the balance sheet is particularly important with penny stocks because so many of them are in financial trouble; by avoiding the weaker companies, you will be able to get involved with those that will still be around in one week, one month, or one decade.

To assess any penny stock, you should look for strength in the balance sheet through the following comparisons:

✔ **Current assets compared to current liabilities:** Make sure that the company has enough money to at least cover its current liabilities. Any company that doesn't have more in assets than liabilities in the coming year could be on its way out or facing a cash crunch. The greater the current asset number, the better.

✔ **Long-term assets compared to long-term liabilities:** Do long-term assets cover the long-term liabilities? Ideally, you want long-term assets to outweigh long-term liabilities, although this is less crucial than making sure that current assets cover current liabilities.

Strong numbers on the cash flow statement

The cash flow statement can be complicated because many companies have money coming in and going out in several different ways, such as financings, returns on stock market investments, and net profits or losses. That complexity is also the reason why the cash flow statement becomes so important — it provides a summary of the final result of all these different events that affect a company's cash.

Look into the following parts of the cash flow statement to assess the strength of a penny stock:

✔ **Operating activities:** You want the penny stock you're reviewing to show profits from its operations, or at very least be able to cover any shortfalls though other categories on its statement of cash flows. While any company reporting a loss from its operating activities can survive by generating funds in other ways, it eventually will need to start producing a profit or run the risk of eventually going out of business.

✔ **Investing activities:** A company that shows no investment income is no cause for concern. Likewise, when the business is generating money through this aspect of the cash flow statement, that's a positive event. However, if a company reports a loss from investing activities, you need to find out how it lost that money, if the amount will negatively and significantly impact its operations, and if it is likely to suffer a similar loss in the future. For example, if the company lost millions speculating on the stock market, find out if it intends to keep trading stocks. If it lost money due to an investment in a subsidiary company that it owns, does it still own it, and will it be investing even more into the subsidiary in the future?

✔ **Financing activities:** Most stocks generate the cash they need to operate by issuing shares of the company, whether through an initial public offering (IPO) or a subsequent offering (flip to Chapter 2 for details on how companies issue shares). Gains from these activities are reported on the cash flow statement. Although it's perfectly acceptable for new companies to rely on issuing shares to generate most of the money they need to operate as long as they are on their way toward self-sufficiency, be wary of companies that continue to operate this way on an ongoing basis.

✓ **Miscellaneous items:** This category is unique to each company and each situation. When reviewing this category, look into any big amounts reported here, note whether they produce or cost money, and make sure that you understand them and whether they benefit the underlying company and its shareholders.

✓ **Net change in cash position:** After taking every factor into account, you should hope for a net increase in cash. If the companies are losing money from their operations, they have hopefully generated all they need to keep their business going through other sources, such as financing or investing.

Trends in financial results

More important than the actual reported numbers in a company's financial statements are the trends in those underlying results. Because investors generally try to anticipate growth rather than react to it, you can get the best investment results by considering where a company is going instead of where it is. This strategy is especially relevant for speculative penny stocks, because so much of their value is based on forward-looking speculation.

By observing, anticipating, and reacting to trends in the financial statements, you can position yourself for success. Whether this involves investing in companies with rapidly increasing revenues or buying stocks that are aggressively paying off their debt or increasing their market share, getting ahead of strengthening fundamentals before they're common knowledge gives you a great advantage over other investors.

Consider a company that has seen 10 percent sales growth every quarter for the last four years. Barring any material changes in the company's fortunes, you may expect similar progress for the upcoming quarterly report. This is a simplified example, but the concept is clear. Anticipate any trends that will show up in revenues, earnings, assets, liabilities, debt load, or any other items tracked on the financial statements. Such trends won't always appear, or even be fully reliable, but when you spot one that could have an impact on the share prices of the underlying company, you have a significant advantage.

Some trends in the financial results that may prove very helpful, and by extension very profitable, include those in

✓ **Revenues:** A sales increase from one quarter to the next, or from year to year, can imply an increasing market share, more widespread adoption of a product, or more frequent or larger orders from existing customers. You want to see growth in revenues. An even better sign is if that growth accelerates to an even greater rate.

✔ **Debt:** Many penny stocks take on a lot of debt early in their life cycle because they don't have significant revenues or they incur costs to get established. Companies with little debt have lower interest payments and the potential to take on debt if they deem it to be required. When you see a company continually pay down its obligation from one quarter to the next, it is becoming fundamentally stronger with each financial report.

✔ **Assets:** In most cases, the asset position of companies will remain relatively stable over the quarters. However, a growing company may see its current and long-term asset positions increase as its inventories, intellectual property, factories, or otherwise, become more valuable.

✔ **Liabilities:** Often a growing company will see its liabilities increase rather than decrease. This is usually due to larger inventory purchases to fulfill bigger orders, or the need for more staff and equipment or a new factory. You don't want to see a growing liability trend if it's not equaled or exceeded by similar moves in the assets.

✔ **The asset to liability mix:** Pay close attention to changes in the mix of assets to liabilities. A trend of decreasing liabilities concurrent with an expanding asset position is a very strong trend for a company. As a penny stock becomes more fundamentally solid, the asset to liability mix should improve.

✔ **Earnings:** Companies report how much money they make in their earnings, the factor with the greatest impact on share price. Anticipate trends in upcoming earnings and you will have a good idea of where shares are heading.

✔ **Profit margins:** Profit margins illustrate how much money a company is making by selling its goods. As it find ways to make greater profits, either by selling for higher costs or enjoying economies of scale to produce products less expensively, its margins will improve. A trend in stronger margins is very positive for a company because it will reflect greater profits.

✔ **Financial ratios:** Financial ratios provide a greater understanding of the business activities by dividing one number from a company's financial statements by another number. For example, the price per share divided by the earnings per share generates the price/earnings (P/E) ratio for the stock; the ratio presents the company's earnings capacity to investors in a clear fashion, especially when compared to the P/E's of other businesses in its industry (see Chapter 10 for details on ratios). If trends in a penny stock's ratios improve quarter after quarter, you know that the company is strengthening.

Finding the trend in the life cycle

Companies have a life cycle, which begins with the start-up phase, and proceeds through growth, maturity, and finally decline. Most penny stocks are in the start-up or growth phase, where they take on costs to get established and post losses while they try to generate enough revenue to cover their bills. Those corporations that make the transition from start-up to growth phase often enjoy the greatest increase in their share price, although many companies in the growth phase end up going out of business if their concept doesn't work. After passing into the mature phase, many companies have captured most of the growth they can, and they enter into a period in which they hold their position or even pay dividends to shareholders with the money they make rather than invest it into further attempts at growth. Mature companies eventually enter a phase of decline, unless they can restructure or reinvest themselves to adapt to a world that may have changed significantly from the time when they first were established.

Acting On Analysis

Doing research (which involves no risk) and actually making a trade (which involves significant risk) are two very distinct activities. Due diligence and your analysis are conceptual. The proverbial rubber doesn't hit the road until you act upon that research, at which point it becomes very real.

The following tools and strategies can help you make the jump from analysis to investment:

- **Specific triggers:** Set a specific target for any penny stocks you're watching. The target can be price, price-to-earnings ratio (see Chapter 10), or some other attractive valuation. As soon as the stock hits that target, take action.

- **Past results:** The more trading you do, the more you build a history of successes and failures. Consider which analytical circumstances resulted in trading profits previously: You may want to act on them each time you see similar situations going forward.

- **Portfolio balancing:** You may decide to buy (or sell) in order to bring your investment portfolio in line with your overall investment goals. For example, maybe you want to have more money in high risk, high reward stocks, or perhaps you want to diversify into new industry groups.

- **Hedging:** *Hedging* involves reducing the risk from one type of investment by buying another that fully or partially acts in a contrary fashion. For example, suppose that you own a technology penny stock that requires silver to create its electronics and that faces financial pressures whenever silver becomes expensive. You could hedge that investment by purchasing shares in a silver production penny stock that benefits from higher precious metals prices.

✔ **Situation timing:** Sometimes an event arises that creates a compelling buying or selling opportunity. For example, a new government is elected, or a new drug is discovered, or war breaks out. Opportunities for trading and profiting from penny stocks exist in just about any situation.

Management Is Steering This Ship

An incompetent leader can bankrupt even a wonderful company. Conversely, a great leader can take an awful company to much higher levels.

Because penny stocks are generally smaller, newer, and more speculative, management can have an even greater impact on them than on larger companies.

When considering which penny stocks to invest in, familiarize yourself with who is in charge and what their leadership style tends to be. Decide how effective you expect their decisions and vision to be in terms of getting share prices to move higher (or lower).

Who's who at the helm

A company's executives and management can be made up of various job titles. For example, a Chief Technology Officer (CTO) may be of paramount importance to an Internet company while a coal penny stock may not have or need one at all. Each company's management team is based on its individual needs, but in general most penny stocks have people in the following positions:

✔ **Chief Executive Officer:** This is the person in charge of all the other officers. The CEO is usually the person responsible for the vision for the company and who makes many of the major decisions.

✔ **President:** This individual is in charge of most of the operations and supervises the vice-presidents. In smaller companies, the CEO often takes on the role of the President as well.

✔ **Chief Financial Officer (CFO):** The CFO is in charge of the financial reporting of the company, is heavily involved any fundraising efforts, and oversees anything to do with a corporation's money flows.

- ✔ **Chief Operations Officer (COO):** The COO is responsible for all the operations of a business, such as product production and delivery, systems development, employee policies, and day-to-day business activities. Often the COO helps the CEO achieve her vision.

- ✔ **Vice-President (VP):** Typically a VP leads each business division. Depending on the company, there may be a VP of marketing, a VP of inventory management, and a VP of operations.

- ✔ **Chief Technology Officer (CTO):** This is usually the individual in charge of all the company's technologies. The CTO answers to the CEO.

- ✔ **Chief Information Officer (CIO):** Corporations with a heavy degree of information technology (IT) typically assign one person to the role of a full-time CIO.

In addition to these roles mentioned, you may see Chief Creative Officers (CCO), Chief Diversity Officer (CDO), and Chief Business Officer (CBO), among others. The breakdown of leadership is less important than their overall effectiveness.

What have these managers done before?

The best indicator of future success is previous success. Investors should look at what a company's top management has done with its other companies in the past.

Companies generally announce new executives by way of a press release, and that announcement usually mentions or highlights the previous experience of the individual. They also tend to post career highlights of the key managers on their websites. If you can't find the information on a press release or website, you can always call the company and ask for details.

Often the executive will have been at a publicly traded company. Pay attention to the time when the manager or executive was with that corporation and check to see how well the shares performed over that time period.

Keep in mind that you can't always pin the previous company's total success or failure on the executive.

Shining a light on executive pay

Publicly traded companies must disclose several facets of their top leaders' compensation, including:

- ✔ **Salaries:** With penny stocks, most annual compensation for the Chief Executive Officer and other top players is close to $200,000 to $250,000, but the amounts can vary widely from one company to the next. Watch for any officers taking massive salaries when the underlying company is struggling.

- ✔ **Current ownership position:** When management has "some skin in the game," a company must make this public. Top execs with significant amounts of shares are more likely to be working hard toward share price gains. Don't always look at this figure as a percentage (for example, the CEO owns 5 percent of the company). Instead, consider it from the perspective of total dollar value (for example, the CEO owns $42 million worth of stock), a figure that more clearly demonstrates the insider's ownership position than is expressed by a percentage. Owning an exact dollar amount worth of shares provides more perspective than saying the percentage value, which can change often and may be very small.

- ✔ **Other miscellaneous factors:** This includes bonuses, stock options, and any payments by way of giving them shares.

It does stand to reason, though, that an executive who was successful at his former company is likely to achieve positive results with this new company. If a chief technology officer completely streamlined the networks of the former corporation, she is very likely to do the same thing again. Moreover, a CEO or president who set the strategic vision for his previous company is likely to enact a similar scenario with this new company, and quite likely will achieve similar results.

The corporate commitment level

If the CEO and most other executives are financially invested in the company, it stands to reason that it's in their best interests for their stock to do well.

The term *insider* can cause confusion among investors because it describes two different types of people associated with a company. Any person or organization that owns 10 percent of a company is considered an insider. They must report their position and trades as soon as they hit that threshold. The other type of insider refers to any individual in a position to have specialized or material knowledge of the operations of a company — for example, the president of marketing, or the chief financial officer, or the CEO. When you hear about insider trading on the news, it is generally based on the latter type, who acted on materially important information before it was publicly available.

Throughout this book when I refer to *insiders,* I am speaking of those key executives who are involved in the day-to-day operations.

When insiders trade shares, they're required to report their activities. Those buys and sells become public record and are generally displayed on any websites or services that provide financial information.

While more insider ownership is generally better than less, people often put too much stake in it. They assume that significant insider buying implies upcoming positive events — and accompanying rise in share price — for the company. On the other hand, many investors see heavy insider selling as a sign of lower share prices to come. Many investors rely heavily on insider trades to give them potential direction of future share prices. I'm not one of those investors.

While my team and I assess insider ownership as a part of our analysis, we are simply looking to see management's level of involvement and commitment and don't consider insider trading as at all indicative of future price direction. To help you understand why, consider that managers are

- ✓ **Generally not good investors:** Top managers may be great at what they do, but they typically aren't good investors. If you look back at insider trades for most companies, you'll see insiders buying at price peaks and selling at price bottoms. If you gauge when to trade shares based on their moves, you'll get the same lackluster results that they're getting.

- ✓ **Biased:** Typically, top executives are very optimistic about the prospects of their company. This is true whether or not they are correct. Insiders buy shares in penny stocks that are nose-diving toward zero just as often as they purchase shares on the upswing.

- ✓ **Real people:** Sometimes a purchase or sale is just about an individual doing what they need to for their nonbusiness life. They may have extra money to invest from other sources, or they may need to raise cash by selling shares so they can buy a boat or pay down their mortgage.

- ✓ **Sometimes new to the company:** Often when new players join the ranks of a corporation, they pick up shares to increase their ownership from zero. Some companies impose minimum ownership requirements on its executive team.

You should hope to see some insider ownership, and usually the greater position by the management, the better. An insider position of 10 to 20 percent is typically a good sign, but be cautious of significantly larger ownership levels.

If the top managers hold control over more than 50 percent of the shares, then they can do whatever they want. They have the ability to control the entire company and pay themselves whatever amount they want, while never facing the possibility of being fired.

In fact, even if they hold only 30 percent, they are still in a control position. Because a large portion of shareholders don't cast their ballots for every vote (such as to replace the CEO), owning a large, albeit minority, position in a corporation very often is significant enough to enable full control.

 Insiders in a company generally sign non-disclosure agreements (NDAs). This demonstrates that they are privy to knowledge that may materially affect the value of the stock but which is not public knowledge. Any violations of their NDA, whether by selling shares before a bankruptcy becomes public knowledge or tipping off their best friend before the company lands a massive contract, could result in that insider going to jail and/or paying massive fines. The only way to protect investors from the significant one-sided advantage that insiders have is by enabling information to come out publicly for everyone at once and to prevent top management "in the know" from acting on their knowledge until everyone has the same chance.

News Releases and Events

Reviewing news items and press releases is a great way to perform research on a company. Especially with penny stocks, major events that can really move the share price around are often first brought to the attention of the public by way of a press release or media article.

Take the news item with a bit of caution because it's usually written and published by the underlying company itself and, as such, should be considered biased. Other times, the article is prepared by a media outlet with a specific agenda, and as such may present the company in whatever specific light best serves them.

With any news item, ask yourself the following questions:

✔ **Who wrote the press release?** A press release prepared by a company will talk its company up in an effort to get investors excited about the stock. Media coverage, on the other hand, may be positive or negative for the company, depending on the story. As such, you can trust third-party media coverage a lot more than press releases issued by the company itself, but you should still review both.

✔ **What are they really saying?** What information can you glean from the article or release that isn't explicitly stated? Look at any release from various perspectives, and pay attention to the details and facts, rather than the opinions or insinuations. For example, is an increased inventory a good thing, or does it mean the company is having trouble selling its product?

Press releases from the company

Press releases generally mention the original source of the document near the bottom. If a release cites the company itself or their investor relations firm as the source, you're looking at a release that came directly from the stock itself.

You can begin to profit from press releases that are issued by a company when you consider:

✔ **Frequency:** Some penny stocks put out hundreds of press releases every year, while others only do a few. Do these articles have any tangible effect on the share price? Does it seem as those shareholders and potential investors have been overwhelmed by too many releases, so much so that even strongly positive news seems to fall flat?

✔ **Style:** Are the releases highly positive or just informative? Does the tone change over time, such as becoming increasingly positive as the company continually improves or lands new contracts and partners? Watch for trading clues in changes in the underlying tone of the releases.

✔ **Effect:** If a penny stock sees shares jump higher with each news item, you can expect that trend to continue and can potentially profit from it. On the other hand, some penny stocks will see no impact from positive news items.

Coverage from third-party sources

As companies grow, they attract more attention from the various media outlets. As a company enjoys more media coverage, assuming the majority of that coverage is neutral or positive, they grow.

You can trust third-party comments about a company — whether a glowing review on a major television program or a single paragraph in an obscure niche magazine — much more than company press releases. Positive media coverage can benefit a company from the perspectives of both attracting customers, as well as attracting investors in their stock.

Follow media coverage of any penny stock you already own or are considering investing in. Using major search engines such as Google, Yahoo!, and Bing are a great way to do this, and many of them will allow you to set automated alerts so that you don't miss any article or coverage.

Consider following any niche trade publication that covers the industries you invest in. The added benefit of doing so is that you will also find out more about the competition, which is always beneficial from an investor's perspective.

The timing of milestone events

Investors can easily anticipate some major events that could have a positive or negative impact on a stock's value. Companies may mention in a press release that they're in the running for a prestigious award and indicate when they anticipate decision to be announced. Companies also publish their financial results in a predictable pattern year after year. And you can probably gauge how long it should take a firm to develop that certain drug or new technology, at which point it will make a public announcement. All these events could have a significant impact on the share price, and savvy investors could have anticipated them before they were actually announced.

To attempt to profit by trading around milestone events, those occurrences must be

- ✔ **Predictable:** You may not know the exact date of a potential milestone event, but you should have an indication of a brief time period when a related release may be issued. Dates for releases of financial results, new customers, management changes, or even anticipated entries into new markets are relatively predictable. Companies tend to telegraph most events, and by anticipating them you increase your chances of profiting over shorter time frames.

- ✔ **Impactful:** Unless an event will have a material impact on the operations of the company or its prospects, the release of information may have little effect on share price. If your intention is to profit from news releases, only play the most significant events.

✔ **Under-recognized knowledge.** I'm not talking about insider trading or knowledge inaccessible to the public. Rather, I refer to events you anticipate based on your own analysis or even events that the majority of potential investors don't take seriously but that could help the stocks trade at higher prices.

You can trade milestone events by positioning yourself ahead of time to benefit from any positive results. Just be cautious in events like this of the "buy the rumor, sell the fact" concept, which I talk about in Chapter 14.

The Outlook for the Sector and Industry

A business *outlook* is a set of expectations for future demand, supply, and prices. Executives generate outlooks for their companies in order to best react to the coming trends; investors generate outlooks so they can profit from stocks in growing businesses.

The outlook for an industry group or economic sector can give you clues as to how well the underlying businesses should perform. Will the company have the wind at its back, or are the coming months and years going to be an uphill battle?

An outlook could involve individual specific aspects for the analysis, such as a rising demand for coal or decreasing automobile sales. Alternatively, the analysis could be very involved and look at every single aspect of an industry and even review each single company operating in that space.

The outlook for any given industry or sector is developed by any and all of the following:

✔ **The companies themselves:** Corporations can justify their actions, vision, and share price by referring to an industry outlook they develop themselves. A uranium mining company may suggest a rising demand for nuclear materials, or a forestry stock could cite growth in home building in their area. Outlooks prepared by specific companies are generally positive about their sector and are often used to justify higher shares prices through the suggestion of growth to come. Outlooks also help companies prepare for and adapt to future scenarios. For example, if oil prices are expected to fall dramatically, an oil production company may lay off workers or presell inventories.

✔ **Analysts who cover the industry or sector:** Major brokerage houses and investment banks typically have analysts who are focused on a specific industry group. For example, one analyst may know everything about the Internet technology industry and all the details of each company involved in that space. These analysts may act on their research, such as by administering a mutual fund. They may also issue their outlook for the industry either publicly or to specific individuals.

✔ **Investors:** If you're going to trade stocks in a certain industry, you may want to develop an outlook for that segment of the economy. By reading trade publications, trusted media sources, and the outlooks issued by professional analysts, you should have a pretty good understanding of what to expect.

Whether you're emboldened by an optimistic outlook for a sector or you see warning signs of slowing growth, proper analysis of what to expect from the space should help you develop your trading decisions.

Changes in the outlook for an industry are even more important than the original outlook itself. For example, there is value in the knowledge that coal demand is rising. But when the outlook changes to falling demand, that information may be even more significant because it represents a change in outlook and may have significant ramifications on stocks involved in the space.

These changes in outlook, or shifts in expectations for an industry, can arise in the short term or long term. Each has specific and different implications. For example, an increase in anticipated global demand for steel might imply higher production costs for those companies that use steel; and they in turn may increase the sale prices of their products.

Microeconomic influences

Microeconomics refers to decisions and purchases by individuals and organizations. For example, the ways a company produces its product, buys the necessary supplies, and prices its wares are microeconomic decisions. Purchase decisions by individual consumers, or hiring decisions by a specific firm, also impact the microeconomy. Individual corporations and people collectively create the microeconomy.

Keep an eye on the microeconomic influences affecting any penny stocks you're interested in. Obtaining new customers, attracting effective employees, and covering expenses such as fuel, property taxes, and rent will drive their success. All these factors, and numerous others, are microeconomic.

Of the numerous microeconomic influences, some that may affect your penny stock investments include

- Purchase decisions by consumers or by corporations
- Attracting or losing customers
- Gasoline prices
- Property taxes
- Commodity prices (steel, oil, silver, and so on)
- Increasing wages
- Commercial rental payments or rental availability

For example, if gasoline prices double, the price increase would be detrimental to courier and transportation companies. Less expensive steel would enable lower costs for vehicle manufacturers, and thus greater profits. If average wages moved higher, employee-heavy businesses would see increasing operational expenses.

Microeconomic influences can impact a specific company or penny stock. In fact, penny stocks get the majority of their price direction from the influences and results of microeconomic factors.

Macroeconomic influences

Macroeconomics refers to the big picture of the economy. Issues that affect the economy as a whole, such as national debt, the unemployment rate, and the growth rate of the entire country's production, are macroeconomic items. In other words, entire nations, trade blocks, or continents — or even the entire world as a whole — are each macroeconomies.

Several macroeconomic factors that may affect your investments include

- Gross domestic product (GDP)
- Money supply
- Taxes
- National savings
- Unemployment rate
- Inflation and deflation

For example, if taxes on corporations are doubled, you can expect profits to fall and growth to slow nationwide. If there is an increase in the average national savings, consumers will have more capacity to make purchases, which could benefit retailers. A spike in the unemployment rate would reflect an increasing number of people looking for work, which may be good for staffing agencies and industries heavily reliant on a larger workforce such as construction.

By taking the macroeconomic influences into account, you should have more clarity with your penny stock investment decisions, and therefore have more trading success. While penny stocks are very small investments, they are affected by major macroeconomic events, and investors who are aware of the interrelationships stand to profit the most.

Keeping your macros and micros straight

In general, a company will have control over its microeconomic choices. In contrast, it will have no control over the bigger macroeconomic events.

By distinguishing between the two types of events, you will be able to anticipate if a company can do anything to change the situation, or if their best approach is to adapt to the larger event that is beyond the company's influence. For example, if a company is having a hard time finding enough workers because it offers a low wage compared to other business in the area (microeconomic situation), it could offer higher wages or hire a headhunting firm. If the unemployment rate drops to 1 percent (macroeconomic situation), there may be nothing that company can do to get enough workers.

Chapter 10

Financial Ratios: Comparing Apples to Apples

*F*inancial analysts and investors use financial ratios to tease out valuable information about companies. A *financial ratio* is simply one value divided by another.

Financial ratios are one of the most important aspects of stock market analysis. They enable an investor to check a company's results for signs of strength or weakness. These ratios also allow investors to compare a company to its peers, competitors, and even shares that in completely unrelated industries.

Analysts take raw data derived from a company's operations and reported financial results and use that information to generate ratios that are more helpful than the original data. For example, it can be valuable to know a stock's price is $2 and its earnings are 20¢ per share. But that same data is more useful when expressed as a price-to-earnings (P/E) ratio (which in this case is 10; check out "Price-to-earnings (P/E)," later in this chapter, for details). The information has more context when expressed as a P/E ratio, because you can see if the shares are under- or overvalued based on their earnings.

Financial ratios may seem complicated at first, but they are actually quite simple. All the major ratios are freely available at any online stock market source that provides financial data. If you prefer to make the calculations yourself, all you need is a calculator and a little knowledge.

Financial ratios can demonstrate the success (or lack thereof) for just about any aspect of a company. Whether you want to see how effective it is at moving its inventory, how much profit it makes from sales, of if the shares are at an undervalued level, financial ratios can tell you all of this — and a lot more.

In this chapter, I show you how you can use financial ratios to compare companies of different sizes directly to each other. I also detail the five categories of ratios and break down the specific numbers and calculations that generate each value.

Leveling the Playing Field with Financial Ratios

Whether deciding between different investment options or industries or choosing among various penny stocks and large cap companies, financial ratios allow you to place them all on equal footing for comparison purposes.

Eliminating size as a factor

Financial ratios allow an investor to compare companies of all sizes directly to one another. Even if your sample has some companies that are 100 times larger than others, you can use ratios to see which shares make the best use of their funds, have the most debt proportionally, or generate the greatest profits from their sales.

By generating ratios, you eliminate company size as a factor. Two companies with a profit-to-earnings (P/E) ratio of 12 are theoretically equally profitable, even if one is a penny stock trading at 40¢ per share, and the other is a large cap company whose stock trades at $500 per share.

With penny stocks, it becomes increasingly important to use ratios in your analyses. Low-priced shares very often have few competitors, let alone those with similar share prices and company sizes. By using ratios, you increase the size of the comparison pool, which in turns makes your data more reliable. It is also important to get an idea of how a penny stock compares to the much bigger players in the industry, to assess what advantages that smaller company has, if any.

Comparing stocks across industries

By using financial ratios, you can also compare companies trading in completely different industries. For example, using ratios you may be able to demonstrate that shares from the mining industry represent much better value than those in the biotech field.

Many investors believe that companies with lower share prices represent better value. Share price is actually a reflection of the worth of the company divided by the number of shares in existence, with additional factors such as growth rate and the future expectations of investors coming into play. As such, attractive valuations can come from shares of any price. By applying financial ratios, you will sometimes see that higher-priced shares represent more compelling value than their lower-priced counterparts.

The Five Categories of Financial Ratios

Investors rely on five categories of financial ratios. Within each category are several calculations to measure the various aspects of a business. You can use each of the following main categories to analyze any type or size of stock:

- **Liquidity ratios:** Also sometimes called "solvency ratios," these calculations demonstrate a company's ability to pay its short-term debts and obligations. If it doesn't have or isn't able to generate enough cash, the company might not be able to keep the lights on long enough to generate a profit.

- **Activity:** Also referred to as "efficiency ratios," these demonstrate how well a company uses its assets to produce revenues. The more effective a stock is at generating sales from the value inherent in the company, the better its activity ratios.

- **Leverage:** Sometimes called "debt ratios," these calculations demonstrate the ability of a stock to repay its long-term debt.

- **Performance:** In some cases, these are referred to as "profitability ratios." They illustrate how profitable a company is at various levels of its sales and fulfillment process.

- **Valuation:** These are ratios derived from the price of the shares and, as such, provide insights into to the value of the stock at those levels.

Within each of these five categories are several financial ratio calculations that you can apply to a specific aspect of the company. For example, the liquidity category includes calculations for current, quick cash, and operating cash ratios, all of which provide different insights into the company's ability to pay its short term obligations. I describe each of the ratios in this chapter.

In this chapter I cover the most popular ratios for analyzing low-priced shares such as penny stocks. Several other financial ratios exist beyond the five categories I talk about; however, analysts use these other ratios far less often, or in relation to larger companies. For example, because very few penny stocks pay dividends, you don't need to calculate the dividend payout rate ratio.

Based on the manner in which the ratios are calculated, sometimes a lower number is stronger than a higher number. For example, a P/E ratio of 8 is much better than one of 16. I always note whether a higher or lower number is preferable when I present the ratio. Make sure that you understand any ratio you're relying on in your analysis, specifically understanding whether a higher or lower number is preferable.

Liquidity Ratios

Liquidity ratios help you determine whether a company can pay its short-term debts and obligations. With many lower-priced shares, you will find that many companies can't! With penny stocks, this category of ratios is the first thing you should check. The good news for you is that liquidity ratios are straightforward calculations.

Any company that's unable to cover its short-term liabilities with short-term assets could be in for some trouble in the not-so-distant future. Even if the company manages to stay out of bankruptcy, it may have to default on payments or find creative (and sometimes detrimental) methods of raising the cash it needs to pay the bills.

You can find plenty of penny stocks in great liquidity situations, though, and liquidity ratios help you identify them.

When a company has a strong position from the perspectives of the following liquidity ratios, you know that it is generating money from its operations or has significant assets to keep operating and advancing its business.

Current ratio

To calculate the current ratio, you divide the current assets by the current liabilities. The result gives you a pretty good indication of a company's ability to pay its short-term obligations, which are due within the next 12 months. Here's the equation:

$$\text{Current Ratio} = \frac{\text{Current Assets}}{\text{Current Liabilities}}$$

This is one of the first ratios my team and I look at in our penny stock analysis. We like it because it is a quick way to eliminate from consideration companies that are already in financial trouble or operationally underwater.

 When calculating the current ratio (or having it calculated for you by any financial data websites), look for a value of one or higher (higher number indicate strength). A current ratio of 0.5 means that the company only has half of the current assets it needs to cover its current liabilities. If that value is 7, then you know that the company's current liabilities are covered seven times over, which demonstrates that the company is in very strong financial shape from this perspective.

Quick ratio

A quick ratio is a more focused look at a company's ability to pay its short-term debt. Unlike the current ratio, which considers all of a company's assets, the quick ratio focuses only on those assets — such as cash, short-term investments, and accounts receivable — that the company can quickly and easily use. Here's how it's calculated:

$$\text{Quick Ratio} = \frac{\text{Cash} + \text{Accounts Receivable} + \text{Marketable Securities}}{\text{Current Liabilities}}$$

Quick ratios are useful because, although a company may have a strong overall short-term asset position, not all those assets are truly liquid. In addition, the assets may decrease in value if the company is forced to sell them. For example, as inventory, short-term assets may be worth a significant amount, but if the company needs to sell inventory to cover its bills, the assets may only generate a portion of that assumed value.

With start-up companies or newer penny stocks that are potentially in their growth phase, the quick ratio is important to assess their ability to pay what they owe in the short term. Look for a value of at least 1 from the quick ratio, but higher values are better.

Financial analysts often refer to the quick ratio as the "acid test." Any company that can pass the acid test, meaning it has a strong enough quick ratio, should be able to pay its bills and obligations and maintain its operations for the foreseeable future. Many analysts and investors are only interested in stocks that pass this acid test and will not get involved with any company that fails (in other words, has a quick ratio of less than one) the test. You should count yourself as one of those people who only invest in stocks that pass the acid test.

Cash ratio

The cash ratio takes accounts receivable out of the equation when considering a company's assets. This removes the uncertainty and reliance on getting paid by customers. You are then left with what I believe is a much more certain and telling number.

You generate a cash ratio by comparing cash and marketable securities to short-term liabilities. Examples of marketable securities include stocks, bonds, and guaranteed investment certificates that are due to mature within the next 12 months. The calculation for the cash ratio is shown in the following equation:

$$\text{Cash Ratio} = \frac{\text{Cash} + \text{Marketable Securities}}{\text{Current Liabilities}}$$

A cash ratio helps you determine whether the company has enough money in the bank and enough easily liquidated investments to cover what they need to have to pay their debts due in the next 12 months.

Look for a cash ratio of at least 1, but much like the other liquidity ratios, the higher the number the better. If you see a cash ratio of 0.5 for example, that means that for every dollar the companies owe in the next year, it only has 50¢.

You will see stronger cash ratios among mature and more-established companies than you will with penny stocks. Newer and smaller businesses are much more likely to have less income, and the money they do generate tends to be reinvested back into research, advertising, and equipment.

With penny stocks, the cash ratio is important from the perspective of making sure that the company will stay in business and advance its operations. The cash ratio doesn't necessarily need to be very strong, however, such as a value of 2 or higher, but look for a value of at least 1. Larger cash ratios are better but not necessarily to be expected in speculative penny stocks.

Operating cash flow

Operating cash flow is a great ratio to watch when dealing with penny stock analysis. The operating cash flow looks only at cash coming in from operations, and divides it by current liabilities. The resulting number illustrates how many times over the cash flow will cover what the company owes in the short term. Here's the equation:

$$\text{Operating Cash Flow Ratio} = \frac{\text{Cash Flow from Operations}}{\text{Current Liabilities}}$$

Unlike the current, quick, and cash ratios, where you should look for a value of at least 1, the operating cash flow could be acceptable at slightly lower amounts. Because other short-term assets could come into play to cover the company's debts, it could potentially do fine even if its operating cash flow doesn't do more than cover the current liabilities.

Although a value of less than 1 isn't a sign for concern, the lower the operating cash flow falls, the more likely it could be a problem. Healthier companies have healthier cash flow and debt coverage, so higher numbers in this ratio are always preferable.

Strong operating cash flow is important with penny stocks because it demonstrates

- ✔ **Income:** Revenues must be coming in to have a strong operating cash flow ratio. To be able to cover short-term liabilities with operating cash alone, independent of other asset classes, is wonderful for any level of company.

- ✔ **Fiscal security:** When a penny stock is able to maintain its own operations, it generally won't need to raise more money. This sort of situation is a good sign for shareholders because it means that the company may be in a position to finance any new undertakings with its own money instead of taking on debt or issuing more shares.

- ✔ **Opportunity:** When cash flow meets or exceeds obligations, the company is in a position to take advantage of beneficial events as they arise, whether that means hiring workers, paying down long-term debt, buying back shares, or other actions.

- ✔ **Demand:** A company with strong cash flow is enjoying sales of its products or services, which means that it has achieved a certain level of demand and acceptance among its market.

Operating cash flow is a great ratio for penny stock analysis. Besides demonstrating the ability to cover liabilities, it also shows income capacity, fiscal security, opportunity, and demand, in relation to that company's operations.

Activity Ratios

Activity ratios demonstrate the effectiveness of a company's operations. The calculations are based on the annual turnover rate of inventory, receivables, payables, and working capital. Generally speaking, the more rapid turnover implies greater efficiency.

For example, a penny stock with a very high working capital turnover uses the money it brings in quite rapidly. A low turnover rate in this same example illustrates slow activity in terms of bringing in and subsequently spending its money.

The expected rate of turnover depends very much on the kind of business you're examining. A fast-food company needs a much higher inventory turnover than a high-end automobile manufacturer. When compared to activity ratios from previous quarters and years, or contrasted with the numbers of competitors, you will have a good idea of how efficient a company is with its operations.

For all the activity ratios I describe in the following sections, you see values for inventory, fixed assets, and accounts receivable, for example. In all cases, for the denominator (the number below the line), it is generally preferable to use average numbers for the year rather than the number most recently reported on the financial statements. For example, instead of using inventory in your calculation, use average inventory. You can get the average by adding the value at the beginning of the year to that of the one at year's end and then dividing by two.

Inventory turnover

Knowing how many times a company turns over its inventory in a year provides excellent insights into the efficiency of a company. The more quickly it can produce goods and sell them, generally the more effective its operations.

You will get very different inventory turnover calculations depending on the specific industry in which a company is engaged. High-end vehicle retailers may turn over inventory once a year or less, whereas a clothing retailer will want to move out their wares seasonally and so desire an inventory turnover ratio of at least 4. You will see different turnover rates within the same industry, and the higher the number — especially in relation to the competition — the better.

Inventory is an interesting ratio, as it calls on both the income statement and balance sheet to get the numbers required for the calculation. To generate the inventory turnover ratio, you divide the costs of goods sold by the value of the inventory, as shown here:

$$\text{Inventory Turnover Ratio} = \frac{\text{Cost of Goods Sold}}{\text{Inventory}}$$

Inventory turnover is a good calculation for penny stocks. When a company is in the early stages, you want to see that it is efficiently producing and selling its wares, especially in contrast with competitors. As well, revenues generated from that turnover benefits other financial ratios, such as the operating cash flow (described earlier in this chapter).

Watching the inventory levels of a company, especially those in the retail space, is the best way to anticipate future success and spot warning signs. When any company sees its inventory levels swell faster than its sales growth rate, it probably indicates a decrease in demand. Inventory levels should hold approximately the same from quarter to quarter or increase at about the same rate as the growth in revenues.

Receivables turnover

Turnover in receivables demonstrates the number of times accounts receivable are collected per year. Companies must keep on top of collections to remain profitable. Problems arise with account receivable when

- Too many customers aren't paying what they owe.
- Too many customers aren't paying in a timely manner.
- A single customer or two owes a significant portion of the accounts receivable. If that account has trouble paying, or is about to go bankrupt, any company that relies heavily on that customer for accounts receivable will find itself in a cash crunch.

The longer the time frame for receivables to be paid, and the greater amount outstanding, the higher degree of payment risk a company is exposed to.

With penny stocks, you will usually see pretty strong receivables turnover rates, such as at least 4, but depending on the industry, perhaps as high as 6 or better. This demonstrates that the company gets paid for its wares four times or six times over the course of twelve months.

More established large cap companies have the luxury of surviving low inventory turnover rates because they aren't as desperate for the short-term cash flow. Penny stocks, on the other hand, generally need access to the cash quickly just to pay their bills and they stay on top of outstanding invoices, which results in higher inventory turnover ratios.

With penny stocks, I look for values of at least 4, regardless of their industry.

Here's how you calculate the ratio:

$$\text{Receivable Turnover Ratio} = \frac{\text{Sales}}{\text{Average Accounts Receivable}}$$

Payables turnover

Payables turnover is a reflection of how many times the company pays the amounts owed to its suppliers. You generally want payables turnover to be equivalent to receivables turnover (which I describe in the preceding section), because money brought in as receivables is used to cover the payables. Because most companies spend money at the same rate they bring it in, the inventory turnover rate should mimic the payables turnover rate.

The company may be experiencing problems when its payables turnover ratio is deceasing. This is especially true when that decrease occurs without a similar drop in its receivables rate. This is sometimes indicative of an inability to pay what it owes.

Penny stocks with very high payables turnover ratios, such as 4 or better, are generally more willing and able to pay their expenses. This has the added benefit of keeping the suppliers happy.

Here's the equation for calculating the payable turnover ratio:

$$\text{Payable Turnover Ratio} = \frac{\text{Sales}}{\text{Average Accounts Payable}}$$

With the payable turnover ratio, higher numbers are better.

Working capital turnover

Working capital is current assets less current liabilities. The working capital turnover ratio illustrates how effectively a company uses its funds. You can generate this ratio by dividing sales by working capital; here's the equation:

$$\text{Working Capital Turnover Ratio} = \frac{\text{Sales}}{\text{Average Working Capital}}$$

When this rate is 15 or higher, it means that the company is very effectively using its funds to generate revenues. When the value is lower, such as closer to 1, it is operating much less efficiently. For each dollar of working capital, the first company is generating $15 in sales, while the second company is generating $1.

The working capital turnover ratio will vary dramatically among companies and among industry groups. The figure is more important in relation to the specific company itself to provide some clarity about the efficiency of its operations; it is less effective when used as a comparative tool.

You want to see that any penny stock you're analyzing is doing a great job of using a small amount of capital in a short time frame to produce revenues. Other companies may have better ratios, but that doesn't necessarily imply that they are a better investment. Look for higher numbers rather than lower, but don't use a higher working capital ratio as a lone indicator of overall value in penny stocks.

Fixed asset turnover

Fixed assets are items such as factories, property, and equipment. These are long-term assets, and generally the company has no intentions of selling them or doing anything other than using them to generate revenues.

Use this equation to calculate the fixed asset turnover ratio:

$$\text{Fixed Asset Turnover Ratio} = \frac{\text{Sales}}{\text{Average Fixed Assets}}$$

By dividing sales into the fixed assets to generate this financial ratio, you gain a reflection of how efficiently the company is using its fixed assets to generate revenues. For example, if it has a $10 million factory, you hope that the high-value asset is contributing to its overall sales.

You want to pay attention to fixed asset turnover rates when considering companies that have a lot of value in fixed assets and are using those assets to bring in money. The ratio becomes less of a factor, or potentially has no importance whatsoever, in cases where the stock doesn't have any significant fixed asset positions.

With penny stocks, use this financial ratio to analyze companies that have factories or expensive equipment related to the production of sales. For penny stocks with few fixed assets, or little reliance on them to produce revenue, you may not need to rely on this financial ratio at all.

Total asset turnover

By dividing sales into the total assets of the company, you derive the total asset turnover. This ratio is a reflection of a company's efficiency in using assets to generate sales. Here's the equation:

$$\text{Total Asset Turnover Ratio} = \frac{\text{Sales}}{\text{Average Total Assets}}$$

The greater the total sales, and the lower the total assets, the higher the value. Larger numbers for this ratio mean that the company is generating more revenues and doing so from a smaller asset position. In other words, it is operating more effectively.

You will sometimes see strong numbers of 10 or even higher from penny stocks, because they tend to have lower assets values. As well, they often start making revenues before they have accumulated many assets of any kind.

Because this calculation is based on total assets, which often don't have much bearing on the survival or short-term operations of the company, total asset turnover isn't usually an important ratio for analyzing penny stocks. It can be helpful when doing direct comparisons with competitors, to assess if the underlying penny stock is running efficiently

Leverage Ratios

Leverage ratios are a category of ratios that demonstrate the mix of equity to debt for a company. Whether focusing on a company's ability to make interest payments on loans or on its percentage of debt when compared to total assets, leverage ratios illustrate the stock's ability to meet its long-term debt obligations.

Although leverage ratios are similar to liquidity ratios, which I describe earlier in this chapter, leverage ratios focus on long-term debts rather than short-term obligations. As an investor, you want to know if a company can carry and finance the loans or mortgages it has taken on in the course of its operations, and you can get that information by using leverage ratios.

Debt ratio

The debt ratio is a very important tool for analyzing penny stocks. It measures how much debt a company has in relation to its total assets. Here it is:

$$\text{Debt Ratio} = \frac{\text{Total Liabilities}}{\text{Total Assets}}$$

A company with $30 million in total assets but with $10 million in debt has a debt ratio of 33 percent ($10 million divided by $30 million = 33 percent).

With penny stocks, you want to ensure that the debt ratio is

- ✔ **Comparable to competitors:** A debt ratio that's approximately in line with the industry average shouldn't concern investors. However, if the ratio is much higher than other players in the same space, that value may be a warning sign.

- ✔ **Shrinking:** Debts have a way of getting out of hand, especially if the company isn't paying the liability down over time. Any debt not being aggressively paid may be one that is too large.

- ✔ **Increasing only for business development:** Debt can be useful, especially to open doors for increased growth opportunities. Any major increases in the debt ratio should be for business development.

- ✔ **Manageable:** Can the company pay interest charges on the debt? Does it have any funds left over to pay the principal amounts?

Keeping these criteria in mind, you should be able to assess a company's debt ratio. Specifically, you want to ensure that it is manageable and in line with the company's prospects and goals, but not burdensome.

With the debt ratio, lower numbers are better.

Debt to equity

The debt to equity ratio compares how much capital has been contributed by creditors (banks, loans from individuals, and so on — this is the "debt" part of the equation) to how much has been contributed by shareholders (the "equity" part of the equation). In other words, how much money does the company owe to creditors compared to how much it owes to shareholders (the total amount invested by shareholders)? The ratio is as follows:

$$\text{Debt to Equity Ratio} = \frac{\text{Total Liabilities}}{\text{Total Shareholder Equity}}$$

For example, if shareholders invested $20 million since the initiation of the company, and the company currently has $10 million in debt, that's a debt to equity ratio of 0.5 ($10 million divided by $20 million).

A weak debt-to-equity ratio, of around 1 or higher, could imply that the corporation may theoretically have difficulty paying its debts and obligations.

On the other hand, a low debt-to-equity ratio indicates that a company could create more profits by taking on more debt. It has the option of increasing its debt load to help the business grow.

Overall, debt-to-equity calculations aren't significantly helpful when dealing with penny stocks. Although they do have some merit for comparison purposes, the cash flow and revenue growth rates have a far more dramatic effect on share prices among penny stocks.

With debt-to-equity ratios, lower numbers are better.

Interest coverage

The *interest coverage* ratio is a measure of how many times a company's earnings (before interest and taxes) can pay the interest expenses on outstanding debt. The more times over a company can pay those specific debt-related obligations, the easier it can carry its debt load and the more likely lenders will be to extend it more credit.

Here's the ratio:

$$\text{Interest Coverage Ratio} = \frac{\text{Earnings Before Interest and Taxes}}{\text{Interest Expense}}$$

To generate the interest coverage ratio, divide a company's net earnings into the sum total of all interest payments it is required to make to all sources for the next year. Generally, you will see high interest coverage values, perhaps as great as 20 or 50 or more, among those corporations that have their debt loads well under control.

Be wary of any penny stock that has an interest coverage ratio of less than 2, and be very worried if that value is falling or sits anywhere near 1.

With the interest coverage ratio, higher numbers are better.

Performance Ratios

Also known as *profit margins,* performance ratios display exactly how much money a company is making at each stage of its operations. The amounts are illustrated as percentages, such as a net profit margin of 12 percent.

Profit margins are often very small and can improve very slowly. This is generally due to the following factors:

- ✔ **Fulfillment costs:** To provide any product or service, there will always be certain costs — which is why you will never see a profit margin of 100 percent. In most cases, the majority of the revenues brought in from sales are eaten up by the costs to provide them. Depending on the specific industry, profit margins of 5 percent, or even less, are not unusual.

- ✔ **Costs of supplies:** The prices of many commodities or supplies required to build a product can often change. These shifts are often beyond the control of the company, such as when a steel shortage doubles prices. Cost increases may detrimentally impact the profit margins for a company.

- ✔ **Currency fluctuations:** Many companies make or spend money in more than one country and so are exposed to fluctuations in the prices of currencies that they deal with. Like the costs of supplies, currency fluctuations are largely beyond the control of the company.

- ✔ **Competition:** There will always be competition, and battling for customers and market share can be very expensive. In addition, any industry that has high profit margins will eventually see new competitors arriving who are trying to take some of that profit.

Even a small improvement in a profit margin can have significant ramifications on a company's results. Bringing an operating profit up from 6 percent to 10 percent can represent millions of dollars in additional earnings, for example.

Ideally, you want to find penny stocks with healthy performance ratios, the higher of which would imply greater profitability. If those profit margins improve even more over time, that is all the better!

Gross profit margin

Gross profit margin illustrates the profitability, and therefore the viability, of a company selling its products or services. The measure is of major importance because the first step for any company is to sell its wares at a profit, and this financial ratio clearly indicates whether a company is doing do.

Here's the ratio:

$$\text{Gross Profit Margin} = \frac{\text{Sales - Cost of Goods Sold}}{\text{Sales}}$$

Gross profit margin is expressed as a percentage. For example, a gross margin of 20 percent means that for every dollar in sales, a company spends 80¢ to produce the product and sell it while taking in 20¢ as profit.

If a company sells widgets for three dollars but it costs them one dollar to make, its gross profit is two dollars per widget. To calculate the gross profit margin, you divide the two-dollar profit into the three-dollar selling price of the widget, which results in a value of 66 percent.

A strong value for this ratio depends very much on the industry in which the company is engaged. An Internet or software company with almost zero costs to provide their digital goods should have a very strong gross profit margin, perhaps as high as 90 percent. A biotech corporation or coal mining operation may see margins of 5 percent or less.

When a company has no revenues or is actually selling at a loss, it will have a negative, or nonapplicable, gross profit margin. Except for possibly serving as a warning to avoid the stock, this ratio is of little value in cases where a company doesn't report any sales.

The gross profit margin ratio is very industry specific. Here are some examples of companies that typically have gross profit margins that are

- ✔ **High (above 70 percent):** Internet hosting, online subscriptions, software, digital files, and computer storage

- ✔ **Medium (near 30 to 50 percent):** Jewelry retailers, clothing, specialty stores, golf supply, and pet stores

- ✔ **Low (less than 15 percent):** Mass market retailers, fast food, movie theaters, farming, electronics stores, and airlines

Gross profit margin is of tremendous use for comparisons against competition in the same industry. For example, if every company in the digital media space has a gross profit margin above 60 percent, you should make sure that any penny stock that you're looking at for that industry has at least a comparable value.

With this ratio, higher numbers are better.

We use gross profit margins as high as 90 percent in our discussion and give examples or various industries with strong values in this category. Keep in mind that for the vast majority of companies you analyze, this financial ratio will come in closer to 10 or 20. Profit margins, whether gross or net, typically are pretty tight, meaning that they will be low. Generally, where an industry enjoys a higher margin, additional companies enter the market to capture some of that profit, thus generating competition and putting pressure on the margins.

Operating profit margin

A company has many more expenses than those it incurs to produce and sell products. For example, it has administrative expenses, rent, and overhead. To take these costs into account, look at a company's operating profit margin.

This ratio is where you will see improvements by companies looking to control their costs. While a corporation can't necessarily do much to reduce the costs of goods sold, it usually has greater ability to push its operating expenses lower.

Operating income is generated after taking all expenses into account, with the exception of interest and taxes. For that reason, operating income is referred to as *EBIT* (earnings before interest and taxes).

By dividing EBIT into total revenues, you calculate the operating profit margin, which is expressed as follows:

$$\text{Operating Profit Margin} = \frac{\text{Operating Income}}{\text{Sales Revenue}}$$

Operating profit margin offers a more accurate view of a company's profitability than gross margin and demonstrates if a company is truly viable. A business may have an 80 percent gross margin, but after it pays for electricity and administration, does it have anything left? To find out, turn to the operating profit margin.

When looking at operating profit margin, higher numbers are better. But because this ratio factors in additional expenses beyond the cost of good sold, the operating profit margin will always be lower than the gross margin. This calculation also brings companies down to more comparable levels, because even businesses with high gross margins will now factor in costs besides those related to goods sold.

Net profit margin

To determine a company's net profit you subtract all the company's costs — costs to produce and sell the products, and the administrative and overhead expenses — from total revenues.

Net profit is the money earned (or lost) after taking every cost into account, with a few exceptions. Specifically, values for interest, taxes, depreciation, and amortization are not included in net profit because they have little bearing on the operations of the company and are based mainly on accounting and financing decisions. Net profit is often referred to as EBITDA, which stands for earnings before interest, taxes, depreciation, and amortization.

 At their simplest, depreciation and amortization relate to the decreasing value of assets over time. For example, a $50,000 vehicle may only be worth half that amount four years later, so the corporate financials need to reflect the changing value. To fully explain the concepts requires at least a chapter or two, but the good news is that you don't need to understand them to be an excellent penny stock investor.

Also called *earnings,* net profit is what can really move a share price because it represents a company's final result after all factors and expenses are considered. Net profit is the reason for any company to be in business in the first place.

The net profit margin is derived from dividing the net income by the total revenue. It shows how much profit was generated from total sales. Here's the equation:

$$\text{Net Profit Margin} = \frac{\text{Net Income}}{\text{Revenue}}$$

A company with $1 million in net profit from $5 million in sales has a net profit margin of 20 percent. That same company, but with $50 million in sales, has a ratio value of only 2 percent ($1 million profit divided by $50 million sales = 2 percent).

Because this financial ratio takes all expenses into account, it is lower than the gross margin and lower again in comparison with the operating margin (see "Gross profit margin" and "Operating profit margin," earlier in this chapter). The net profit margin is often very small; in the cases of companies losing money, it can't even be calculated.

Ideally, a company has net profits at the end of the day, and those companies that do hopefully can show healthy profit margins in the single digit (1 to 9 percent) range. Higher ratios are better, but you will usually see very small net profit margins regardless of the industry. Look at the direct competitors of all sizes to gain insights into the strength or weakness of the net margins for any penny stock.

Return on assets

The return on assets explores the amount of earnings generated from the total asset position of a company. The equation is as follows:

$$\text{Return on Assets Ratio} = \frac{\text{Net Income}}{\text{Average Total Assets}}$$

The higher the ratio, the better. A corporation may report $1 million in earnings compared to $50 million in assets, for a return on assets of 2 percent (1 divided by 50). What would be even better is if they achieved $1 million in earnings from a smaller asset base, such as $8 million. In that case, the return on assets would be 12.5 percent (1 divided by 8).

With penny stocks, return on assets is sometimes a useful analysis tool, but not in the majority of situations. Newer and lower-priced companies often don't have either earnings or assets of any significant amount, and you will not see shares trading in speculative companies based on their return on assets.

Like most financial ratios, the most effective use of the return on assets calculation is as a comparative tool against other companies in the same industry. Watch for any major discrepancies (such as the value being dramatically off the industry average), but don't read too deeply into this ratio for most penny stocks.

Return on equity

The return on equity ratio measures how much profit the corporation has generated from the money shareholders have invested. Here's the formula:

$$\text{Return on Equity Ratio} = \frac{\text{Net Income}}{\text{Average Shareholders Equity}}$$

Higher ratios are desirable, but this ratio is of limited value for evaluating penny stocks. Most start-ups and newer corporations have a large equity position and low or nonexistent profits. This ratio will become more relevant after a company matures and has been around for a longer period of time; it is not valuable when applied to most penny stocks.

Valuation Ratios

Successful investing comes down to buying stocks at the right price. Even shares in the best company in the world can be too expensive or overvalued and may be a disappointing investment if you pay too much.

Valuation ratios give you an understanding of how attractive shares are at current prices. Based on the current cost per share, you can see if the stock is relatively expensive or if you're getting a bargain.

All valuation ratios are derived in relation to share price, and as such, lower results are superior and, ostensibly, imply better value in the shares. A P/E of 8 is more attractive than one of 17, while a price-to-sales value of 1.2 is more attractive than one of 4.3.

Stocks tend to move back and forth from overvalued to undervalued levels. When they represent very attractive valuations, the theory is that the shares will increase in price as more and more investors recognize the value inherent in the company. This will push share prices to — and even beyond — this intrinsic value. This investment theory also holds true in reverse, when stocks that are overpriced cause more and more investors to look for companies not selling at a premium.

Price-to-earnings (P/E)

Price-to-earnings (P/E) is the most common and widely known financial ratio. It simply divides the price of the shares by the earnings the company has generated over the last 12 months and is derived by using the following equation:

$$\text{Price-to-Earnings Ratio} = \frac{\text{Current Share Price}}{\text{Earnings Per Share}}$$

P/E is a way of seeing how much earnings power you can buy for the money. It will take less total investment capital to buy more earnings capacity in companies with lower P/E ratios.

Like other valuation ratios, the lower the P/E value, the better. For example, if Company A has a P/E ratio of 8 and Company B has a P/E ratio of 24, it means that it costs one-third as much to buy a dollar of Company A's earnings as it does to buy a dollar of Company B's earnings.

Although P/E is a simple and common calculation, you should keep in mind some important points when using P/E ratios:

- ✔ **No earnings:** A fraction can't be divided by zero. If a company didn't produce earnings, or operated at a loss, you can't generate the P/E calculation. What is $2.25 per share divided by earnings of zero? You can't derive a result; on financial websites, this is usually displayed as "not applicable."

- ✔ **Looking backward:** Because P/E is based on a company's earnings over the previous 12 months, the ratio is really displaying whether the shares are attractive at current prices based on what they have done in the past. It doesn't take into account what the company may do going forward, and unless the stock maintains earnings at former levels, the P/E will not be as useful.

- ✔ **Corporate life cycle:** Expect to see higher P/E ratios for companies in their growth phase of the corporate life cycle. Investors are looking to invest in growing companies, and as such they pay more for the shares. While a mature and predictable corporation may have a P/E of 14, a rapidly growing or start-up penny stock could see P/E ratios higher than 80.

While lower P/Es theoretically demonstrate better value, there is a major difference between blue-chip companies on the New York Stock Exchange, for example, and a tiny 25¢ penny stock that's seeing its first sales. Your reliance on P/E depends greatly on the nature of the investment.

When a company is expected to produce significant earnings in the future, investors often pay more for the shares. This drives up the price, while the earnings for the P/E ratio don't change. The end result is a much higher P/E ratio, because investors in the know ignore the theoretically high valuation on the shares and are willing to pay more.

Lower P/E's are better in theory, but when they are too low, view them as a major warning sign. You may see a P/E ratio of 4 or even 1, for example. What this is really telling you is that investors aren't willing to pay for the shares, and as the stock falls in value, the P/E ratio falls along with it. This is generally a result of issues with the underlying company. For example, when the mines of a highly profitable gold production company run dry. Or perhaps investors do not trust the reported numbers coming out of a specific country and they stop buying shares, while that nation keeps providing false, although very strong, earnings data.

Price-to-earnings-to-growth-rate (PEG) ratio

The price-to-earnings-to-growth-rate (PEG) ratio is great for analyzing penny stocks because it factors in the company's growth rate. The calculation is generated by dividing the P/E ratio by the anticipated annual growth rate in earnings per share. Here's the equation:

$$\text{Price-to-Earnings-to-Growth (PEG) Ratio} = \frac{\text{Price-to-Earnings Ratio}}{\text{Annual Earnings Per Share Growth Rate}}$$

With PEG ratios, lower numbers are stronger. Anything below 1 should be considered compelling, while PEGs approaching 3 or higher may imply overvalued shares.

For a company with a P/E of 10, with annual earnings per share growth of 20 percent, you divide 10 into 20, for a result of 0.5. That represents a very healthy PEG, and as long as the anticipated earnings growth used in the calculation is reliable, the shares represent significant value.

Price-to-sales

The price-to-sales ratio compares the current trading price of the stock against their total sales. Here's the equation:

$$\text{Price-to-Sales Ratio} = \frac{\text{Current Share Price}}{\text{Earnings Per Share}}$$

You can use this ratio to assess how much money you have to invest in exchange for what level of revenue generation capacity.

The price-to-sales ratio is an effective analysis tool for use with penny stock research. As newer and smaller companies generally don't have earnings, ratios such as P/E and PEG can't be applied. Because they also have fewer assets, and their shares trade more on speculation and the potential for growth, many of the ratios are not applicable. And so tracking the sales is a more appropriate analysis approach. You want to see revenues in these newer businesses to demonstrate the demand among customers and consumers.

With the price-to-sales ratio, lower numbers are stronger. A two-dollar company with one dollar in sales per share would have a price-to-sales ratio of 2. On the other hand, if that same company in had four dollars in sales per share, the ratio would stand at a stronger 0.5.

By comparing the price of the shares to the sales levels, you get an idea of how expensive or inexpensive the share may be at its current price. The ratio is even more helpful when compared with the company's direct competitors, because it will demonstrate how much you would need to pay for shares and for what degree of revenues.

While the ratio varies greatly by industry, generally you won't see a price-to-sales ratio of less than one. When it's that low, the value will be clear to investors, who will generally start paying more for the shares. Share prices will in turn increase, resulting in a higher price-to-sales value.

With penny stocks in their early stages, the price-to-sales ratio is one of the most important analysis tools. A strong value near two or less generally implies that the shares represent strong value.

Price-to-cash flow

The price-to-cash flow ratio tracks how expensive the shares are in relation to the company's cash flow. Like the other valuation ratios, lower numbers represent better value. This ratio is generated by taking the total cash flow over the previous 12 months and dividing that by the number of shares outstanding, to provide the total cash flow per share. Then divide the price per share by the cash flow per share. Here's the equation:

$$\text{Price-to-Cash Flow Ratio} = \frac{\text{Current Share Price}}{\text{Sales Per Share}}$$

A company trading at $2.50, with a cash flow of $5 per share would have a strong price-to-cash flow ratio of 0.5. If those shares increased to $10 over a few months, without any change in cash flow, then the ratio would become two (10 divided 5 equals 2), and represent significantly less value from the perspective of the price-to-cash flow ratio.

Chapter 11

The Abstract Review in Penny Stocks

The concepts in this chapter can help you find really profitable penny stocks, which is why I'm surprised that more investors don't understand or apply them in their research. The purpose of a business is to make money and when it generates those profits, the shares very often trade at higher prices. The ideas presented here help a company increase its profits and lift itself above its competitors.

Although you can uncover great stocks without any of the knowledge I share with you in this chapter, without this information you will never truly understand the underlying businesses. By getting a grasp of the abstract review and applying it during your due diligence, you will have a tremendous advantage over any investors who don't take the time to glean this information.

I introduce you to what proper branding looks like and why it is the first competitive advantage for any business (of any size)! I review the Unique Selling Proposition that a product can offer and how its positioning can be the most important aspect in the success or failure of any company.

I also examine advanced concepts such as product acceptance, market share, and barriers to entry, to give you an understanding of the ways in which they are important to you and your investment decisions. The marketing strategy a penny stock employs, and its customer loyalty and attrition, are of monumental importance to its success.

Making Products Meaningful with Branding

Branding is the single most important aspect of any business. A *brand* is the concept or unique image of a company and its products or services.

Brands have the unique ability to hold certain beliefs or expectations in the minds of individuals. For example, you may think certain countries make inferior cars, or a certain politician is dishonest, or a specific restaurant chain provides healthier options than the rest. Branding plays a major role in all these notions.

Branding is the act of developing or directing a brand so that customers react positively to the underlying company and its wares. Brands hold certain connotations — whether positive or negative — among consumers and have impacts on all aspects of their interactions with a company.

McDonald's — along with its Golden Arches logo — is an instantly recognizable fast-food brand. Apple's brand differs significantly from that of IBM, even though both companies make computers.

Any time you have opinions about a company or product, they're probably a result of branding (or a lack thereof). Many people think that they know the best vacuum, or motorcycle, or smartphone, even though they've never even tried all the options. That is branding at work.

A brand can improve in the eyes of consumers. When a retailer gives one dollar to charity with each purchase, it is trying to burnish its brand by generating feelings of goodwill with its consumers. Brands can also fall out of favor (and pretty quickly, too), such as when a car company's latest model has sudden engine fires.

Most companies try to improve their brand and by extension, their sales, through various means. Here are some of the most popular:

- ✔ **Provide superior customer experiences.** Branding occurs at every touch point between a consumer and the company. This includes customer service personnel, the experience with the product, and even the ease of navigating it website.

- ✔ **Make visual cues.** Easily recognizable brand logos and colors help customers associate connotations with a company. The Peter Leeds brand uses a specific shade of red on all our publications so that there is a cohesion and consistency across all touch points. Banks tend to use green to represent wealth; many retailers like to use yellow because it grabs your attention.

✔ **Manage reputations.** Companies try to address any detrimental perceptions by improving the way they interact with people or going after those who besmirch their reputations. Some firms specialize in helping companies manage their reputations.

✔ **Improve accessibility.** Some of the best brands are more accessible or accountable to consumers. Even having enough customer service personnel to answer the phone lines so that customers don't have to wait on hold is enough to improve a brand's image.

✔ **Play into their strengths.** Brands that know what customers like about them and work to make that aspect of their business even better, are likely to succeed. For example, if a company is known for having the lowest cost offerings in its market, it often can improve its brand by doubling down on that strength and dropping prices even farther. I like to think of this as the best getting better, the fastest getting faster, and the loudest getting louder.

 Pay attention to branding all around you. I can guarantee that there are dozens of brands within 12 feet of you, and you may have a certain opinion of all of them. This even includes many of the brands whose products you've never even tried.

Why branding is more important with penny stocks

Branding is more important with penny stocks than it is with larger, more established companies because it represents a way for newer and smaller companies to compete and maybe even have an advantage. Established companies are committed to how consumers already see them, which opens angles and opportunities for younger and unknown companies to use solid branding to take market share.

Newer companies also have the advantage of developing their brand from scratch, devoid of any preconceived notions. They can look for what is missing in a market and position themselves to be that missing link — whether that link is the "fastest," or "friendliest," or "simplest," or "cheapest."

With smaller companies, the brand is often their only asset. When handled properly, though, that brand enables little companies to compete and survive among the big boys.

When branding is done well

Unfortunately, far too many companies do a bad job of handling their brand. In such situations, the brand is actually costing the company in terms of revenues and reputation.

When branding is done properly, however, it can lead to easier and more numerous sales, higher customer loyalty, and increases in word-of-mouth referrals. A strong and effective branding strategy must

- **Remain consistent.** Every time a customer sees or interacts with a brand, it should be obviously similar. A company's colors, logo, and even its style must remain consistent.

- **Add value.** Each time a consumer interacts with a brand, it should provide some value. Better software, an easy-to-navigate website, great fashions for the money, or whatever the deliverable.

- **Maintain communication.** Successful brands continually connect with customers to see how they are feeling about the brand. They conduct focus groups, monitor customer reviews, or simply keep clear contact channels open so they can ask questions or provide feedback.

- **Continually improve.** While it is best to never change a brand in terms of appearance or focus, companies must constantly work to improve their brand. The main concept should remain consistent, but there are lots of things around the brand that a company can always improve. Examples include an improved social media presence, value-added features to new products, or even free customer appreciation gifts.

- **Appear unique.** A great brand stands out from very other business operating in the space.

- **Focus on fewer attributes.** He who is friends with everyone is ultimately friends with no one. A strong brand conjures up, and goes after, only one or two attributes. The least expensive, healthiest, best-tasting hamburger will never outsell a hamburger that only claims to be the best tasting, or only claims to be the healthiest.

When analyzing a penny stock, pay attention to its branding and that of its competitors. While the operations of a business are not at all important for very short-term trading, they are of paramount importance when investing for more than a few weeks.

In addition to scrutinizing the operational results of any business, having an understanding of the ways in which a company's brand helps it perform will provide excellent insights into the future of that company. And when you know what that should look like, you're in a better position to anticipate future share prices.

Harnessing a Unique Selling Proposition (USP)

The unique selling proposition (USP) is the value that a product or service offers to its customers that can't be matched by any offerings from the competition. Think of it as the "only," the "first," the "leading," the "cheapest," or the "loudest" whatever.

For example, the fastest car available has the USP of speed, and if the boast is legitimate, competitors will never be able to claim that same USP. Enter the customer who wants to buy the fastest car, and he will be looking in the direction of that particular company.

Every company should have a USP to help them stand out among all the marketing noise consumers are faced with every day. Just about all businesses have a USP, whether they recognize it or not. If a business doesn't leverage a strong USP, it may have a harder — and more expensive — time capturing prospects and converting them into customers.

Done properly, leading with a strong USP can represent a tremendous competitive advantage for a company; as a matter of fact, it may be the most important part of its marketing strategy. With smaller and newer penny stock companies, a USP takes on even greater significance because they need to generate sales and survive against larger competitors, and an effective USP is a way to do exactly that. The quality of a USP can be measured on the following factors:

- **Significant benefit:** Only if the USP represents a significant benefit to the consumer will it have any value. A USP may be "the only shoes with 7 percent silk in the laces," but that's a very weak boast that will generate no benefit to the purchaser or the company. On the other hand, "the largest toilet seat," has an instant market and provides value to anyone who finds standard toilet seats too small.

- **Unique:** Unique is the first part of the USP. A product or service must be something that no other company is offering, or else the whole concept is derailed.

✔ **Being leveraged:** Companies need to communicate the benefits of their USPs to the prospective customers in order to get any value out of them. If a company has a great USP but isn't marketing it, they aren't leveraging it.

✔ **Easily communicated:** Simple ideas are much more effective. Being the only neurological drug that targets scarred myelin in patients who have been on beta-blockers for less than 12 months but more than 3 months is far too complicated of a message. Being the world's most expensive licorice is straightforward and clear, with no room for confusion.

Pay attention to the marketing messages you see each day. Watch for companies with USPs and see if you can differentiate the weak ones from the strong ones. This approach may lead you to some potential investments, but it may also help you improve your understanding to apply to your short list of penny stocks when you perform your due diligence.

Superior logistic networks or variety of offerings almost always trump the better product when an upstart goes head to head against engrained competition. Most new business people, and the vast majority of investors, don't realize that having the best product matters little. In fact, the superior product often fades away, taking the company with it. Lots of businesses can make a cola that tastes better than Pepsi or Coke. There are better-tasting hamburgers, friendlier gyms, more enjoyable board games . . . you get the idea. New companies selling these products or services almost always blow their budgets trying to educate the market, but at the end of the day, nobody cares. Consumers do what's easiest for them or take the familiar route.

Ensuring Product or Service Acceptance

For penny stocks, especially those with brand-new products or services, acceptance of those wares by customers is of paramount importance. The demand will tell you everything about the company, from its potential future revenues to its chances for increasing its share price.

To gain an understanding of the acceptance of the wares and improve your own knowledge of the upsides and downsides of their offerings, you should do the following research:

- ✔ **Find out what customers are saying.** You can go online and read customer reviews and comments. Look at message board posts, blogs, surveys, and online reviews.

- ✔ **Find out what the competition is saying.** Even more telling than what a company says about its own product are comments made by its competitors. You don't have to worry about bias in favor of the product, but you may need to filter out the standard competitor-induced negative positions. The best way to get a competitor review is to call that competing company and ask for help in deciding between the various options of product.

- ✔ **Try out the wares.** When possible, try the product or service the penny stock is selling. Besides making for great due diligence and potentially revealing aspects of their wares you may not have anticipated, you will have the added benefit of getting to use the product.

Keep a very close eye on the acceptance and benefits of any product or service the penny stock is offering. Customer appreciation and demand are the first steps to uncovering a profitable penny stock investment.

Market Share

Market share is an indication of what portion of a total market a company owns. In other words, a company's market share tells you the percentage of its total sales within an industry. If the total sales in the market for hot sauce remover spray are $100, a company selling $20 worth of the stuff would have a 20 percent market share.

The ideal is for a company to have 100 percent of a huge and rapidly expanding market. (Good luck finding that company.) Smaller markets and smaller shares are less desirable, and if the industry is shrinking, that's an even worse situation for the company.

With market share, it is important to know these factors about a company:

- ✔ **Total market size:** How much money are consumers spending on a particular service or product, in total? Larger markets generally mean that there are greater opportunities for generating revenues but that there are also more competitors.

- ✔ **Potential market size:** Especially when dealing with a growing market, such as many penny stocks are involved with, the potential size is particularly important. An industry may only sell a small number of its wares right now, but if that market is expected to grow many times larger, the penny stocks already engaged in the space will benefit.

✔ **Ownership by each competitor:** Besides the market share owned by the company you're interested in, you also want to know the share claimed by each competitor. One company owning 95 percent of the market has different implications than if that 95 percent is divided among 40 companies.

✔ **Change in market share:** Changes in market share can reveal effectiveness of marketing efforts, product acceptance, and company progress. When a penny stock sees its share go up 5 percent at a time when its competitor's share declined by the same amount, perhaps it is stealing customers away from that competitor.

Any time a company is selling something, it has a share of the total market. You can add a lot of clarity to your investment research if you know what percentage each player in the industry lays claim to, how large the market is and may become, and what changes are evident in terms of total share.

How to find out the market share for a penny stock

As with most concepts mentioned in this chapter, the quickest and best way to find out a penny stock's market share is to call the investor relations of the company. Any business worth its salt should know what share of the market they capture, as well as the total market size. (For details on investor relations, head over to Chapter 6.)

Sometimes companies comment on their market share in their quarterly financial reports. Keep an eye on this percentage and watch especially for changes from one period to the next. You can also get the total market size estimates from competitors in the same industry.

To calculate the percentage of market share for a company, divide the company's annual revenues into the total market size in terms of sales.

Profit from changes in market share

For penny stock investors, a much more important value than a company's market are changes and expectations in that value.

When a penny stock reports increases in its market share, that movement can imply higher revenue levels, as well as a greater degree of customer acceptance for its wares. When those gains come in line with other competitors losing ground, it can suggest a shift among consumers.

 Whether the bigger players are losing business on their own, or the smaller companies are taking those customers away, this could be an opportunity for penny stock investors. There will be a lag between when a penny stock sees an increase in its market share and when the stronger financials that result from that increase are reported. Investors who buy companies that are enjoying an expanding market share, but who do so before the financial results are reported, may benefit from an upward move in the share prices when the increased revenue numbers become public.

 Watch for improving market share in companies, and expect improved results to help the stock prices after they're eventually reported.

Barriers to Entry

The more difficult it is to enter an industry or market, the greater the barriers to entry. These barriers can make it impossible for some companies to start operations in a certain space, but they also can help companies already selling to that market because they reduce the likelihood of new competition arising.

Imagine if you are running a weight-loss website. You could have a dozen new competitors today alone because it would be very simple for them to get up and running.

On the other hand, a nuclear power plant construction firm will likely see very few competitors enter the market. Due to the high barriers of entry, which include technical knowledge requirements, expenses, and regulations, the industry may never see a new competitor enter the market.

Many potential barriers to entry exist within any market. Here are some examples of industries with high, medium, and low barriers:

- ✔ **High:** Nuclear power plants, pharmaceutical, banking, satellite and space travel, airports, automobiles, telecommunications

- ✔ **Medium:** Restaurants, insurance, mass-market retail products, alcohol, consulting, hotels

- ✔ **Low:** Web retailers and services, hairdressers, niche publications, lemonade stands, board games, bed & breakfasts, low-end retail products, hot dog vendors

If a penny stock you're interested in is already operating within a certain industry, then the higher the barriers to entry the better. Ideally, you want the companies you're investing in to have a toe-hold in industries where it would be close to impossible for any new competition to arise.

If a company you like is entering a new industry or business line, you want the barriers to entry to be low, or at least easily manageable. As soon as the company is established within the space, you want to see the barriers to entry increase dramatically and thus lock others out, such as a new regulation or requirement that would be too difficult for new entrants to attain.

Consider the barriers to entry for any penny stock in which you are interested. Pay attention to the obvious major ones but also notice the medium and smaller ones, because they all have some impact. Generally, many more barriers exist than you may notice on first glance.

Because barriers keep competition out but also make the path for new companies more difficult, they can be either (or both) a blessing or a curse. Newer penny stocks will have difficulty clearing whatever hurdles are in their way, but each hurdle also represents a stumbling block for new competition.

Gauging barriers to new competition

One way to assess what the barriers to entry are, and thus to extrapolate whether a particular penny stock should be able to clear them, is to imagine yourself in the shoes of that company. To eventually enter the market, what barriers to entry will you need to overcome? Barriers include

- **Regulations:** If a company needs approval of an organization or regulatory body to operate, that represents a barrier to entry.

- **Preexisting competition:** Entering a market that is already saturated with large competitors will be extremely difficult.

- **High customer loyalty:** If most customers are happy with their current providers, the task of winning market share will be a hard one.

- **Technical requirements:** Technical roadblocks include finding specialized staff and highly refined product specifications.

- **Material availability:** If a company needs resources that are in high demand, ensuring adequate supplies serves as a barrier to entry.

By asking yourself what hurdles lie ahead for a penny stock, you can get a better understanding of how long and complicated the road may be. You may even recognize that the company will not succeed in its efforts, and so you can avoid a long and drawn-out investment failure.

The best first movers are the small ones

Being a *first mover,* which means the first company to sell a certain type of product or operate in a specific industry, can be a massive advantage. The very act of being first is a marketing angle in itself, but the new market is also wide open and devoid of any competition, at least at first.

Eventually, other competition will enter the market. Any time there are profits to be had, other businesses will crowd around to try to take a share.

Consider a (fictional) company that produces a breakfast cereal that is eaten with water rather than milk. Being the first business to offer such a product gives the company a 100 percent market share initially. As the concept becomes more well known, and the company starts generating sales, it needs to expect competition.

The first mover in any new industry should

- **Move quickly.** The instant the first mover releases the new concept or idea to the public, it will be chased by competition battling for the newly created market share. The first mover needs to drive forward and never lose the leading position because being the leader is always a major advantage.

- **Lock in its market.** Through trademarks, employees, patents, and aggressive branding and marketing, the first mover should solidify its position. By properly establishing itself in the infant industry, a company increases the difficulty for others to enter the space, while strengthening its own position.

- **Hope for numerous competitors.** If only one new competitor enters the new market, then it will go head to head against the first mover. If dozens enter, they will all battle each other, dispersing the footprint of each of them, and leaving the spoils primarily in the hands of the original company. The marketing efforts of the follower businesses have the added effect of spreading the word about the new industry, with the majority of new customers going to the first mover.

Penny stocks that achieve first mover status are very often capable of achieving massive returns for investors. When they create a new industry concept, and therefore have 100 percent market share, they could be in for dramatic growth (in demand, sales, and earnings).

Being the first mover isn't an advantage when the company needs to educate the market. Even a great idea needs to be introduced to consumers when it's new, and nothing is more expensive than trying to educate the market. Many times the first mover will aggressively spend to present its new product or service concept, and nearly run into bankruptcy in the process. Then the second mover can just step in and start competing for market share, without all the associated costs and efforts.

Marketing Strategy and Results

Any business that intends to engage in marketing, which can consist of things like ads, public relations, press releases, or media interviews, should have a single, thoughtful, and carefully monitored strategy.

Ask the company you're interested in for a copy of its marketing strategy. It may not provide you with it, but it does not hurt to ask. At least discuss its plans and results with the company's investor relations contact (for insights into dealing with investor relations personnel, check out Chapter 6).

You want to ascertain

- ✔ **The percentage of expenses represented by marketing:** This will give you an idea of how aggressive the marketing plan is and whether it represents a realistic portion of overall expenses. Depending on the industry, marketing generally should be between 5 and 20 percent of total costs, but there are no rules set in stone.

- ✔ **The effectiveness of its efforts:** Is the business spending money and time on an average campaign with mediocre results? Ideally, the marketing efforts of a company will augment sales or at least improve positive brand awareness among consumers.

- ✔ **Future plans and expectations:** Find out the company's marketing plans for down the road. And after it undertakes those new efforts, ask what sort of results it anticipates achieving.

Marketing isn't about spending a dollar to make a dollar or more. Many aspects of advertising are actually expected to produce a loss. For example, a company may be using its marketing efforts to block out a competitor or to put its brand name in the forefront of people's minds, or even just to test a new marketing message.

Poor marketing is bottomless

A company can burn up millions of marketing dollars very quickly and have nothing to show for it. Advertisements can be extremely costly, and even some superior strategies don't always come close to covering the time and expense involved.

A funny Super Bowl ad doesn't necessarily translate into hundreds of thousands of customers clamoring for a company's wares. The reality is that the majority of people don't even see or pay attention to the commercial, and those who do don't care about the product the company is pushing. Generally, consumers need to see an advertisement several times before they even consider taking any action.

If a company spends $1 on advertisements, it can just as easily spend $500 million. When management of a penny stock puts too much faith into the power of commercials, they're likely to dramatically overextend themselves. Ads that fail to translate into equivalent revenues can sink a company with unrealistic marketing goals.

Marketing has a place, as long as it is

- ✔ **Part of an overall strategy:** Strong marketing involves public relations, media coverage, word of mouth, advertisements, and product experience. Any approach that relies exclusively on only one of these aspects is doomed to failure.

- ✔ **Profitable:** Marketing involves many expenses beyond the obvious. For example, when considering reinventing a brand, companies should factor in the cost of producing new ads that feature the new brand identity (art work, actors, production), a new presence (website, brochures, letterhead), and the time and salary involved with replacing any use of the former brand.

- ✔ **Tracked:** Any marketing strategy needs to have realistic goals so the company knows what success looks like. In terms of commercials, for example, expenses and results should be tracked for every individual ad, in terms of placement and time.

- ✔ **Adjusted:** The best marketing plans involve dropping ineffective strategies immediately, while increasing spending on those aspects that are effective. For example, if improved customer service is helping sales, while changes to the product seems to be detrimental to sales, the marketing approach should put more resources into the former and less into the latter.

✔ **Within budget:** Companies that keep their marketing expenses within a strict and realistic budget will have the best results.

Any business can spend millions on marketing, but only a few will actually generate those millions back.

Marketing is hard to track with penny stocks

Many smaller businesses don't track the results of their marketing strategy. This failure to pay attention to what works and what doesn't makes it nearly impossible to ascertain costs of various advertising channels, the effectiveness of particular types of marketing, and results from each method.

Even those penny stocks that do closely observe and detail their marketing efforts may not want to share that information with the public. In some cases, they may be trying to prevent their competitors from acquiring the details, while in others they may not yet have the information.

With advertising spending on commercials, there is a major delay between when (and even if) a spot runs and when the company receives the results. That delay is usually weeks, but can often be a month or more, depending on the media-buying agency the company is working with.

In terms of other marketing channels, such as social media efforts, word-of-mouth conversations, and branding efforts, the companies themselves typically track them — if they're tracked at all. Ideally, each company provides details about its marketing efforts, and the results derived, with their quarterly financial results. Unfortunately, penny stock companies rarely provide these details, which increases the amount of work for the investor conducting due diligence.

Often, the best way to track the marketing results of penny stocks is to speak with the investor relations contact. Also, keep an eye on any press releases or management statements for clues.

Loyalty and Attrition

The degree to which customers stick with a company's products or services is their *loyalty*. The portion of a company's market that stops being customers is called the *attrition rate*.

Picture a penny stock with a million clients. The next year, it only has half that many. That company then has 500,000 loyal customers and also suffers a 50 percent attrition rate.

With any business, you want to see very high customer loyalty and very low attrition. This is even more important with penny stocks; they generally have a smaller customer base to begin with, and their wares are newer and need to survive the test of attrition, which could stand as testament to the acceptance of the customers.

When a company has a very high loyalty rate, it is able to focus on capturing new clients instead of putting resources into changing their offerings in an attempt to hold on to existing customers. A high loyalty rate also lowers a business's cost of customer acquisition because the easiest individual to sell to is the one you already have.

In businesses with recurring billing, such as those with monthly subscription fees, loyalty is of extreme importance. Any client attrition represents declining revenues, while those who remain loyal ensure the upcoming sales base.

Customer turnover

One goal for every company is a very low (or nonexistent) customer turnover rate. Any lost business needs to be replaced, and the greater the turnover, the greater the resources required just to break even.

High customer turnover also indicates issues with the penny stock's products or services. If the users aren't happy, they will take their business elsewhere.

 With penny stocks that are just bringing their wares to market, watch the customer turnover very closely. This number will provide you with insights into product demand and future financial results that the majority of investors do not have.

Like many of the abstract review concepts in this chapter, the best (and possibly only) method to find out the customer turnover details may be to call the companies and ask. They will tell you.

Doing so will provide you with information that most other investors don't have.

You can also keep an eye on press releases, public comments from management, and financial results for clues to client turnover. Generally, when the rate of customer turnover is low, companies will make a point of bringing that news to the attention of investors. If this aspect of the business is problematic, they may not make any public statements on the topic, which is why the quick phone call can be particularly effective at getting this information.

Relative order sizes and frequencies

Besides standard customer loyalty, a business should also want its clients to place larger orders and to do so more frequently. By keeping an eye on the average order size and frequency, you can potentially predict which penny stock will be enjoying increased revenues.

A great way to find details about these specific factors is to call the company and ask directly. I walk you through the process of speaking with executives or investor relations contacts in chapter 6.

Many companies issue press releases announcing significant orders. These may provide direct details about larger or more frequent contracts.

Chapter 12

Technical Analysis with Penny Stocks

. . . .

In This Chapter

▶ Using trading patterns to predict future penny stock prices

▶ Understanding when technical analysis does not work

▶ Profiting by spotting specific trading patterns

▶ Trusting technical indicators

▶ Knowing when a trading pattern is failing

. . . .

*I*f you could predict where share prices would be in the future, you'd do pretty well with your investments. With penny stocks, many clues are available by analyzing the trading chart. By analyzing the chart to see how the shares have been trading up to this point, you can often predict where they will go next.

In this Chapter I introduce you to technical analysis (TA), a way of studying stocks that is based entirely upon the activity of the trading price. I show you how a simple review of the trading chart can help you predict where prices are heading. I tell you which TA indicators work well with penny stocks and which don't. I also help you discover how to gauge the reliability of a chart pattern based on the total trading volume.

TA has no connection to the underlying company's fundamentals or operations. TA doesn't care about who's on the management team, or how quickly a company's revenues are growing, how much debt they have, or the percentage of employee turnover. By using TA properly, you can find out how to spot buy and sell points, know where the shares should be heading from here, and generate a hefty profit without ever needing to know the details of the inner workings of the companies.

When Technical Analysis Is Good

Most investors do their research on the basis of fundamental analysis (a topic I cover extensively in Chapter 9). They want to invest in healthy companies with proven management teams, positive news releases, and increasing market share. A good fundamental review will tell you all of that.

Other investors want to predict where the share price is going simply by reviewing the trading chart (as illustrated in Figure 12-1) and applying TA. These investors are less likely to worry about the fundamentals of the company and, in fact, probably don't care about the management team or market share or anything that the financial reports might tell them.

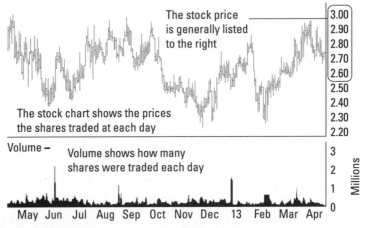

The stock price is generally listed to the right

The stock chart shows the prices the shares traded at each day

3.00
2.90
2.80
2.70
2.60
2.50
2.40
2.30
2.20

Volume —

Volume shows how many shares were traded each day

3
2
1
0

Millions

May Jun Jul Aug Sep Oct Nov Dec 13 Feb Mar Apr

Figure 12-1: An example of a trading chart, displaying the price action of a stock over time along with each day's trading volume.

TA, when done well, has tremendous advantages over the more conventional fundamentals-based research approach. However, this trading technique also has numerous downsides, and you should consider the pros and cons before you proceed.

Although you can use TA on its own, without any fundamental or abstract reviews (flip to chapters 9 and 11, respectively), many investors prefer to use it in combination with the other research approaches. You may want to apply TA to your research in some combination with a full fundamental and abstract analysis review, to give you the most clarity from your research approach.

TA can be highly effective, and most appropriate for you, in specific situations, such as:

- ✔ **You want to eliminate all the work required for fundamental analysis.** With TA, you don't need to worry about a company's market share, revenue growth, debt load, profit margins, or anything else. You're not investing in a company, you're trying to squeeze gains out of the action of the share price based on what it has done immediately leading up to this point.

- ✔ **You're a short-term trader, not a long-term investor.** Most investing is about fundamental analysis, and that involves buying into a great company and hoping to profit as the operations improve over time and the share price eventually increases as a result. If the patience game isn't for you, and you want to see changes in share prices much more quickly, TA is much more appropriate for you. TA profits and losses generally come in the short term.

- ✔ **You need more clarity about good buy and sell opportunities.** By watching trading volume, chart patterns, and price direction, TA often reveals pretty accurate buying and selling points. Read on to see how a huge drop-off in volume, or shares approaching a resistance level, or an upward trend, can clearly indicate when it's time to trade a penny stock.

- ✔ **You want to minimize your investment exposure.** Every minute you have dollars in stocks, they're exposed to events that may play out on the market. By trading short term based on TA, you theoretically should have fewer dollars sitting "out in the open" at most times. Keep in mind, though, that although this shorter time frame limits your exposure, it doesn't limit your risk. TA can be more risky than investing based on fundamentals, and downside losses often come very quickly when the share price doesn't act as the TA had predicted.

If the points mentioned appeal to you, then so will TA. You don't necessarily need to go 100 percent into TA for all your investment decisions, but you can use it as a tool to augment your trading in fundamentally solid penny stocks. However, for some investors, based primarily on the trading results derived from it, you may find that TA is all you'll ever need.

Many investors who trade stocks based on TA don't want to own their shares overnight and certainly not over a weekend. Because events can occur when the markets are closed, and those events may impact share prices when the markets open, it leaves the day traders and TA investors exposed to losses. Because these investors aren't buying based on the underlying fundamental strength of the companies, they're often more cautious about issues that may impact the share prices when they're unable to react immediately.

The Peter Leeds Approach

For the Peter Leeds Penny Stock Newsletter, our analysis is comprised of approximately 80 percent fundamental review because we put a lot of weight on making sure that the penny stock is financially and operationally solid. We then apply 10 percent to TA, in order to uncover opportune buying and selling prices. (The other 10 percent of our review is what we refer to as Abstract Review, as is discussed in Chapter 11).

The most effective research approach usually involves a combination of both a fundamental and technical review. By using fundamental analysis, you can locate high-quality, well-run penny stocks whose operations are moving in the right direction. By applying TA to the trading charts of those stocks, you can uncover great buying and profit-taking opportunities. You need to decide on the analysis mix that works best for you.

TA has a lot of benefits, but the approach also has a pretty serious downside. Understanding the shortcomings helps you recognize how to perform TA wisely, if it even turns out to be appropriate for you at all. Consider that TA

- ✔ **Has nothing to do with the actual underlying company:** You aren't buying shares in a company as much as buying shares in a potential price direction. As a trader, not an investor, you may not be watching when the company is growing, or increasing its profits, or if its biggest competitor goes out of business. This may result in you selling at some of the wrong times. TA will often fall short of what a good fundamental analysis review would have told you.

- ✔ **Involves a tremendous amount of work:** Day traders, short-term traders, and others relying mainly on TA typically look at hundreds of trading charts per week. Out of all those charts, they may not identify any good trading opportunities because most TA will not show any predictable patterns most of the time. The traders who put in all that time researching trading charts tend to do much better than those who do not.

- ✔ **Takes a significant amount of time:** Besides work, TA also involves a big investment of time. Sometimes that means 5, 20, or even 40 hours per week! Most of the time spent needs to be when the stock market is open.

- ✔ **Is unpredictable:** All investor use different TA tools and use those tools differently. They also have their own ideas of which chart indicators work best and what level of gains to take. If you adopt this approach, you will need to decide on your own indicators and adjust your TA methods as you go, and even then there is no certainty that it will be effective.

✔ **May result in missing the really big gains:** Because most TA involves taking smaller gains more frequently, you could miss out on the big 50 percent, 100 percent, and even 2,000 percent moves. A single penny stock that triples in price may generate more profits than years of taking 20 percent gains and losses.

Done well, TA can turn an average investor into a master of the markets.

Having been an investor since I was 14 years old, I have been involved with all forms of trading. Whether it was stocks, bonds, warrants, options, real estate, debentures, day trading, long term, short term, large stocks, penny stocks, international investments, or otherwise, I was right in there. I came to the conclusion that long-term investing in high-quality penny stocks is by far the most lucrative. A half-million-dollar profit off a $20,000 investment here, a $200,000 profit off a $30,000 trade there, five baggers, ten baggers. . . . The biggest gains always came from fundamental analysis on penny stocks that I held for the long term. Although everyone is different, just like every investment is different, you may come to the exact same conclusion with your own investment path.

Why TA Often Doesn't Work with Penny Stocks

The more trades and investor activity involved in establishing a TA pattern, the more reliable that pattern will be. Whether you find a resistance level, a price dip, or any of the other indicators I describe later in this chapter, the TA will be more trustworthy in direct proportion to the amount of trading volume that established it.

Think of political polls. If the results were based on the opinions of 20 people, most folks would put less stake in the findings than if the results were generated from the answers of 2 million people. The more answers behind a survey or poll, the more likely the findings will be representative. TA is very similar, and the reliability increases hand in hand with the amount of trading volume that generated the pattern.

Similarly, the lower the trading volume, the less a TA pattern should be trusted. As penny stocks are generally subject to less investor activity, meaning fewer trades, the majority of TA techniques shouldn't be used, and wouldn't be consistently reliable even in the cases where the patterns implied a future price direction.

Having said that, a few TA indicators can provide hints at future price direction in penny stocks, but even those only apply when the underlying shares have been enjoying enough trading volume. What constitutes "enough" trading volume, or critical mass, to generate a TA pattern that you can trust? It depends greatly on the stock and the situation, but in general consider these factors:

- **Percent of shares trading hands:** If about 1 percent of total outstanding shares trades on any given day, there will not likely be any reliability to patterns that may seem to form. On the other hand, if the penny stock shows an optimistic indicator on 5 percent of shares each day, then the reliability of that indicator is very high. I start feeling more confident in TA when the daily percentage of shares traded is 3 percent or more.

- **Turnover of total shares:** Calculate how many days it would take at current trading volumes to turn over an amount equivalent to all the shares one time. If a penny stock with 100 million shares trades 1 million a day, that is a total share turnover rate of 100 days. The shorter that turnover becomes, the more reliable the underlying pattern will be. Personally, I start trusting TA patterns for stocks that have turnover rates of 50 or less

- **Daily trading volume:** Watch the number of shares trading hands each day. You want to see hundreds of thousands of shares being bought or sold each day to be able put any trust into the underlying TA pattern.

Also consider changes in trading volume. If buying and selling activity suddenly starts increasing day by day, some great TA patterns may be forming from all the new investment activity. Although indicators become more reliable with high trading volume, they are even more trustworthy when that trading volume is not only high, but getting higher.

TA with penny stocks is a very involved concept. What works with some shares won't work with others, and what constitutes enough trading volume to make the patterns reliable for each situation is difficult to state in general.

Each stock and each situation is very different, and the effectiveness of various indicators can vary significantly from one penny stock to the next. Like most aspects of investing, you'll get much better at it as you proceed.

Use Technical Indicators to Spot Trading Opportunities

TA is the study of the trading chart. In its pure form, TE eliminates all consideration of the actual underlying company and its operations. TA can be used on its own or with a solid fundamental research review, but either way, when you apply TA, the trading chart is your best friend.

Before getting familiar with the individual TA indicators, and before you look for and apply them, you should first gain an understanding of how TA helps you spot future directions of prices and, therefore, trading opportunities.

Specific patterns on a trading chart imply certain actions in the share price. For example, a consolidation pattern suggests that the shares are about to spike higher. So you will either notice a pattern in the chart of a penny stock you already own, or you will look through (potentially) hundreds of charts and act on any optimistic patterns you find.

After you know about the major TA patterns, you can apply them to your trading in a number of ways:

✔ **Sift through hundreds of charts.** You will no doubt have your favorite TA patterns (which will generally be the ones that help you make the most profitable trades). Use a stock screener and a charting website (both discussed in Chapter 6) to go through the charts one by one, looking for patterns with positive implications.

✔ **Study the chart of a stock you already own.** You gain a lot of information about your current holdings by reviewing the trading chart. Maybe the patterns suggest that you sell, or maybe they imply that you should buy more before a big run-up. The chart you already hold could have both good and bad indicators; when you feel familiar with the patterns and know what to look for, the subsequent trading decisions will be clear.

✔ **Choose between companies.** Whether you're deciding between two or more companies from a peer group or from vastly different industries, TA can often solidify your final decision. This is especially true when conventional due diligence still leaves you sitting on the fence about which stocks to purchase.

✔ **Know when to sell.** This is one of the top questions we get from our subscribers. TA can help you make or solidify your choice to sell and will help you with the timing and the price.

> ✔ **Watch the progress of your purchase.** By keeping an eye on the trading chart, you get an idea if your penny stock is moving in the right direction.
>
> ✔ **Spot buy opportunities.** If you've wanted to get involved with a specific penny stock, and TA shows that a current price dip will be temporary, it may be a great time to purchase.

TA is an important part of most investing, and for some traders it is the only part. Decide for yourself how and when to use it, and adjust your TA approach as you gain understanding and see some results.

All Patterns Break Down

TA isn't just about spotting a bullish indicator but also knowing when that indicator still applies and when the pattern is breaking down. The moment when a TA indicator breaks down, it no longer provides any clues as to future share price direction.

Even when TA indicators play out exactly as you had hoped and predicted, their impact will only be temporary. TA is about spotting trading opportunities at a moment in time, and those opportunities will change or fade away, and likely very soon.

Later in this chapter, I discuss TA indicators such as trends, support levels, and consolidations. While each of these indicators demonstrates where shares of a penny stock may go, they also eventually break down. Perhaps the trend reverses and shares start moving in the other direction. Perhaps the support level stops supporting the shares any longer, and the stock plunges through to lower prices.

Often a pattern will break down, and no tangible or useful indicators replace it. Other times, a new pattern will take the place of the old, and you need to adjust your outlook based on these factors. For example, a strong downtrend may reverse and be replaced by a gradual uptrend. Perhaps share price momentum fades away, but nothing appears to replace it. A perfect consolidation pattern may suddenly break down and no longer be at all predictive in regard to share price activity.

 Always watch the TA patterns for signs that they are holding up or breaking down, as described for each individual pattern later in the chapter. No longer relying on a TA indicator that has broken down is just as important as finding it in the first place.

For each penny stock, watch for multiple TA patterns. For example, you may find a support level, a bottoming out indicator, and strong relative strength, with all three suggesting higher share prices. The agreement of multiple indicators should increase your clarity of your trading decisions.

Trading patterns are elusive, and that is even more true with thinly traded penny stocks. If you see a technical pattern or indicator on one out of three charts, then you're not doing it right. You may look at 20 or 50 charts and only see a couple of solid TA indicators that have enough trading volume behind them to suggest that you can trust them. However, if you do look at fifty charts and find only a couple of indicators, you will probably do very well with those trades.

Technical Analysis That Will Work with Penny Stocks

Everyone's TA will be unique. As you find what works for you through trial and error, the indicators you use and the types of stocks you apply them to will be very different from the next person.

Specific TA indicators can be highly successful with penny stocks. These will be easy to spot, and if trading volume is high enough, they will also help you predict upcoming price moves.

The following TA patterns have proven effective and reliable for penny stocks. They can help you pick out attractive buying and selling prices, predict future share price direction, and even identify warning signs before you risk your money and time.

Clues from trading volume

Trading volume is one of the most important considerations for any TA investor. By watching how many shares are trading hands and changes in that activity, you can spot trading opportunities and have a better understanding of the reliability of other TA indicators on that penny stock.

Compare a penny stock's daily trading volume for the last few days or weeks to the daily average for the previous weeks or months. Daily trading volume and average trading volume are available through many free websites, such as www.Finance.Yahoo.com. By comparing the average to the current activity levels, you can easily see if buying and selling activity is increasing or decreasing, and to what degree.

A *significant increase* in trading volume means that more than double the average amount of shares are trading hands. You can ignore anything less than a significant increase. Likewise, when trading volume experiences a *significant decrease,* such as cutting down by more than half, it may imply an issue that shareholders should watch.

The sustainability of the change in trading volume also matters. If buying and selling activity doubles for a day but then returns to normal the next day, the activity may be a unique and meaningless event. When trading volume dramatically increases or falls for days or weeks on end, you can conclude that specific events are causing the unusual trading activity.

You can draw a lot of conclusions about the shares of a penny stock based on its trading volume. Here are some volume indicators and what they may be signaling:

- **Increases suddenly:** A sudden increase in volume may be due to a specific event or issue, such as the release of financial reports, FDA approval, CEO resignation, or any other material event. Be aware of the cause for the investor interest, whether based on optimism or pessimism, so that you can make appropriate trading decisions.

- **Increases gradually:** If the increasing activity coincides with rising prices, the penny stock may be getting increased attention by investors, gaining market share for its products, or producing improved financial results. Alternatively, gradually increasing trading volume with falling prices may imply that shareholders are dumping their positions and going for the exits.

- **Neither increases nor decreases over time:** Consistent trading volume over time does not reveal much from a TA standpoint.

- **Decreases suddenly:** A sudden decrease in trading volume is a rare event. If a material issue scared investors away, you would expect it to come with an increase in trading volume, rather than a decrease. While the cause for a sudden drop-off in trading volume may be hard to understand, the situation generally is negative for the shares in the longer term simply because there is less investor interest.

- **Decreases gradually:** When a penny stock falls out of favor with investors, you'll see a gradual decrease in trading volume over time. This can warn you that shares may drop next, if they haven't already, as fewer traders are interested in buying and selling the shares.

Trading volume is simple to monitor and can provide you with more clues about future prices of a stock than most other TA factors. Of course, when combined with some of the other TA indicators, trading volume really demonstrates its importance.

Support levels

A support level is a price at which shares see increasing demand, which in turn holds the stock above that level. For example, a penny stock may keep falling toward one dollar, but the shares bounce back to higher prices each time the price gets close to one dollar due to increased trading volume. See Figure 12-2 for a chart illustrating support levels.

While support can form at any price for any stock, with penny stocks it's much more common for supports to form at round number prices. Investors generally buy or sell at threshold levels, such as $4.00 or $1.50, as opposed to $4.12 or $1.44. Because many investors buy at these round number prices, and penny stocks have low trading activity, support levels often form.

The beauty of a solid support level is that it theoretically limits your downside. Buying shares at $1.02, when a strong support level exists at $1.00, can be a good strategy.

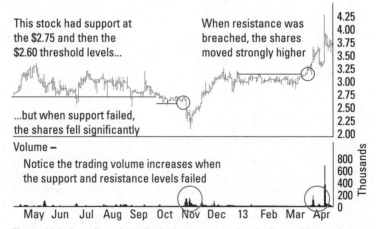

This stock had support at the $2.75 and then the $2.60 threshold levels...

When resistance was breached, the shares moved strongly higher

...but when support failed, the shares fell significantly

Volume –

Notice the trading volume increases when the support and resistance levels failed

May Jun Jul Aug Sep Oct Nov Dec 13 Feb Mar Apr

Figure 12-2: A trading chart displaying a support level, along with a resistance level which is eventually breached, clearing the way for higher prices.

To trust that you are seeing a support level — and one which seems likely to hold up — you want to witness the following characteristics on the trading chart:

> ✔ **Increasing trading volume at support:** A true support level is based on increasing demand at certain prices. If you see an increase in trading volume when shares fall to the support level, then that TA pattern is more likely reliable.
>
> ✔ **Multiple attempts at break down:** The more times that support gets tested without failing, the more reliable the support level will be. You can't assume support exists at any certain price if the shares haven't tested that level. However, if the stock fell toward support twice, or three times, or eight times, and the support level held up, you have a more trustworthy support level pattern.

Like any TA pattern, support levels are prone to break down or fail. This can be costly to investors who trust the pattern because they aren't expecting that downside.

When support fails, the shares sometimes fall significantly lower. A company may have held up above a $3.00 support for a long time, but when events induce enough selling that the shares break below $3.00, they very often will continue down toward $2.50, $2.00, or even lower.

If you're relying on a TA support level pattern you've found, as soon as it breaks down, you need to reconsider the stock. After a support level gets broken, it no longer applies. Support can re-form, but there are no guarantees that it will, and it may take a long time before a trustworthy pattern surfaces again.

When support levels get broken, they often "flip" and become resistance levels at the same price. In other words, shares have difficulty trading *above* a specific price. For example, a $2.25 support level gets breached as shares fall toward $1.70. The $2.25 level may then become resistance, and the shares that were once held up by the support level will have difficulty trading above the $2.25 range. See Chapter 15 for more on when support and resistance levels flip.

Sometimes the penny stock company buys back its own shares on the open market (See Chapter 3 for more on buybacks). This buying pressure is often significant enough to create a support level in the stock. When a company buys back its own shares, it makes this information publicly known, and you can bring that into your support level consideration.

Resistance

Resistance is the opposite concept to support levels. When shares have a resistance level, they have difficulty trading above a specific price due to increasing selling pressure. For example, each time the shares approach $2.50, volume increases as shareholders sell their stock, and the price drops back from the $2.50 range under the weight of the selling.

Resistance levels are prone to form at round number and threshold prices, such as $2.00 and $1.50. Resistance levels are characterized by increasing trading volume at the resistance price and multiple failed attempts to break above that level. Refer to Figure 12-2 to see a resistance level in action.

Resistance keeps shares contained below a certain price and, as such, can be most effectively used to show investors where to sell. If the TA pattern demonstrates that your specific penny stock faces a major resistance level at four dollars, you may want to take profits as the shares approach that level.

When a resistance level gets breached as the stock breaks through to higher prices, those shares very often power to much higher levels. It would have taken a major wave of investor buying to break through the resistance level and that buying may continue, and it may be based on materially positive events.

When resistance levels are breached, they very often become support levels. For example, a $3.00 resistance level may hold up for months, but after shares finally trade at $3.01 and above, that $3.00 level now becomes support.

Identifying resistance levels can be useful for investors who watch the TA pattern and only buy penny stocks that break through. They also serve those traders who want additional clarity of what price to sell shares.

Trends are friends

When something is in motion, it is more likely to continue in the same direction than any other trajectory. This is true in physics, and it is just as true in the stock market. In the market, these motions are called *trends*.

In terms of probability, shares in a steep downtrend over the last two weeks are most likely to go even farther down today. Shares trending sideways will probably keep going sideways; shares trending higher will probably continue their climb.

As long as the shares maintain their trend, they will move at approximately the same speed. A slow, gradual trend will continue on slowly and gradually. A strong downward trend will continue on a strong downward trajectory.

When a trend shows signs of changing, whether in terms of direction or speed, it may signal that you shouldn't rely on or trust this particular TA pattern any longer.

You can spot a price trend very simply. Draw a straight line on the trading chart over the share price of the stock for the last few weeks or months. Ignore temporary price spikes or dips, and just identify the general direction of the shares. If your price trend line is angling upward, the stock is experiencing an uptrend. If the line is flat, you've found a neutral trend; a downward trend will show a downward line on the trading chart. Figure 12-3 illustrates both downward and upward trends.

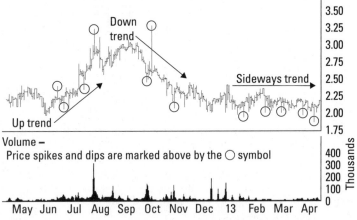

Figure 12-3: A trading chart displaying up and down trends, along with some price spike and dip anomalies.

Based on this approach, an unusual or sudden price move isn't a trend. Price jumps and collapses, or strange share price activity that's out of the norm for the time frame that you're looking at, shouldn't be considered a trend.

If you have trouble identifying the price trend, there may not be one to be found. Alternatively, try adjusting the time frame that you're looking at, either longer or shorter term. For example, sometimes you won't see the price trend if you're looking at a yearlong trading chart, but a month-long chart may reveal a trend much more clearly.

With the concept of trends alone, you can pretty accurately predict future share price movements if you follow these three steps:

1. **Spot or identify a price trend.**

   If the trend over the last weeks or months is going up, shares have a high probability of moving higher. If the trend is going down or sideways, you're most likely to see downward or sideways price activity.

2. **Position yourself to benefit from the trend.**

   Generally, you want to buy shares that are on an uptrend. As the trend is most likely to continue higher, your investment is most likely to increase in value.

3. **Identify if the trend is breaking down.**

   Some trends will play out for a short time, and others will last for a long time, perhaps even years. However, they all eventually end. Shares going up will not go higher forever. The moment the trend breaks down, you need to stop relying on it.

Trends are usually in relation to share price. However, trends can also relate to trading volume. For example, if shares of a penny stock continually see greater trading volume from one week to the next, this may represent a trend of increasing volume. This trend would demonstrate increasing investor interest and may forecast higher levels of investor activity and, therefore, higher prices going forward.

Price spikes

Penny stocks are prone to spikes in price, which can sometimes be a sign of even higher prices to come but is most often a profit-taking opportunity. Sudden and dramatic leaps in the price of shares often come back down just as suddenly and dramatically.

As penny stocks have fewer buyers and sellers, the likelihood of a price spike is higher than with most other forms of investment. When several investors buy at the same time, whether it's based on coincidence or Internet hype or otherwise, they may outnumber the sellers, resulting in the shares suddenly being much more expensive.

As these price spikes are most often based on the technicalities of trading rather than on any underlying materially beneficial events, you should consider them artificial and temporary. As such, they're very often profit-taking opportunities for alert shareholders. Refer to Figure 12-3 for some examples of price spikes on a trading chart.

You should assess any price spike based on the following criteria:

- ✓ **Trading volume is below average.** If the upward move was on lower than average trading volume, it is likely to reverse.

- ✓ **The upward price move is significant.** A true spike will see gains of at least 20 percent above the pre-spike prices and perhaps as much as 100 percent or more.

- ✓ **The spike was not based on any news or event.** When the shares trade higher without any tangible reason, you can expect that they are likely to come back down to former levels.

- ✓ **Shares immediately begin to reverse.** A true price spike won't last long. Sometimes the shares fall back from the higher levels within minutes and hours — and certainly within a day or two.

When shares leap to much higher levels on low trading volume, and you find no news to justify the price increase, you're dealing with a temporary price spike. When the shares immediately begin to reverse and trade lower, you can be even more certain — especially if you've taken your profits already!

Price dips

Much like price spikes, penny stocks are subject to a similar effect to the downside, called a *price dip.* When the buildup of sellers overpowers the number of investors looking to buy, the shares of the underlying penny stock can sometimes drop significantly.

Investors who understand that the price dip is a temporary event will be able to buy shares at discounted prices and will benefit as the shares snap back to realistic valuations. Figure 12-3 illustrates what some price dips may look like on a trading chart.

A price dip can be identified as follows:

- ✓ **Trading volume is lower than average.** Unless shares are falling on average or greater than average trading volume, the move is likely to reverse.

- ✓ **Downward price move is significant.** In terms of percentage, the drop-off greatly outweighs the average change in share price. For example, a 10 percent drop when the average price change from day to day is closer to 2 percent is a significant downward price movement.

- ✓ **No news or events created the drop.** When shares fall but no news or material events are pushing the stock lower, you may be seeing a temporary technical dip and potential buying opportunity. Just make sure that you're not missing any publicly available event that could have significantly negative impact.

✔ **Shares begin snapping back higher.** A price dip is temporary, and the stock will snap back to realistic valuations rather quickly, often within a matter of hours. The investors who profit from price dips are often the ones who were already watching the shares and were ready to take advantage of just such an opportunity.

When shares drop significantly (in terms of percentage), on low trading volume (in terms of daily averages), with no detrimental news to be found, you can expect the shares to snap back to higher prices. In fact, investors who accumulated the penny stock at these new and temporary lower prices should do very well with their investment.

Topping out patterns

When shares enjoy a long and gradual price uptrend, the trading chart may show a *topping out pattern.* Such a pattern indicates that that the prices won't go any higher from here and are about to start falling lower. Figure 12-4 shows a topping out pattern.

When you spot a topping out pattern, it may be a good time to take profits. Further upward moves in price will be hard to come by, and the probability of shares sinking is high.

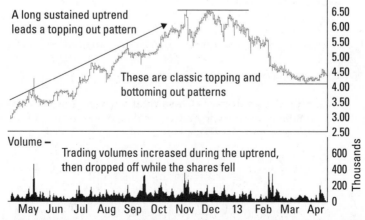

Figure 12-4: A trading chart displaying both a topping out pattern and a bottoming out pattern.

A topping out pattern can be indicated when all the following situations play out:

- **Prices gradually increase.** An upward price trend is a necessary part of any topping out pattern. Ideally, you will see several months of gradually increasing prices; the longer the uptrend, the more likely a topping out pattern will form.

- **The upward trend turns sideways.** The shares next need to turn into a sideways trend. Shares have stopped their gradual advance, and now they close with very minimal gains or losses from day to day. For example, if the shares were generally up about 2 percent every week during the uptrend, they may now close up or down about 0.5 percent on a week-by-week basis.

- **The number of down days increases.** In the uptrend, the penny stock may have closed higher twice as often as it closed lower. As the shares near the topping out point, you will see a higher closing price about as often as a lower closing price. Right before the shares start falling lower, the number of trading days in which the shares close lower will reach about two or three for every day that the shares closed higher.

- **Volume decreases.** The total trading volume will decrease as the shares approach their topping out point. The number of shares trading hands will fall to a fraction of what it had been during the uptrend. This lower trading volume is one of the most important aspects of a topping out pattern and will be the best indicator of when the shares are about to fall. Investor buying drove the upward trend, and as soon as that buying dries up, there is nothing to hold the shares at the higher levels.

Treat a TA indicator as a topping out pattern only if it meets all four of the criteria listed above. Many situations resemble topping out patterns, but unless they meet all four criteria, you can't expect them to play out like one.

Penny stocks often rise in share price over time, then "take a breather," or slow down for a while. The shares may trade sideways or even fall off under the weight of profit takers who are selling into these new higher prices. This activity isn't the same as topping out, and the share price weakness may be temporary or not at all indicative of what to expect next.

You won't see topping out patterns very frequently; however, you might see them quite a bit among penny stocks that have had months of of upward trending prices.

Bottoming out patterns

A *bottoming out pattern* illustrates when shares are about to trend higher. Bottoming out is about spotting those shares that have been sliding lower for a long time, only recently have flattened out and stopped falling, and may be setting up for a long and sustained uptrend.

When a penny stock company has fallen out of favor with investors, or the company's operational results have been looking weak or is experiencing other detrimental issues, the stock may begin a long, downward slide. Not until the company corrects these issues will it be back on the right track, and generally that won't be until it reports its financial results two months after the end of its next three-month quarterly reporting period.

It takes a long time for shares to change their trend from downward to sideways, and then again from sideways to upward, after events entice investors come back to the shares. In other words, you have plenty of time. Until the bottoming out pattern shows itself and shares begin to reverse to higher levels, there may be any number of investors getting in too early and taking losses by trying to pick a bottom. You can see an example of a bottoming out pattern in Figure 12-4.

Bottoming out patterns are great when you want to get involved very early in a brand-new uptrend with a long way yet to run. You can spot a bottoming pattern only when all the following criteria are met:

- ✔ **Predicated by a long decline**. A bottoming out pattern can only exist after a long, sustained, and significant decline. Just make sure that the decrease in share price isn't related to a detrimental material event that hasn't been, or has no way of being, resolved. For example, if a new law or massive competitor is putting the future of this particular penny stock in doubt, rather than setting up a bottoming out pattern, you may be witnessing shares on their way to zero.

- ✔ **Set up by a sideways trend.** Shares rarely go from sliding straight down over time to turning straight up. Expect a long a transition period, in which some shareholders are still selling when others start to buy at these lower levels. This will result in a sideways trend, where shares are neither heading higher nor lower.

- ✔ **Frequency of up days improves.** As you transition from downtrend to sideways trend, you may see an increase in the number of days that the shares trade higher and a decrease in the number of days that the shares trade lower. A ratio of one up day for every two down days may become one-for-one. An average ratio of two higher closes for each down day indicates that the bottoming out pattern has formed and will send shares higher.

✔ **Trading volume increases.** Trading volume needs to rise, putting it at least 50 percent but as much as 100 percent or more, above the daily average during the sideways trend. Keep in mind that these new lower prices should see higher trading volumes, simply because it takes less money to buy more shares. For this reason, the higher the trading volume increases, the greater the likelihood that the bottoming out pattern is about to turn into an uptrend.

The most important aspect of any TA pattern is timing. With bottoming out patterns, don't act until the shares are well into their sideways trend, the ratio of up-to-down days turns in a positive direction, and the trading volume swells.

When all the criteria mentioned above occur, you're very likely to be witnessing a bottoming out pattern. When shares bottom, they eventually enter an uptrend, and take astute investors along for the profitable ride.

You may have heard the popular stock market term, "Don't try to catch a falling knife." This refers to trying to pick the bottom price on shares as they have been falling. Many investors think that "now" is finally the lowest the stock may drop, and they get burned more often than not. If shares are falling, let them finish their price slide and level out before you get involved. Remember, even shares that have already fallen 80 percent still could go lower. Just ask the investor who bought after they had fallen 65 percent!

Consolidation patterns

Consolidation is about the turnover of shareholders, first and foremost. When the investors who bought more recently replace those who want to sell (and by implication have high expectations for the shares to go higher from current levels), downward pressure on the stock is replaced by demand.

This TA pattern predicts a sudden and sharp price increase, and when formed properly is one of the more reliable indicators. While not always present in most stocks, when you're certain that a consolidation pattern has formed, it can represent an opportunity to take significant profits.

On the trading chart (see Figure 12-5), the share price will look like it's forming a cup and handle. The indicator is generated in the following phases, and in this exact order:

1. **Before the cup forms.**

   Shares first approach what will eventually become the cup pattern. This approach is flat and sideways trading, in a very tight price range.

2. **Shares fall steeply, forming the left side of the cup.**

   Shares fall relatively steeply and quickly in price as some investors grow tired of the lack of volatility in the stock. This drop usually occurs in a matter of days and forms what will eventually look like the left edge of the cup and handle pattern.

3. **Sideways trading after the drop forms the bottom of the cup.**

   Shares eventually stop falling and enter a tight sideways range for several weeks. During this time, many sellers stop selling because they're unwilling to unload their shares at these prices. At the same time, buyers see value, thus creating a price floor that limits any further downside. Shares neither spike higher or lower as the bottom of the cup forms.

4. **Share price rises, forming the right side of the cup.**

   For almost the exact amount of the fall (which formed the left side of the cup), and just as quickly, shares will jump higher. The trading chart will now show price activity that looks as if a cup pattern has formed. Sudden demand overpowers the last of the sellers who would take the lower price, and after they are gone, the shares respond to even minimal buying by moving higher.

5. **Reactionary fall.**

   After the sudden price spike, some shareholders who had been on the sidelines move back in to take advantage of the price jump. Even the buyers get spooked by the speed of the move and aren't interested in paying these comparatively "expensive" prices. Shares fall back lower, although only partially. They settle slightly lower than the high in the latest price spike, yet well above the bottom of the cup pattern.

6. **The handle forms.**

   After the spike and the reactionary sell off, shares enter a narrow sideways trading range, forming the handle of the cup pattern. During this time, old shareholders turn over in favor of new ones, so that an increasing percentage of investors in this company expect good things from the share price going forward and aren't likely to sell.

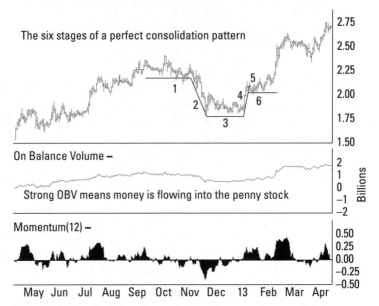

The six stages of a perfect consolidation pattern

On Balance Volume –

Strong OBV means money is flowing into the penny stock

Momentum(12) –

Figure 12-5: A trading chart illustrating the six steps of a consolidation pattern. Across the bottom of the chart two other TA indicators, specifically on balance volume (OBV) and momentum, are also displayed.

Think of the handle of the consolidation pattern like a spring that is slowly coiling. The greater percent of shareholder turnover during this time period, the more pronounced the subsequent upward move will be and the more reliable the indicator.

Check the daily trading volume as the handle forms. If 100 million shares are out and 1-million shares trade in a single day, that's a trading volume of 1 percent. If approximately the same number trade each day for the next three weeks, that's a trading volume of 15 percent.

I've seen perfect consolidation patterns play out with only 10 percent of shares turning over during the handle-formation period. However, I've felt a lot better about the pattern when closer to 20 or 35 percent of shares were bought and sold.

For shares to trade, there must be both a buyer and a seller. Of course, a seller one moment can be a buyer the next. While this fact makes it impossible to accurately gauge shareholder turnover, for the purposes of TA it is sufficient to count a share traded as a share turned over to a new owner.

On balance volume

On balance volume (OBV) is an indicator illustrating the flow of money into and out of a stock. OBV can be very useful when predicting future prices of penny stocks, especially because lower-priced shares are generally more sensitive to even small amounts of buying and selling.

The OBV value is derived by keeping a running total of shares traded. Each day in which the shares close higher, all of that day's trading volume is added to the running total. Each day in which the shares trade lower is subtracted from the running total.

The OBV displays as a line, and starts at a value of zero. It rises and falls over the period of time you select for your trading chart. The day's total trading volume either adds to (on days when the shares closed higher), or subtracts from (on days when the shares closed lower) the OBV value. Figure 12-5 illustrates OBV across the bottom of a trading chart.

The farther into positive territory the OBV line rises, the more money is moving into that penny stock. When the OBV line is in the negative, it illustrates money flowing out of the penny stock.

You can see an OBV line by using any TA charting website. It usually displays across the bottom of the chart near the trading volume indicators.

Here are several important OBV considerations:

- ✔ **Time frame:** OBV displays for the time period of your trading chart. A two-month chart shows OBV for that two-month period, while a three-year chart displays OBV for a three-year period.

  When you switch between various periods of time, you see different OBV values; when you compare those values, you can get important clues. For example, if OBV shows positive 45,000 for a two-month period but negative 2.5 million for a three-year period, you can surmise that there has been a recent increase in buying, whereas most investors have been selling over the last several years.

- ✔ **Correlation with OBV and share price activity:** Because OBV is a measure of buying or selling, and shares are priced based on those trades, you often see a close correlation between OBV and share price. As OBV rises, shares are likely to rise, and vice versa. Therefore, if OBV is trending up or down but share prices haven't yet followed suit, you can usually expect that they will in the very near future.

✔ **Slope strength:** When OBV is rising or falling very sharply, the activity indicates that money is flowing in or out of the stock very strongly. The steeper the slope, the greater the relative number of shares of that stock being bought or sold.

✔ **Slope magnitude:** A slight positive or negative OBV value isn't significant in terms of TA clues, but a more substantial value can be quite useful. For example, OBV of 2,000 implies that only 2,000 more shares were traded on up days than down days during the entire time period of the trading chart. On the other hand, an OBV value of 65 million for that same stock is much more significant and could provide helpful trading clues.

✔ **Mid-chart trends.** The most important OBV analysis clue isn't necessarily its final value but rather the strong and significant up- and downtrends that occurred at various times during the trading chart's time period. For example, if a one-year chart shows a massive OBV drop-off halfway through the year, you can assume that shareholders were unloading their positions at that time.

Momentum indicators

The determine a stock's *momentum,* compare the current price of a stock to its value on a previous date. For example, if you set the momentum indicator to 12 days, momentum will show as the difference between the current day's share price compared to the share price 12 days prior.

Momentum is typically displayed across the bottom of the trading chart as a line that rises and falls, as demonstrated in Figure 12-5. This indicator can help investors make buy and sell decisions in penny stocks with greater clarity when used to identify

✔ **New price trends:** When the momentum indicator turns higher from a bottom, the trend may imply a good buying opportunity. When the indicator starts dropping from a peak, it suggests selling the underlying shares.

✔ **Trend changes or reversals:** If the momentum indicator drops sharply but then starts climbing (before prices do), it could imply a bottom in shares price and the beginning of a brand-new uptrend. When the indicator spikes but then starts sinking (before prices sink), it may signify a top in the underlying share price.

Each TA investor needs to decide what time frame works best for them. While by no means an indicator with perfect accuracy, it can provide investors in penny stocks with a great deal of clarity for their trading decisions.

Moving averages

Moving averages (MA) are valuable tools for generating clear buy and sell signals. They are simply the representation of the average price of the shares over a time frame that you select. For example, a nine-day MA displays the average price on any given day from the nine days prior to that day.

The MA is displayed as a line across the upper portion of the trading chart (see Figure 12-6), overlaying the stock's price line. Generally, multiple MA's are applied at the same time to provide the greatest amount of clarity for your trades.

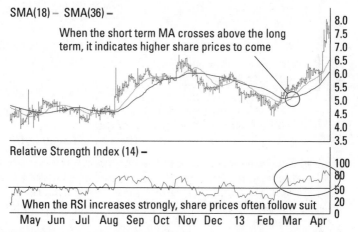

Figure 12-6: A trading chart displaying the use of moving averages (MAs) and the relative strength index (RSI).

MA's are backward looking, meaning that they're displaying what prices have done up until this point rather than predicting what the shares will do going forward. However, by spotting shifts in price momentum of a stock, illustrated by MA lines of different time lengths crossing, you can theoretically spot trends when they begin.

The logic behind this TA indicator is that when shares begin to increase or decrease significantly, their new prices will outpace the lagging MA. This outpacing is displayed by the MA breaking away from the price of the shares. For example, when a major uptrend begins, the share price will start moving higher. This will then be followed by a rise in the shorter MA over the following days, as average price over the MA span begins to increase. Finally the long-term MA will begin to float upward, lagging the short term MA.

Any investor using MAs should consider the following concepts associated with MAs:

✔ **Various lengths of time:** Choosing the duration of the MAs is the most important part of using them successfully, and there is no single correct answer. Instead, finding an effective duration comes down to finding what is most reliable for you. The shorter the MA time frame, the more responsive to price moves it will be at first, because fewer days are used to calculate the average. Some common MA time frames include 9- and 27-day MAs, or 8-, 13-, and 21-day MAs, or even 8-, 34-, 55-, 89=, and 144-day MAs.

✔ **Number of MAs:** Most technical analysis involves two MA lines. Some investors use only one MA, while others find that three or more are most useful.

In my experience, two MA lines is the only consistently effective and reliable approach when dealing specifically with penny stocks.

✔ **Buy signals:** Any time a short-term MA crosses above a longer-term MA, it implies a buy. This is because the action of the MA indicators is displaying that the short-term prices are trending up, and, therefore, the stock is in an uptrend.

✔ **Sell signals:** When the shorter-term MA crosses below the longer term MA, it suggests a sell. The action of the MA lines is displaying that prices in the shorter term are moving lower beneath the longer-term average price and, therefore, the stock is in a downtrend.

Relative strength

The *relative strength index* (RSI) provides buy and sell signals, which are based on whether the underlying shares are in an overbought or oversold position.

Overbought refers to any stock that has increased in price beyond its appropriate value and so is due to come back down. *Oversold* refers to shares that are trading well below their appropriate value and are due for an increase in price.

Whether shares are overbought or oversold is very subjective, and the tools and criteria vary from one investor to the next and one stock to the next.

RSI is displayed in the lower portion of the trading chart. It is represented by a line that oscillates between 0 and 100. Generally, when the line breaks above a value of 70, the shares are considered overbought, indicating that lower stock prices may come soon. When the RSI line slips below a value of 30, the shares are considered oversold and have a high likelihood of trading higher. Notice Figure 12-6 for an example of the RSI indicator.

While no TA technique is accurate in all instances, history shows that overbought stocks have higher likelihoods of declining in price, while oversold stocks represent good value and are most likely to increase going forward. This makes a simple TA tool, like relative strength, very valuable and effective for investors.

Part IV
The Part of Tens

Enjoy an additional Part of Tens chapter online at www.dummies.com/extras/pennystocks.

In this part . . .

- ✔ Use the life cycle phase of a company to determine whether it's a good investment.

- ✔ Find out what insider and institutional ownership tells you about a company.

- ✔ Discover the major influences affecting all corporations.

- ✔ Go from average investor to expert by discovering a few surprising concepts.

- ✔ Quickly improve your odds by adhering to some simple trading guidelines.

Chapter 13

Ten Rapid Result Tactics

In This Chapter

▶ Getting to know the product or service being sold

▶ Comparing the penny stock company to the competition

▶ Gauging where a company is in its life cycle

▶ Adapting your portfolio to best capture stock market gains

*I*n this chapter, I discuss ten tactics that, if you deploy them regularly, should produce results in no time. None of the strategies I describe here require a significant investment of time or effort but will nonetheless have a beneficial impact on your investment results.

By applying these ten rapid result tactics to your investment strategy, you will have a better understanding of what is moving the prices of stocks as well as a deeper knowledge of exactly what wares a company is producing and selling to the masses. I also challenge some long-held beliefs about the optimum make-up of an investment portfolio, and provide some opinions about my personal approach and why it is effective.

Of all of the strategies I describe in this book, the ten rapid result tactics may have the biggest (and quickest) impact on your investment successes with penny stocks. The concepts are straightforward, their application is intuitive, and the impact of each can be significant.

Although these concepts aren't exclusive to penny stocks, they are especially effective with these newer and smaller companies and their low-priced shares. As soon as you're acquainted with these rapid result tactics, you'll probably never invest without them again.

Call the Company

One of the most important things you can do when considering whether to invest in a company is to pick up the phone and call it. Never invest in any penny stock until you have spoken to, and asked questions of, the management or at least its investor relations contact.

You can discover more in a twenty-minute call than you might find from hours of research. In fact, some of the information you glean from that call isn't available through more conventional means.

Ask the person on the other end of the line what the company's competitors are saying about it and its products. You can also get an idea of difficulties the business may be having attracting and maintaining employees. See if its growth strategy for the next two and five years is the same as you had believed before you made the call.

You can gauge many intangibles — passion about the products, employee morale levels, and even the professionalism with which the representative treats you — more easily through a conversation than by reading publicly available press releases and financial reports.

If you're new to the process, the idea of making that call may be intimidating. Although you may feel awkward at first, you may surprise yourself by how quickly you improve and how comfortable you become with the process.

Most investors never call the company. Those who do end up having additional information that most people aren't necessarily privy to, and therefore enjoy a competitive advantage when it comes to trading the shares.

Average Up

Savvy investors *average up,* meaning that they buy more shares when their investment increases in price. After their initial purchase, the rising share price vindicates their beliefs and expectations about the company and the prospects for the shares, and they increase their position in the company as it rises. Their average price per share will increase because they bought more at this higher price, but they don't mind paying a higher average price for a stock that's moving in the right direction.

Less experienced, and generally less effective, investors tend to average down. *Averaging down* is the process of buying more shares of an investment that is falling in value. In other words, when they see the value of shares they have already bought sinking, they purchase more to lower their average price per share. For example, they buy shares at two dollars, which then fall to one dollar. Investors average down by buying more at the one-dollar level, bringing their average price per share down, while increasing the total amount of their investment.

In theory, averaging down sounds like a good strategy. If you have 500 shares of a stock whose value has dropped by 40 percent if you buy 500 more shares, your total investment is now down only 20 percent.

The problem with this strategy is that you may be doubling down on your original mistake. After all, you were wrong about the shares in the first place, so why should you invest more money in the stock?

Typically, investors who average down lose, especially when the shares keep on falling. I have personally had friends who went bust averaging all the way down with a doomed company. (They didn't listen to me!)

Contrast this approach to successful investors. They *average up*, meaning that they buy more shares in a company as it grows in value. As the initial purchase grows in value, their original expectations are confirmed. The shares may be on the way up, and buying more of a corporation that is growing in both share price and fundamental strength tends to be a very rewarding strategy.

Don't Confuse Market Risk with Company Risk

When you invest in any stock, you want to be sure that you understand the difference between the two types of risks involved. These are as follows:

- **Company risk.** This type of risk involves anything related to the specific stock of the corporation you're investing in. Examples of company risk include the company losing a big customer, losing a court case, or posting very weak financial results.

✔ **Market risk.** Market risk is based on the potential downside for any shares when the overall stock market declines. If all investments suddenly crash in value, even excellent up-and-coming companies will drop. This risk isn't based on the operations of the underlying company, and frankly there is nothing they could have done to curtail the weakness in their shares that resulted from market risk.

Market risk can affect the entire stock market or impact individual sectors or industries. These effects are still market risk, because they are based on entire groups of companies, and not specific individual investments. If the entire energy sector drops 10 percent, even some great companies within that group will be brought down with the others.

Watch the competitors and the industry, because if a specific stock is trading in line with the rest of the stocks in that industry, you can safely assume that any downside move is based on market risk. On the other hand, whenever a company is trading very differently than the rest of the group, you can probably attribute it to company risk.

Pay close attention to the differences between these two types of risks. You don't want to get scared out of a stock market investment when it is simply experiencing market risk — in other words, when it is trading in line with its peers (unless you see a material issue with the entire group). You should, however, pay extra attention to any price move that shares make that is independent from the industry and is instead due to company risk. You will do much better in your trades when you are able to assess when weakness in share prices is market based or company based.

Try the Product, Use the Service

Using a company's product or service can sometimes be more effective due diligence than analyzing the financial results. Especially with penny stocks, where the adoption and early usage of the wares can make or break the company, you want to know exactly what they're selling.

I'm always puzzled by how many people buy shares in a penny stock company but never purchase one of its $20 products. You will find out a lot about the company, develop a feel for how well their sales might do, and be able to make a more fully informed decision about investing in the shares.

Taken in reverse, you may even decide to invest in the company because of a great experience with their product or service. If you see the value in what it sells realize the superiority of its wares or services, its penny stock might be a great investment.

If you have difficulty getting a company's product because it keeps selling out, this may indicate demand. If you try its wares and are left thoroughly disappointed, that should be cause for concern. If the sales staff is rude or unhelpful, the company may lack effective managerial oversight or suffer poor employee morale.

 Never invest in a company without trying its products or services, assuming that doing so is a realistic option. Giving the products a test drive is often a low-cost form of due diligence that could provide greater clarity than the majority of Wall Street analysts derive from the lifeless numbers on the company's financial reports.

Compare the Wares

To go a step beyond trying a penny stock's products or services (as discussed in the previous section), take a look at what the competition is offering. When considered in a vacuum, a company may have a great technology or franchise restaurant or motorcycle helmet, but as soon as you look at the alternatives that are available from other sources, you may change your mind (or reaffirm your original assessment).

For example, to truly do full due diligence on a company's new software program, you need to assess it in relation to the alternatives. You may find strengths and weaknesses that you hadn't noticed before.

An added bonus to assessing the merits of the competition is that you may discover superior products and services. Through the process you may end up with a much better potential investment, which you may not have been aware of when you started looking into the original company.

Paper Trade

I became an effective investor when I had no real money to invest by making paper trades. *Paper trading* is a form of virtual investing that gives you the opportunity to learn the ropes: You get to see how your penny stock trades would have done without risking any capital. I walk you through the process of paper trading in Chapter 5.

The benefits of paper trading are many, and the downsides are few. The technique gives you a chance to improve your skills without risking a single penny and to refine your strategy by investing an imaginary portfolio that is many times greater than the actual amount of money available to you.

If you make a mistake with real money, you may be out of the game before you know it. If you buy the wrong thing with imaginary cash, the "loss" will simply serve as a valuable lesson.

Aside from the minimal amount of work involved, there really aren't any downsides to paper trading. Some investors may caution that you'll miss out on actual gains when a penny stock you're paper trading increases in value, but that virtual success should actually inspire you, because it affirms your ability to pick companies that are on the way up.

Newer investors absolutely should start by paper trading. Even more experienced traders can benefit as well. This approach helps lead the way to finding those penny stocks that will produce significant returns, while insulating against mistakes and downside risk.

Know the Corporate Life Cycle

All companies go through what's called the *corporate life cycle* — the transition from start up to growth and then into maturity and, eventually, decline.

By knowing where a company is at in its corporate life cycle you can really get a leg up on your investment decisions. Specifically, being aware of the phase a company finds itself in will shed light on what to expect from the stock and where the company's corporate priorities lie.

As the company moves through the phases of the corporate life cycle, it has very different strategies and goals, which will be reflected in how you should value and treat its shares.

- ✔ **Start-up phase:** During this phase of a company, most people base the share price on its speculative potential: What "could" it do? How big might it become, if everything goes according to plan? At this phase, the price of shares and the total market capitalization are generally far above realistic valuations.

- ✔ **Growth phase:** As the company grows, fundamental strength takes a back seat to percentage increases in revenues. Double-digit sales growth can easily distract investors from huge debt loads and weak financial positions.

✔ **Maturity phase:** Mature companies typically have their finances in much better order than when in earlier phases, but they've also captured the majority of the market share available to them. Growth slows, and the shares are valued based on earnings capability. Profits are spent on maintaining their position, rather than capturing more customers.

✔ **Decline phase:** Whether it takes 10 years or 100, all companies end up on the down slope. New technologies arise, consumer tastes change, competitors rise up, and so on. In the decline years, a company is uncertain of which actions to take, very few of those actions seem to work, and it expends most of its energy and money trying to curtail fading away.

The good news is that a declining company can reinvent itself. By stepping away from the waning aspects of the corporation while doubling down on its strengths and adjusting its focus, it can reverse the decline phase and instead move back towards growth, which is where there were the greatest gains in their share price.

As an investor, you need to consider various financial factors based on where the company is in its corporate life cycle. For instance, you shouldn't get scared out of an investment because of operating losses and a high debt load if the company is a start-up or just entering their growth phase. On the other hand, the exact same company might be a poor stock to own if they are in or near the end of their mature phase.

Awareness of the corporate life cycle, especially with knowledge of where on that life cycle your stock sits, will go a long way to helping you make the right investment decisions.

What's Really Driving the Share Price?

Sometimes the shares of a stock change in price for reasons you're not aware of or haven't even considered. Taking the time to figure out exactly what is driving the shares, as opposed to what the majority of investors are assuming is moving them, gives you a major trading advantage.

Tracking the source of price movement is a particularly effective strategy when trading penny stocks because, unlike with larger investments, a single obscure blog comment or new release or lawsuit can significantly affect the value of smaller companies.

Picture a company with great fundamental strength, excellent financial results, and impressive growth. If the shares suddenly start falling and the trading volume is far above the daily average, it is very important to assess exactly the reason for the weakness.

Perhaps a major lawsuit was launched against the company, or the top managers all suddenly quit, or they had an explosion at one of their mines, for example. These events may not yet be public knowledge, but they will have material impacts on the function of the company going forward and on the price of the shares.

On the other hand, perhaps the sell-off was from an ill-informed comment on some blog, or statements made by a competitor, or even the result of a major mutual fund rebalancing its holdings for year end. In cases like these, the weakness in the share price may represent an undervalued buying opportunity rather than a cause for concern.

How do you get to the source of the movement? Do some extra web and media searches, call the company and ask, and even connect with some other investors in the same company if possible.

Any time there is unusual trading activity with no clear basis, do whatever you can to source the reasons. Search for media coverage, especially that which is presented to the mass market. Check for coverage in recent issues of trade publications. Try to see if all the selling or buying is from a single trader or dozens of them. All of these are clues that can help you find out what's going on and, in turn, make correct trading decisions.

Be like a stock market private investigator, because once you know what's really moving the share price, you will clearly see buying and profit-taking opportunities that others won't. Just like a company can have a competitive advantage, knowing why the shares of penny stocks are moving can be your investing competitive advantage.

Watch the Short Interest

The *short interest* demonstrates what percentage of shares in a company is held by short sellers, who profit when the stock decreases in value. I discuss short selling in Chapter 6.

Short sellers expect the price of shares to decrease. They profit when this occurs by selling the stock first and then hoping to buy those shares back later at a lower value.

Large short interests may indicate that a significant portion of investors have reason to expect that the shares will decrease in price. For example, if the short interest is over 20 percent, a potentially negative event for the shares is widely expected and publicly known.

You can easily check the short interest of any stock through any online financial portal like Yahoo! Finance. Short interests will typically be below 10 percent, and any values higher than that may indicate a cause for concern among investors.

The most a short seller can make is 100 percent, and that's only if the stock drops to zero. However, they can lose unlimited amounts of money because there is no ceiling to how high the price may rise. If an investor sells shares short at one dollar and then watches that stock increase towards five dollars, he'll have to pay five times his investment amount.

For that reason, combined with difficulty of finding shares that can be sold short, as well as forced trades and restrictions on short sales by your broker, this is not an appropriate avenue for the majority of investors.

There will usually be a "short interest" in a stock, which is the percentage of total shares that have been sold short. It stands to reason that the more investors believe that the stock price is too high, the higher the short interest will climb.

When shares are sold short it's a healthy event in the market, because the activity helps increase the efficiency of valuing stocks. Shares shouldn't only go higher, and in addition to sellers who think that the value is getting too high and so unload their positions, some short sellers go a step further and bet that the stock is coming down.

Many believe that short sellers push the stock price lower, but this is not the case. Rather, when the short interest position gets significant — for example, anything above 10 or 15 percent — you can take that as a sign that more and more investors are expecting the price to decline.

While rarely having much impact on where the shares go, there is value in keeping an eye on the short sellers. Whether they are right or wrong with their bet, you should find out why they hold this belief. If you aren't sure why they are betting against the company, and that short position just keeps increasing, you will want to understand their logic to ensure that you have full clarity in your investment decisions.

Don't Diversify, Pinpoint Invest Instead

Financial advisors like to tout the merits of diversification. The idea is to spread your investments out among several stocks as a means of minimizing the overall impact of a dropping price on your portfolio. In many cases, diversification is a great strategy; however, if you divided your money between eight stocks and one slid lower, it would only have a negative impact on one-eighth of your portfolio. Compare that to putting 100 percent of your money into one stock, and that investment dropping. Your resulting downside would be significant because the portfolio isn't diversified.

Investors can diversify in many ways. Besides buying a greater number of stocks, they often choose shares from different industry groups, various ranges of price per share or company size, or even spreading their investments between companies from different countries. Many people also like to own various investment types, such as some index funds, some bonds, some individual stocks, and some precious metals.

Although diversification is a smart and seemingly logical approach for most investors, the strategy presents some problems. For one thing, the more an individual diversifies, the closer to average returns she will achieve. This is great for those who want the same profits (and losses) that the overall stock market generates, but it's not as attractive for anyone who wants her investments to out-perform the market. And considering that you're reading this book, I assume that you want your returns to be above average.

Diversification also increases your odds of getting an investment that performs poorly. When you buy a dozen eggs, there is a chance that one may be cracked in the carton. If you're worried about getting a cracked egg, you could buy five dozen. That strategy increases your odds of having a carton without a broken egg, but it also increases the probability (by a factor of five times) that you'll get a cracked one.

Instead of diversifying, embrace a strategy that I call *pinpoint investing*. This strategy involves buying fewer stocks, with a greater percentage of your total portfolio invested in each. With a seven-figure trading portfolio, the most individual stocks I buy is seven, but I sometimes buy even fewer than that. And yes, in my case most of those investments are penny stocks.

Depending on your own investment portfolio, whether it's worth $1,000, $50,000, or otherwise, you may also perform better with pinpoint investing than you would with diversification.

Picture a $20,000 portfolio. You could diversify into 20 stocks, but that would bring you closer to the average stock market returns than if you had invested in only 5 of them. As long as you keep a very close eye on those 5 companies, and your analysis is effective, the portfolio with fewer stocks could greatly outperform the more diversified one with 20.

Pinpoint investing isn't an appropriate strategy for beginning investors, and keep in mind that I personally have an advantage in terms of experience and knowledge. Unless you're a very experienced and effective trader, then diversification is certainly the best approach for you.

Having cautioned you to be careful, pinpoint investing can be very effective as long as the individual has a high risk tolerance, only invests risk money, and has a strong knowledge of how to monitor and analyze companies. When you make the right calls with your investment decisions, pinpoint investing can produce dramatically superior results.

Chapter 14

Ten Trading Truths

In This Chapter

▶ Arming yourself with secret weapons for investing

▶ Gaining insights into the true workings of the stock market

▶ Finding profits in the movements of shares

S ome realities in the stock market aren't common knowledge even though they should be. With an understanding of the ten trading truths I reveal in this chapter, you'll make more timely buy and sell decisions, bring greater clarity to your research, and reap more rewarding returns.

Investor Sentiment Is Contrarian

Stock prices change based on the buy and sell decisions of the masses, and a cold, hard fact is that the mob, aka the majority of investors, is usually wrong. Whether you're talking about penny stocks or regular stocks, most people lose more money over time than they make. Most people buy shares at price peaks and sell them at price bottoms.

This is why investor sentiment is a contrarian indicator, meaning that the more investors who believe that the stock market is going higher, the more likely it is going to fall. Similarly, the more investors there are who expect a crash, the higher the probability of shares increasing in price.

When investor sentiment is highly optimistic, traders anticipate higher share prices to come. As a result, demand for stocks increases, pushing prices higher, until they are overvalued. During periods of investor optimism, stocks generally trade well above realistic values and so are due for a correction or price meltdown to return to realistic levels.

When everyone and their grandma is telling you about the next hot stock pick, you should be ready for a possible market dip, if not a full-fledged crash. When the market feels like a feeding frenzy, be very cautious.

Highly negative investor sentiment is usually matched up with a distaste for stocks, along with a good degree of fear and panic selling. Shares may come closer to being given away, let alone trading for fair valuations. Shareholders do not mind unloading their positions at rock-bottom prices, especially since they can't comprehend how the stocks will ever have any value again.

When no one wants to talk about stocks, and any comments you do get out of them are very negative about investing and the direction the stock market is heading, it is a great predictor of coming upward momentum. With highly negative investor sentiment, it's time to hunt for bargains.

Watching media coverage of the market is a great way to monitor investor sentiment. Media outlets not only provide data on investor sentiment from surveys they conduct but also demonstrate actual sentiment. If the cover and every main page of a newspaper are talking about how the market is roaring higher, then expect a fall. You can track investor sentiment through any number of sources, with details often released through articles published by outlets such as Barron's, CBS, and CNBC. Alternatively, you can go straight to the American Association of Individual Investors for their ongoing survey results, which are available at `www.aaii. com/sentimentsurvey`.

Keep in mind that the media is reactive, not predictive. They don't tell you what to expect but instead report on what has already happened. An article about the stock market going up is really just telling you that it already has. What the same article won't tell you in all of its cheerleading is that now you're in more danger of a stock correction or market drop.

There have been hundreds of times when market sentiment warned investors to be cautious, or to look for opportunities to buy, and there will be hundreds more in the future. Whether it is the dot-com bubble (which burst after the feeding frenzy of investors), or people paying ten times their annual income for a single bulb at the 1637 height of the Dutch tulip mania (which also burst after the feeding frenzy), you will see sentiment spikes and dips very frequently in the days to come (albeit to much smaller degrees than the examples we've used above).

You can have great investment success by playing sentiment. When you develop a good understanding of mob mentality, you may find that you can use it alone to guide your trading decisions to great result.

Big Moves Occur During Brief Trading Windows

Successful penny stock investors recognize that shares make their greatest moves in small amounts of time. About 80 percent of changes in price, whether to the upside or downside, occur over approximately 20 percent of the time.

You can verify this by looking at just about any trading chart. Measure the big moves, and you will see that when a penny stock changes markedly in price, it typically does so over the course of weeks, if not days.

To take advantage of trading windows, you should only put money into penny stock shares immediately before corporate events or news that could benefit the stock. You can then reinvest any profits into other trading-window opportunities, thus only risking your money for short periods before major events. With this technique, you avoid leaving your money exposed on the markets for longer time frames, during the weeks or months when you don't expect any major corporate events. Check out Chapter 8 for a full discussion of trading windows.

Greater Volume Means Greater Sustainability

The more trading volume behind a price move, the more likely it is sustainable. If a penny stock sees its shares go up 40 percent on a $500 purchase of 20,000 shares, the price is highly likely to come right back down. On the other hand, if the shares rose 40 percent on $3-million-worth of purchases for a total of 8 million shares from dozens of different buyers, you can rest assured that the strength is more likely to remain.

Each share purchased is a vote of confidence in the underlying company, just like each share sold is from a shareholder who has lost faith. The more investors behind a move, the more probable the price change will be sustained.

Always watch volume to assess which price moves to take seriously. Price changes due to light trading from fewer investors for smaller dollar amounts are very likely to reverse. So you shouldn't worry about downward price moves that don't have much behind them, as they almost always reverse pretty quickly. Similarly, don't get excited by upward spikes that don't have a good portion of the masses behind them.

Making Up for Losses Is Harder than Preventing Them

A stock that has lost 50 percent of its value needs to increase by 100 percent from its new, lower level just to get back to where it started. I call this sad mathematical truth of the stock market the *half down principle.*

Picture a share of your favorite penny stock, which is trading at $2. If that stock falls to $1 per share, that slide represents a 50 percent decline. To return to the original $2-level from this new low point, it would need to increase by $1, or 100 percent.

It takes any stock a percentage rise that is greater than the original percentage decline to climb back to break even. Shares that lose 10 percent need a recovery of 11 percent to get back to predecline levels. Shares that fall 25 percent would need to increase by 33 percent to reach break even. If you own shares that sink 85 percent, they need to rise 460 percent from that level to regain their original value.

This mathematical reality makes avoiding and curtailing losses extremely important. React quickly when your penny stocks are going the wrong way, and pay special attention to the discussion on limiting losses in Chapter 8.

Bigger Things Take More Energy to Move

Larger companies are generally more stable. They are less influenced by events like contract wins, lost customers, the resignation of a top manager, or the appearance of a new competitor.

On the other hand, even minor events can significantly affect penny stock companies. Consider the impact of a corporation worth $5 million landing a $7 million contract versus that of a $500 million corporation landing the same contract. Obviously, the smaller company will be much more strongly affected by the event. The same principle applies to negative events, such as lawsuits or losing clients.

While this can be a cause for caution among investors, it can also be an opportunity for significant profits. Because events of lower relevance have the capacity to drive penny stock shares, and these same events can telegraph the potential direction of the company well into the future, shareholders positioned in the right stocks stand to profit to a much greater degree.

It would take a series of significant events to cause the share price of a $1 billion corporation to halve or double in price. With a penny stock, a single event may be enough to shake things up.

Rapid Rise, Rapid Fall

Price increases are generally sustainable if they develop over longer periods of time. On the other hand, the quicker and more dramatic a price spike, the more likely that these higher levels won't be sustainable. For example, a stock that quadruples in price in a day is more likely to fall all the way back down than a stock that quadruples in price over a full year.

Based on this reality, you ideally want to own stocks that enjoy a gradual and sustained uptrend, because the gains achieved will probably be maintained. In contrast, while stocks that spike dramatically in short time frames are great for investors who sell quickly and near the peak, the stocks don't usually hold those gains for more than a couple days (if that).

This concept is especially important in relation to penny stocks, because major and sudden price moves are more common among low-priced shares than other types of investments. To be a successful penny stock investor, when you see a massive price spike, consider taking profits rather than expecting the shares to keep on soaring.

Because penny stocks are thinly traded, they are also often targets for manipulation. Promoters drive the prices higher through free newsletters and dishonest message board posts. When the promoter has taken enough profits, they stop pumping the shares and the penny stock collapses.

News items and events can really drive penny stock prices higher. Often the reactionary buying frenzy among investors drives the stock well above levels it should be trading at, even with the great news or press release. As shareholders let the news digest, and the buying stampede calms down, the shares often come right back to Earth.

Beware of sudden and pronounced price spikes in penny stocks. Put much more trust in slow and gradual price increases, because they may remain for a long time.

Dilution Disguises Losses

Some penny stocks have done a lot worse for their shareholders than appearances may seem to indicate. Most investors look only at the price of the stock, or the trading chart, and if the price of the shares is up, they assume that everything is fine.

Unfortunately these same investors may not be looking at the total number of shares trading on the market. Because most companies raise money by selling more shares, the total number outstanding increases. The end result is dilution of the company's stock — because there are so many more shares, the proportionate value of each is less. As the total number of available shares increases, the value of each gets watered down. Flip to Chapter 3 for a full discussion of dilution.

For example, each of the 10 million shares available for fictional FFFF Corporation entitles the holder to one ten-millionth ownership of the company. If FFFF creates and sells 5 million more shares, each stock now is entitled to one 15-millionth of the company. At the same time, each share will generally (but not always) decrease in price.

Suppose that FFFF posted an annual loss of 1¢ per share back when it had only 10 million shares out. Then the company diluted the stock by putting out an additional 5 million shares. If FFFF reports losing 1¢ on its next financials, that actually represents a 50 percent larger loss.

The total loss is greater (1¢ per share on 15 million shares compared to 1¢ per share on 10 million shares), but the number for the loss per share did not change because more shares are outstanding.

 Penny stock companies often need to do two things: raise money and hide losses. They can accomplish both via issuing more shares, and this dilution often misleads investors as to the company's actual progress.

Buy the Rumor, Sell the Fact

Shares often react exactly the opposite way that you expect. The stock welcomes great news with a major sell-off, or answers bad news by increasing in share price.

The phrase that best captures this stock market activity is "Buy the rumor, sell the fact." In other words, as traders position themselves to benefit from an event, they tend to push shares higher (or lower in the case of pending negative news). The shares often over-extend beyond what the actual event justifies, so that the result of the official news or occurrence is a falling stock price despite the positive (or rising stock price despite the negative) information.

You can profit by purchasing stocks that will rise along with a growing rumor. The trick is to be ready to take your gains out before the actual fact occurs, because even seemingly positive events may result in a sell-off of the shares.

When fictional FFFF company is widely expected to report 100 percent increases in revenues on its next financials, the shares may trade higher leading up to the actual release of the numbers. As more investors become aware of the anticipated financial results, they bid the shares even higher.

Upon the release of the official report of 100 percent revenue increase, short-term traders take profits, especially as the underlying stock starts to move in the wrong direction. There are also very few buyers, since the majority who wanted to get into FFFF have already done so in anticipation.

The same could occur in reverse, with FFFF shareholders selling leading up to a widely expected loss of a major customer, for example. FFFF stock may be so battered down that the actual event of the customer leaving results in the stock popping higher.

Anyone who wanted to sell probably already has, and the shares now have gotten to highly undervalued levels. In addition, the negative overhang of the customer potentially leaving is now done, removing some uncertainty around FFFF.

When trading penny stocks, keep the fact that most people "buy the rumor and sell the fact" in mind. You may then turn surprising and unexpected stock price moves into profit opportunities.

Don't Try Catching Falling Knives

When a penny stock falls from $2 per share to 25¢, does it represent a good value? That depends on the reason for the fall and the strength of the underlying company. Even at 25¢ it could still go lower, and you may lose 100 percent of whatever money you invest in it.

Trying to buy shares as the stock is falling is referred to as "trying to catch a falling knife." As long as the trend of the shares is heading lower, you should wait before you invest. Only after the downward slide stops or reverses, should you consider getting involved.

Keep in mind that a $2 stock had investors who thought they were getting a deal when it was trading down to $1.75, and then again when it hit $1, and yet again when it was down to 50¢. Don't be the investor who comes along to make the same mistake as they did, by believing 25¢ is a great value considering that the stock used to be a worth eight times that much.

The former value, whether it was $2 or $55 per share, is absolutely meaningless. The current value of any stock is whatever someone is willing to pay you for it — and not a penny more — right now.

Resistance Levels Can Flip

Resistance levels are price ranges above which a penny stock's shares may have trouble reaching (I explore this concept in detail in Chapter 12). Very often these levels occur at key price points in penny stocks, such as $1.00, $1.50, $1.75, and other significant numbers because many shareholders sell at threshold prices, rather than mid-range levels, such as $1.07, $1.23, and $1.72.

Because breaking through a resistance level is difficult, when shares do push into higher prices, investors can be more certain that the underlying stock has significant buying demand behind it.

After shares break through a resistance level, that level often *flips,* or transforms into a support level. Picture a stock that breaks through a resistance of $1 after ten months. That $1 level very often becomes a support level, where shares remain above for the indefinite future.

The same concept holds true in reverse, where support levels fail and then become the new resistance level. Shares may remain above $2 for years, but after the stock dips below that price, they may never be above $2 again for just as many years.

Look to a trading chart (and Chapter 12) to identify support and resistance levels. Use them to gain an understanding of how the share's prices may act, but be aware of their potential to flip and the resulting ramifications.

Chapter 15

Ten Key Considerations for Companies

. . . .

In This Chapter

▶ Understanding abstract concepts that have major corporate impacts

▶ Discovering forces that can dictate success or failure for stocks

. . . .

*A*lthough the share price of a penny stock is often dictated by the results of the company's financial reports, those financial results are ultimately derived from operations. And so it only makes sense that you need to pay close attention to a company's operational factors and related concepts when making your investment decisions. In this chapter I describe ten key concepts that can have a major impact on the success or failure of a company.

By understanding these key considerations, you get a much clearer picture of any corporation's longer term potential and, by extension, get a better sense of where the stock price may be heading.

Barriers to Entry

A *barrier to entry* is any issue or obstacle that a company must overcome in order to sell to a specific market. For example, if a company wants to sell a new prescription drug, getting FDA approval represents a barrier to entry. To open a factory in a town with a workforce shortage, a barrier to entry may be getting enough employees.

The higher the barriers to get involved in an industry or business line, the harder it will be for the company to get started in that space. That's why you won't see more than a few companies building electronic components for satellites, but you can find hundreds of companies selling weight loss systems — the barriers to entry are much lower for entering the weight loss market.

Barriers to entry can be based on many factors, including high regulations, lack of specialized workforce, governmental requisite approvals, pre-existing competitors, materials costs, and more. Anything that makes it difficult for a company to establish itself and sell specific products to a specific market acts as a barrier to entry.

One of the greatest barriers to entry is a solid patent. If a company has a patent to a specific product or technology and they defend it legally against competitors that try to violate that patent, then that patent is a significant barrier to entry.

Ideally, you want to invest in companies that are established and doing well in an industry with very high barriers. This limits the amount of new competition it has to face. Picture a penny stock with FDA approval for a drug that fights a major disease. The company has already cleared the biggest hurdle, and any companies looking to take on the same market will have to achieve the same clearance. And even if they clear that barrier to entry, there may not be much market left.

The worst-case scenario is when a company is trying to break into a market with high barriers to entry and several other companies have already cleared all the obstacles. Picture all the energy drink inventors who came along for the first time after the major companies had already saturated the market.

Companies can navigate barriers to entry, but you need to consider how much time, effort, and money they need just to get established in a market where competitors are already operating.

Competitive Advantages

A *competitive advantage* exists for a company when it finds itself in a beneficial situation not shared by its competitors. Picture a corporation that has better access to a skilled workforce, is able to produce products for less, or makes greater profits from its services.

For example, China has a competitive advantage of producing products at much lower costs due to the availability of its expansive and low-cost work force. A widely sought-after fashion brand has a competitive advantage because consumers are more likely to pay more to own products from that maker.

Not every company has advantages over the competition, but the majority of businesses can point to at least a few ways that they have an edge. Corporations that leverage those advantages have the potential to do very well, especially in relation to their competitors who don't enjoy the same benefit.

For example, if only one mining company in America is finding and extracting rare earth metals, they have an advantage over all the other mining companies in the United States that don't have those resources. That company also has at least one other competitive edge: They don't have to import the rare earth metals from overseas, and so they have much lower shipment costs to bring their commodities to market.

 Look for penny stock companies that are aware of and leverage their competitive edge. Be cautious of those companies that don't seem to be benefiting from any specific advantage or are not aware of and leveraging it to the fullest.

Market Share (and Room for Growth)

Every company selling its products or services has a portion of the total available market. For example, if a penny stock sells half of the total worldwide stock of waffle makers, it has a 50 percent market share.

You definitely want to know what share of market a company enjoys, but you're in an even better position if you understand whether that percentage is increasing or decreasing over time. Growth in a company's total market share every year demonstrates expanding customer adoption of its services.

Pay attention to changes in market share not only for the company you're interested in but also for the competition. If your penny stock loses 15 percent of its market share over the same time that its competitor gains 15 percent, you can assume that the competition is winning or stealing away customers.

You also want to understand the total value of the market. If you're able to forecast that customers are going to spend $600 million on security consulting services in the next year, and your penny stock has 10 percent of that market, then you have a pretty good handle on how much money your company is going to make. Contrast that with an even higher share of a smaller market, such as 90 percent of a $1 million market. This company, despite the much higher market share, would make significantly less money.

The sizes of the markets can change, too, which will impact the stocks in that industry. If the market for fur coats was $2 billion worldwide 20 years ago but then slid to $3 million this year, every company in that industry is going to do very poorly, regardless of their market share.

Ideally, you want to own penny stocks in growing industries that are also expanding their market share by taking business away from their direct competitors. As long as the company maintains those trends, and the industry maintains its growth, your investment could perform very well.

Customer Diversity and the Company's Reliance

Some companies have one or two customers; others have thousands. By having a greater diversity of clients, the company is insulated from shocks that can come from the loss of a few of them.

Picture a website design firm with 3,000 customers. It won't get derailed by losing one or two customers — and may not even notice the loss!

Contrast that with a military weapons designer with only two customers, both of which come from contracts with the government. If the government cancels one of its contracts, the event would decimate the company's stock and possibly put it out of business.

Every industry is different, of course, but it's generally better to have more customers than fewer. Ideally, companies shouldn't be overly reliant on any one of those customers, so that their comings and goings don't leave the company — and therefore its shares — vulnerable.

For certain penny stock companies it's just not realistic for them to have numerous clients. For example, a mining surveyor won't have hundreds of customers. However, they could have dozens, which would be better than if they had only seven or two.

You also want to beware of penny stock companies with many clients but that get a significant portion of their business from only one or two of those customers. Anytime a corporation is reliant primarily on a smaller number of customers, they are exposing themselves and their shareholders to risks.

Allies

We all need friends. That claim is just as true in business as it is in our personal lives, because the proper connections and allies can open doors, assist in landing contracts, and even provide guidance and staff.

Allies are more important with penny stock companies than larger corporations. When a business is in the early stages of its life cycle and is trying to survive, the advantages that strong alliances provide can have the greatest impact.

Picture the nephew of the President of the United States running a business. The newsworthy relationship alone could open opportunities.

Or consider a company in the digital advertising space. If it has cooperative agreements with the top five media outlets, it will have a major advantage in contrast with any competitors who don't have similar arrangements.

Some of the greatest companies of all time leaned heavily on their alliances with other strong players in their industry. With the right corporations, organizations, or individuals in its corner, a stock can advance very quickly.

Insider Ownership

When executives and managers of a company own a high percentage of the shares, that's generally a good sign. Called *insider ownership,* it means that management is financially vested in the fortunes of the shares and, as such, has an additional motivation for the company to do well.

Insider ownership positions, just like corporate financial reports, are a matter of public record. You can easily see the exact percentage of insider ownership from anywhere financial information is displayed, including `www.finance.yahoo` and `www.marketwatch.com`.

Insider ownership of 10 to 30 percent is generally a positive sign. If that ownership percentage is increasing over time, that's an even better sign, because it means that key players are accumulating shares.

Keep in mind that insiders can sell, too, and if they start liquidating their positions it could have a negative impact on the shares. Such actions also illustrate a manager or executive who is lowering their exposure to the company, which gives rise to numerous questions.

You don't want insider ownership to go too high, though. Avoid companies where a controlling percentage of shares, or close to it, is in the hands of the key executives. Any time insider ownership gets higher than about 30 percent, the key players will have a much easier time controlling the company. An ownership stake higher than 50 percent gives management the power to do whatever it likes without fear of losing their jobs.

By watching for a healthy amount of insider ownership, with that percentage increasing over time, you can know that insiders are committed to the company. While insiders are often wrong with their buying and selling timing, it can still add to your due diligence when analyzing any penny stock.

Institutional Ownership

Companies must disclose the level of *institutional ownership*, or ownership by institutions such as mutual funds, hedge funds, investment banks, and other professional investors. Most of these institutions move around tens of millions of dollars with each trade.

You can view institutional ownership anywhere financial data is displayed, such as www.finance.yahoo and www.marketwatch.com. A very high degree of institutional ownership is a good sign, because it demonstrates that the stock is worthy of interest by professional analysts. When a top-level analyst working for a multi-billion dollar mutual fund buys 5 percent of a company's shares, most investors believe that he did extensive due diligence and feels the shares are a good investment. Sometimes such actions turn out to be wise, but not always.

Keep in mind that most institutional investors manage hundreds of millions, if not billions, of dollars. They usually have restrictions on the size and types of the companies they can invest in, and they are rarely allowed to invest in penny stocks. Because of this, you will often see penny stocks with no institutional ownership at all, but that situation isn't necessarily a warning sign or indicator that the company is a poor investment choice.

When deciding on the merits of an investment, check out the level of institutional ownership. If institutional ownership constitutes at least 15 percent, and perhaps even 50 percent or more, view it is a good sign. An even better sign is if you see that amount is increasing from one month to the next.

Positioning

Every company fights for a position in your mind. You may have opinions about which fast food tastes best, which cereal is healthiest, or which cell phone company provides the most reliable service. These companies hold a space in your mind, and even when your opinions aren't right, you act as if they are.

I just described the concept of *positioning,* which was first developed by marketing professionals Al Ries and Jack Trout. When a company understands how it and its competitors are positioned in the minds of prospects and is able to adjust that positioning when necessary, their actions can have a significant, albeit somewhat intangible, advantage.

Consumers want to buy coffee from Columbia, wine from France, military items from America, and cigars from Cuba. Companies from these nations have a positioning advantage to sell the goods just mentioned when compared to purveyors of coffee from Canada, wine from Honduras, military items from Laos, and cigars from New Zealand.

When a penny stock is enjoying a strong position in the minds of prospects (assuming that position is a positive one), then it has a competitive advantage. If customers believe that the penny stock's software is fastest, or its vitamins are least expensive, or its mountain climbing gear is safest, then they should see increased sales to anyone looking for the fastest software, inexpensive vitamins, or safe mountain climbing equipment.

Look for penny stocks that hold a position in the minds of prospects or that are culturing and developing one. For example, consider whether a company is promoting its new product in a way that it could establish a place in the minds of prospects. At the same time, avoid those penny stocks whose companies don't seem to represent anything noteworthy.

The Secret of Flag Fall Fees

You incur an initial charge, called a *flag fall fee,* when you first get into a taxi. That fee is in addition to and independent of the subsequent distance charges.

Many industries charge flag fall fees. Any time a customer incurs a set initial fee, regardless of expenses thereafter that are based on time, distance, or amount, that is flag fall in action.

You may have been victim to flag fall already if you've set up a new mobile phone account. Most mobile phone companies require customers to pay "an account establishment fee" or "initial activation fee." Every new customer pays out that amount, regardless of the phone plan they purchase or how much they use the phone.

Flag fall fees show up under various names in many different industries, including airlines, health care providers, and cable television companies, just to name a few.

When a company charges flag fall fees that are cleverly hidden or in a way that doesn't seem to bother their customer base, such fees can be a significant and reliable source of additional revenue. When that company also has some room to increase those rates without significant detriment to its sales, it will probably do so, which results in a relatively cost-free method of increasing revenues.

Regardless of what the companies imposing the fees might tell you, the flag fall or account establishment costs are generally not necessary. There also aren't many expenses involved in collecting them, so that they represent a revenue stream that will eventually apply to profit.

Any penny stock that increases its flag fall rates without impacting its new client numbers should see a jump in its revenues. As long as the penny stock is collecting higher amounts as a means to increase profits or income, as opposed to being a desperation move due to financial issues, then that company may represent a strong investment prospect.

It's All About Recurring Revenues and Attrition

A company that enjoys recurring billing, such as monthly membership fees, is easier to analyze than businesses with unpredictable sales or no recurring revenues. If it charges ten dollars a month, and it doubles its subscriber numbers, you can anticipate that its revenues will also double.

Recurring revenues make it easy to analyze a company because you can know how much money will be coming in. As long as the company keeps its subscriber count growing, it should also grow as a company and see the benefits in its share price.

Anytime you're looking at a business with recurring revenues, the most important factor is its *attrition rate,* which indicates how many customers it is losing. Ten percent growth in new subscribers is great, but not if it has a 20 percent attrition rate.

Attrition also tells you a lot about the experience and loyalty of customers. If most of the attrition occurs within the first two months of trying a product, it implies that those customers either did not find much benefit from using it, didn't like the item, couldn't afford it, or found better alternatives elsewhere.

With any business that derives revenues from recurring billing, pay special attention to its new subscriber growth rate and to its attrition rate. A recipe for success in penny stocks is strong growth in customers with very low customer loss.

Index

business outlook, 174–177
businesses. *See* companies; small businesses
"Buy the rumor, sell the fact," 267
buying known quantities, 123
buying opportunity, recognizing, 71
buying stocks, 95
buyouts, 46

• C •

candlestick charts, 99
cap stocks, investing in, 23
cash flow statement
  categories, 157–158
  example, 158
  financing activities, 163–164
  investing activities, 163
  operating activities, 163
  strong numbers on, 163–164
cash ratio, 184
CDs (Certificates of Deposit), 22
CEO (Chief Executive Officer), role of, 167
CFO (Chief Financial Officer), role of, 167–168
chat rooms, researching, 104
choosing penny stocks
  company size, 127
  industry, 127
  market, 126–127
  share price, 127
  trading activity, 127
CIO (Chief Information Officer), role of, 168
commission schedule, asking broker for, 82
companies. *See also* small businesses
  calling, 250
  growth of, 19
  market capitalization, 12
  quality of, 11, 27
  size and stability, 264–265
  total value of, 12
company financials, researching, 99–100
company versus market risk, 251–252
company-specific risk, 120–122

competition, barriers to entry, 212–213
competitive advantages, 270–271
competitors
  acquisition by, 69
  comparing offerings of, 253
  dealing with, 69
  impact of changes on penny stocks, 20
  poaching, 69
consolidation patterns, relationship to TA, 238–240
COO (Chief Operations Officer), role of, 168
corporate commitment level, 169–171
corporate life cycle
  decline phase, 255
  finding trend in, 166
  growth phase, 254
  maturity phase, 255
  start-up phase, 254
cost of sales, reflecting on income statement, 153–154
CTO (Chief Technology Officer), role of, 168
current ratio, 183
customer changes, impact on penny stocks, 20
customer diversity and reliance, 272
customer loyalty, 69
customer turnover, 217–218

• D •

DCA (dollar cost averaging), 140
debt ratio, 191
debt to equity ratio, 192
derivatives, investing in, 23
diluting shares, 40–42, 45
dilution, disguising losses, 266
discount broker, 81
diversification
  explained, 146
  versus pinpoint investing, 258–259
diversity and reliance, 272
downturn, occurrence of, 149
due diligence, doing, 58, 93–96, 136